ethics
FOR PUBLIC SAFETY
Ethical & Moral Decision Making

SECOND EDITION

CARL J. LOFTHOUSE

MORGAN PETERSON, Ed.D

Kendall Hunt
publishing company

Kendall Hunt
publishing company

www.kendallhunt.com
Send all inquiries to:
4050 Westmark Drive
Dubuque, IA 52004-1840

CONTENTS

PREFACE

Perhaps more than ever, the topic of "making ethical decisions" needs to be discussed and even learned. We want to believe that ethics can be learned or are we wasting our time writing books and studying the topic? The news is full of behavior that is far from ethical, moral or even legal. Then, throw in the popular reality shows; are they "real", or are they just made for entertainment? It's in our political arena. We see it in our Presidents, our Governors and our Senators. It seems that we can't turn on the news without hearing another story of unethical behavior. We see people who are entrusted with investing our money, and turns out, they aren't investing our money at all but taking it from us. In fact, they were stealing millions of dollars from many hard working people.

We're then disappointed when we see behavior that the public is not proud of and neither are the ones that made the poor decision. This includes actors and world class athletes. These are athletes who are considered to be at the top of their game, the best in the world. But they have made such a poor decision that they feel the need to go into "hiding" leaving the public to wonder what went wrong. Many of their sponsors are then left to debate if they want to keep this person as a sponsor to uphold the image of their company.

This book discusses the unethical decisions made by entrusted Public Safety Officers. These kinds of decisions leave many asking "What were they thinking?" or "What happened to our heroes?"

Ethics for Public Safety covers the history of ethics from the days of Socrates through examples of poor ethical decisions with police, fire and EMS departments. Discussion and scenarios are intended for the student to look at our every day ethics from the time the alarm goes off in the morning until we fall asleep at night. This book looks at the ethical process. It goes even a step further for the Public Safety Officer because, after all, it's expected that we are ethical, moral, and obey the law 24/7. There are no breaks and there is "no free lunch". The public is watching (and so they should). We're always on stage and once we lose that trust it is very difficult to redeem.

We need to monitor ourselves and each other. The public expects it and we must remember they pay our salary. The community holds police officers, firefighters, and EMS/Paramedics in higher esteem than it does other professions. We are an example, good or bad, to the public and to children who may look to us as heroes.

The authors hope that after reading this text you carefully reflect on your personal behavior, not only when you're training in an academy, responding to a medical aid, apprehending a suspect, extinguishing a fire, or building a fence with your neighbor, that you take the time to make ethical decisions all the time.

Public Safety Officers need to constantly think about ethics because ethics is what they should use when faced with a decision. Being almost ethical doesn't cut it, "sounded like a good idea at the time" may be too costly. That decision could very well end your career, injure someone, or worse yet take someone's life.

Carl J. Lofthouse
Morgan Peterson

ACKNOWLEDGMENTS

Photo by Melinda Finn

CARL J. LOFTHOUSE

In 2009, Jason and John with Kendall/ Hunt contacted me about writing an emergency management textbook. We discussed my thoughts and ideas of writing an "ethics" textbook from a public safety officer perspective instead of emergency management. I believe my passion for the subject matter came through because after an initial discussion of the book, I was given a green light for the "go ahead". Immediately, I knew I wanted my co-author to be Professor Morgan Peterson. This book would not be possible without his life experiences and passion for the subject. I want to thank Professor Peterson for joining me in making this journey enjoyable and educational. Thank you also Morgan for your patience!

I especially want to thank my wife and best friend Terri. Other publishers have approached me in the past about writing a textbook and somehow life's responsibilities prevented me from writing. She insisted this time that I go forward with writing an "ethics" textbook (third time's a charm!) This book could not be complete without her support, our marriage of 35 years and her understanding of my desire to write this book. She understands the importance to me of seeing the fruition of this book after a long career as a firefighter, public servant and college professor.

I would also like to thank my family as well for their love and support for me during this journey. Since the first edition was published, I am also proud to announce the birth of our granddaughter. Thank you all and a big thank you to Uncle Jerry for his positive encouragement for the team.

Since the First Edition, I have learned more from my students about ethics on a daily basis. One doesn't need to watch the news to see unethical decisions because it is all around us. I refer to it in my classes as the "the good, the bad, and the ugly". All you have to do is go to work, the store, or drive your car to experience bad behavior. Are we trying to stay off the slippery slope? Let's not regret "sounded like a good idea at the time".

My students have commented:

- I didn't know there was so much to study about ethics . . .
- The best class I've ever had . . .
- Made me think of things I never thought of . . .
- I think differently now . . .
- Ethics can teach you right from wrong and how to keep your job . . .
- Because of this class, I feel more prepared to be a firefighter . . .

I'd like to thank Lara Sanders, Acquisitions Editor, Linda Chapman, Senior Project Coordinator, and Carla Kipper, Permissions Editor at Kendall/Hunt for their guidance. Your kind words, help and insight are much appreciated!

Photo by Melinda Finn

MORGAN PETERSON

A few years ago Carl Lofthouse came to my office and floated the idea for a public safety ethics book. I had been teaching criminal justice ethics for about 3 years and he was interested in starting a fire ethics course, so we decided that they were enough alike to marry them in a textbook. I thought this was a great idea so we wrote the book. I'll say it again . . . good idea, Carl.

I would like to thank my wife JoAnn for a couple of things. First for putting up with me; whenever I get started doing a project such as this I have a tendency to neglect other things and one of them is my wife. She has put up with this while I was an inspector in the San Francisco Police Department, during graduate school, and while I was writing my doctoral dissertation. Secondly, she also reads my work, offers constructive criticism, and sometimes corrects punctuation that I neglect during the heat of writing.

I would also like to thank the rest of my family for their patience and support. Thanks Shannon, Casey, Aidan, Iva and Jeff, and my dog, Cassie, who had to give up more than a few walks.

Casey turned me on to Tom Deierlein and Pat O'Hanlon, who were very helpful and provided me with answers to some difficult questions regarding ethics and terrorism.

Another guy who is always there when I need encouragement is Professor Kevin Barrett, a friend and colleague that I can bounce questions and ideas off of when I need a critical opinion.

The publishing staff at Kendall Hunt has been very helpful to me in the writing of this book. I would like to thank specifically Lara Sanders, Acquisitions Editor, Linda Chapman, Senior Project Coordinator, and Carla Kipper, Permissions Editor.

History of Ethics

1

CHAPTER OBJECTIVES

1. What is the definition of ethics?
2. Identify historical philosophers.
3. Explain contributions of historical philosophers to modern-day ethics and morals.
4. Why are there religious laws?

Let us begin our discussion of ethics with the question "What do ethics mean to you?"

_____

_____

_____

_____

_____

_____

There are many interpretations and theories on the topic of ethics. Many of us combine the idea of ethics with morals, and while they may be related, there are differences. Some of us say that ethics dictate the difference between right and wrong. While others say it is "doing the right thing." We get these ideas from our parents, church, school, and friends.

We also are bombarded by the media, such as television news, newspapers, and the social media. Then you can throw in a few reality shows and the waters are really muddied.

> If you don't read the newspaper, you are uninformed; if you do, you are misinformed.
>
> —Mark Twain

It would be nice if we had a show that depicted people acting ethically and doing the right thing on a regular basis, where no one got their feelings hurt, and there was no hate and anger. It may provide a balance, and we would get the idea of how to behave civilly toward one another.

However, the reality is many people today do not behave ethically and that is the problem. Public safety officers come into contact with people who do not behave ethically on a daily basis, and they sometimes lose their focus on the fact that they are the role models and should exhibit the way to do the right thing. It is for this reason that we endeavor to enlighten public safety officers to the importance of behaving ethically. We will begin with a look into the history of ethics.

DEFINITION OF ETHICS

Ethics {eth-iks}
-plural noun

1. (Used with singular or plural verb) a system of moral principles: the ethics of a culture.
2. The rules of conduct recognized in respect to a particular class of human actions or a particular group, culture, and so on: medical ethics; Christian ethics.
3. Moral principles, as of an individual: His ethics forbade betrayal of a confidence.
4. (Usually used with a singular verb) that branch of philosophy dealing with values relating to human conduct, with respect to the rightness and wrongness of certain actions, and to the goodness and badness of the motives and ends of such actions.[1]

Ethics

Eth'ics = (noun)

1. Study of moralities effect on conduct.
2. The study of moral standards and how they affect conduct.
3. A system of moral principles governing the appropriate conduct for a person or group.

Morality

Mo'ral'ity (noun)

1. Accepted moral standards, standards of conduct that are generally accepted as right or proper.
2. How right or wrong something is the rightness or wrongness of something as judged by accepted moral standards.
3. Virtuous behavior, conduct that is in accord with accepted moral standards.
4. Moral lesson, a lesson in moral behavior.[2]

Conceivably, the best place to begin the study of ethics is the past. History will repeat itself, both the good and bad, and, hopefully, we can learn from those, particularly the bad decisions. In order to fully understand what the future holds, we must explore the past.

When we look at our family ancestry, genealogy for instance, we not only find things of interest about our families, but also find stories that show us why our lives are the way they are and how they got that way. So we are about to embark on a journey that began long ago. Socrates, Plato, and Aristotle are historical philosophers considered to be the forefathers of ethics and morality by many, which by the way is still referred to and used today.

Life and the societies were much different then. The conveniences and modern modes of communications of today were nonexistent, yet there was a universal thread of community among the people of the time. Socrates, Plato, and Aristotle are sometimes referred to as "the big three," and they were fans of critical thinking. In other words, identify the issue, gather all of the information, make the best decision or solution, and be ready to defend that decision.

Socrates said, "Not life, but good life, is to be chiefly valued." He also believed "that life is not worth living if it goes unexamined." Life today is so fast-paced that many of us don't take time to contemplate our world. We have immediate worldwide information at our fingertips: if something happens thousands of miles away, we know about it instantly; as a result, our lives are more complex and subject to change on short notice.

Back in the day, much of our time was spent hunting and gathering food and water, preparing the food, and working hard to make a warm and secure home. Socrates was just simply referring that life should be examined and thought about thoroughly before, during, and after any actions. The big three believed that society must examine and inquire into our daily thoughts and how those ideas related to the common good of people and society. This thought process is not that much different than the modern-day philosophers or ethicists, such as Immanuel Kant. Kant said, "Two things fill the mind with ever new and increasing wonder and awe—the starry heavens above me and the moral law within me." Albert Einstein was quoted saying, "try not to become a man of success, but rather try to become a man of value." From more recent history, Martin Luther King Jr. said, "The ultimate measure of a man is not where he stands in moments of comfort and convenience, but where he stands at times of challenge and controversy." As we take a closer look at these three quotes, we can see the significance of their thoughts; they were profound then and are still today. There are many wise philosophers and ethicists in our history. We will study only a few of those to get a better idea of the significance of ethics and morals in our societies—past, present, and future. We will start with Socrates, Plato, and Aristotle and the birth of ethics.

SOCRATES

The unexamined life is not worth living.

—Socrates

Not life, but good life, is to be chiefly valued.

—Socrates

The philosopher Socrates was born in 469 BC and died in 399 BC. He is considered one of the most important philosophers of all time and the first Greek philosopher to concentrate on ethics. He followed his father's profession and was a stonemason.

His approach to philosophy is known as the Socratic method. It is interesting to note that Socrates never reduced to writing any of his thoughts. Because of this, much of his life's work is disputed. Socrates' thoughts are alive today because of the writings of Plato and Aristotle.[3]

Plato was a student of Socrates and is generally accepted as the most reliable source. His trial and death at the hands of the Athenian democracy is nonetheless the founding myth of the academic discipline of philosophy. His influence has been felt far beyond philosophy itself. Socrates basically believed that we should do our own thinking and question ourselves. He once said, "I know you won't believe me, but the highest form of human excellence is to question one's self and others."

Many were impressed with him, and yet, many found him, his personality, his behavior, and his views and methods strange He helped others recognize on their own what is real, true, and good. This was a new concept and approach to education for its era. Not everyone liked to be challenged by Socrates. This was a busy and advanced civilization for its time. He was known for confusing people by the way he structured his conversations. Perhaps Benjamin Franklin said it best, "I found the Socratic method the safest for myself and very embarrassing to those against whom I used it; therefore, I took delight in it, practiced it continually, and grew very artful and expert in drawing people, even of superior knowledge, into concessions, the consequences of which they did not foresee, entangling them in difficulties out of which they could not extricate themselves, and so obtaining victories that neither myself nor my cause always deserved." This quote fully describes Socrates' unique ability to make his conversationalists think about what they were thinking or saying or eventually drive them to frustration. Socrates appeared to have a higher opinion of women than his colleagues during that time in history. He spoke to everyone: men, women, young, old, rich and poor. Socrates could be found in the marketplace and other public areas conversing with a variety of different people. He would talk with virtually anyone he could to try and persuade people to join with him in his quest to get the answers to important questions. Socrates' lifework consisted of examining his and others lives as he believed that

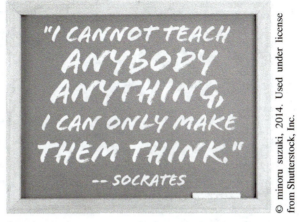

Socrates-quote.

"the unexamined life is not worth living for a human being." Socrates pursued this task single-mindedly, questioning people about what matters most as examples on how to groom, love, respect, moderations, and the state of their soul. He did this regardless of whether they wanted to be questioned or not; and Athenian youths imitated Socrates' questioning style, much to the annoyance of some parents. He had a reputation for sarcasm and said that "he knew nothing of importance and wanted to listen to others," yet keeping the upper hand in every discussion. Politically, he did not align himself with oligarchs (rule by the few) or democrats; he had friends and enemies among both, and he supported and opposed actions of both.

The Socratic method, which is an examination of moral concepts of good and justice, is still used today. To solve a problem, it would be broken down into a series of questions, the answers to which would gradually arrive at the solution. This approach most closely resembles today's scientific method, in which a hypothesis is the first stage. The development and practice of this method is one of Socrates' most permanent contributions and a key factor in earning his place as the father of ethics or moral philosophy, political philosophy, and as a vital figure within Western philosophy. To this day, the Socratic method is still used in classrooms and schools of law as a way of discussing complex topics to expose the underlying issues.

The Socratic paradoxes are as follows: no one desires evil, no one does wrong willingly or knowingly, virtue—all virtue—is knowledge, and virtue is sufficient for happiness. Some believe that these conflict with common sense. A famous Socrates quote: "I know that I know nothing." He often said his wisdom was limited to an awareness of his own ignorance. He believed bad behavior was a consequence of ignorance and those who did wrong knew no better. He never actually claimed to be wise, only to understand wisdom.

Socrates believed the best way for people to live was to focus on self-development rather than the pursuit of material wealth, and he always invited others to try to concentrate more on friendships and a sense of true community because Socrates felt this was the best way for people to grow together as a populace. His actions lived up to this; in the end, Socrates accepted his death sentence when most thought he would simply leave Athens because he felt he could not run away from or go against the will

© Georgios Kollidas, 2014. Used under license from Shutterstock, Inc.

Socrates drinking the Conium

of his community. At seventy years of age, he was found guilty by a jury of five hundred of corrupting the minds of the youth of Athens and interfering with the religion of the city. The trial which took approximately ten hours was held in the people's court of Athens. The jury consisted of five hundred male citizens chosen from volunteers. The jurors received payment for their service of three obols. The prosecution presented their case first in three hours, measured by a water clock. No record of the prosecution's argument against Socrates survives.[4]

Following the prosecution's case, Socrates had three hours to answer the charges. At his trial, he was alleged to have given the following speech in his own defense:

I shall never stop practicing philosophy and exhorting you and elucidating the truth for everyone that I meet. I shall go on saying . . . Are you not ashamed that you give your attention to acquiring as much money as possible and similarly standing and the perfection of your soul? And if any of you disputes this . . . I shall question him and examine him and test him . . . I shall do this to everyone I meet.

The five hundred jurors voted on his guilt or innocence by dropping bronze ballot disks into marked urns. Socrates was found guilty on a relatively close vote of 280–220. The jury voted for the prosecutions' proposal of death by a larger margin of 360–140.[5]

He was sentenced to death and died drinking a mixture containing the poison hemlock. Socrates' morals and ethics were so high he accepted this outcome with remarkable grace. He drank the hemlock and died in the company of his friends and disciples.

Having served with distinction as a soldier at Delium and Amphipolis during the Peloponnesian War, his reputation for valor on the battlefield by many was without criticism. It appears his life ended in a similar way with grace and honor.

PLATO

A hero is born among a hundred, a wise man is found among a thousand, but an accomplished one might not be found even among a hundred thousand men—Plato was a historical Greek philosopher, writer, and mathematician. He founded the Academy of Philosophy in Athens in 388 BCE, the first institution of high learning in the Western world, which lasted over nine hundred years. Plato's academy was not like the universities that we are familiar with today. It did not have organized classrooms and degrees. Instead, it was a place to exchange ideas with fellow intellectuals and Plato. He was born in 427 BC and died in 347 BC, and is considered one of the three forefathers of Western philosophy. His birthplace and time are not exactly known; however, it is believed he belonged to an aristocratic, wealthy, and influential family. It is generally believed he was born in Athens. As a boy, Plato was praised for his hard work, the love for study, shrewdness, and modesty. It is also generally accepted that Plato was instructed by highly regarded teachers in grammar, music, and gymnastics.

Plato was a student of Socrates and is considered one of the leading trustworthy sources for his mentor's life. Plato became a student of Socrates in his early years and was influenced by the philosophies of Socrates. Plato also taught the character-based ethics in which people should pursue virtue and happiness. After his mentor's death, it is believed that Plato traveled to Sicily, Italy, and Egypt, teaching and advising. It is generally accepted that Plato was twenty-eight when Socrates was put to death in 399 BC. Although many written versions of the defense at the trial of Socrates circulated, only two have survived, one by Plato.

He returned to Athens many years later—that is, when he founded and organized the Academy (academic), which operated until AD 529. Plato was a sophisticated writer and also lectured, studied, and wrote while at the Academy. The Academy was closed in 529 CE by the Roman emperor Justinian, because of the advent of Christianity after having had been in operation for over eight hundred years. Plato, of course, employed the Socratic style of thinking through mathematical learning and to achieve the philosophical truth. Plato taught four cardinal virtues: justice, wisdom, courage, and self-control. His teachings included subjects such as philosophy, mathematics, logic, and rhetoric (expression—public speaking). It is generally accepted that Plato's writings included thirty-five dialogues and thirteen letters. These written dialogues are still referenced today and were his ongoing life's work at the Academy. Some of his writings continued the Socratic idea that "no one knowingly does wrong," but then later asks the question "can virtue be taught?" Perhaps, one of his most famous writings is *The Republic*. It begins with a Socratic conversation about the nature of justice and then proceeds to the discussion of virtues of justice, wisdom, courage, and self-control. The idea of combining these virtues in people would then create the ideal society. The knowledge and educational programs taught at his Academy to both men and women alike would be a powerful educational tool to make this "ideal society." The dialogue later concludes that philosophers are the only fit citizens to rule such an ideal state. The philosophers are the only ones who truly understand the virtues of justice, wisdom, courage, and self-control. According to Plato, a state/government that is made up of different kinds of souls will decline overall from the aristocracy (an hereditary ruling class), to a timocracy (a state being governed by honor and military glory), then to an oligarchy (government by a few, a small group or class), then to a democracy (government by the people or elected representatives), and finally to tyranny (a single leader has absolute power).

Plato's "ideal society" was an interesting concept that promotes women in government and then "eugenics". Eugenics, according to the dictionary, is "a science that deals with the improvement (as by control of human mating) of hereditary qualities of a race or breed.[6]

Plato's later writings changed and often modified or completely abandoned the formal structure of the dialogue. It should be said the exact order of Plato's

© Algol/Shutterstock, Inc.

Ruined City of Atlantis

dialogues are not known; however, it is generally accepted *The Republic* was written in Plato's middle period.

Plato is considered by many philosophers to be one of the most influential authors of philosophy. His works regarding political events, intellectual movements of his time, and perhaps the questions he raised are rich and challenging even in regards to today's ethics. Plato is considered to have conceived a thorough and organized examination of ethical, political, metaphysical, and epistemological issues armed with a distinctive technique; this is considered to be his invention and legacy. Few authors in the history of philosophy are comparable: Aristotle and Immanuel Kant are generally agreed to be two of them.[7]

Plato also, in his writings, refers to platonic love, which means involving in friendship, affection, or love without sexual relations between people who might be expected to be sexually attracted to each other. Plato is also credited with the famous Greek mythology of Atlantis, an idyllic island that sank below the sea in an earthquake. These writings are in the dialogue called *Timaeus*.

Plato's influence has been especially strong in mathematics and the sciences. He helped distinguish between pure and applied mathematics by widening the gap between arithmetic, now called number theory and logistic. He regarded logistic as proper for businessmen and men of war who "must learn the art of numbers or he will not know how to array his troops."[8]

ARISTOTLE

We are not concerned to know what goodness is, but how we are to become good men, for this alone gives the study (of ethics) its practical value.

—Aristotle

Aristotle was born in northern Greece in 384 BC and died in 322 BC. He was a student of Plato at the Academy. Plato's thought is often compared to his most famous student, Aristotle. After his father died in 367 BC, Aristotle migrated to Athens, where he joined the Academy of Plato; he was seventeen at the time. He remained at the Academy for twenty years as a student and colleague of Plato.

Aristotle had a vast intellectual range that included the arts, biology, botany, chemistry, ethics, history, logic, metaphysics, rhetoric, and philosophy of mind, philosophy of science, physics, poetics, political theory, psychology, and zoology. He was the founder of formal logic, devising for it a finished system that for centuries was regarded as the sum of discipline, and he pioneered the study of zoology, both observational and theoretical, in which some of his work remained unsurpassed until the nineteenth century. But he is, of course, most outstanding as a philosopher. His writings in ethics and political theory as well as in metaphysics and the philosophy of science continue to be studied, and his work remains a powerful current in contemporary philosophical debate. Aristotle is considered by many to be the most intelligent person who ever lived.

Aristotle was the first professor to organize his lectures into courses and to assign them a place in a syllabus. His lyceum was the first research institute in which a number of scholars and investigators joined in collaborative inquiry and documentation. Finally, and not least important, he was the first person in history to build up a research library, which was a systematic collection of the works to be used by his colleagues and to be handed on to posterity.

The scope of Aristotle's scientific research was amazing, much of it concerned with the classification of animals into genus and species: more than five hundred species in his writings, many of them described in detail. The myriad items of information about the anatomy, diet, habitat, modes of copulation, and reproductive systems of mammals, reptiles, fish, and insects are part of his investigation. In some cases, his unlikely stories about rare species of fish were proved accurate many centuries later. In other places, he states clearly and fairly biological problems that took millennia to solve, such as the nature of embryonic development.

Aristotle believed that all human beings are born with the potential to become ethically virtuous and practically wise. To achieve these goals, they must go through two stages: (a) develop proper habits during childhood and (b) combine ethical virtue with practical wisdom once reason is fully developed. He believed that every ethical virtue is an intermediate condition between excess and deficiency. For example, fear isn't bad in and of itself; it's just bad when felt to excess or deficiency. A courageous person judges that some dangers are worth facing while others are not—the levels of fear are appropriate to the circumstances. The coward flees at every danger, although the circumstances may not merit it. The foolhardy person disregards all fear and dives into every danger regardless of the consequences. Aristotle identifies the virtue as being "the mean of the situation." Thus, there is no way to form a strict set of rules that would solve every practical problem. "The virtuous person sees the truth in each case, being as it were a standard measure of them." He sets certain emotions, such as hate, envy, jealousy, spite, and certain actions, such as adultery, theft, murder, as always being wrong regardless of the situation or the circumstances.

Depending on the level to which a person is able to use reason, they may fall into one of four categories: (a) virtuous, those who truly enjoyed doing what is right and do so without moral dilemma; (b) continent, does the virtuous thing most of the time, but must overcome conflict; (c) incontinent, faces the same moral conflict, but usually chooses the vicious thing; and (d) vicious, sees little value in virtue and does not attempt it.

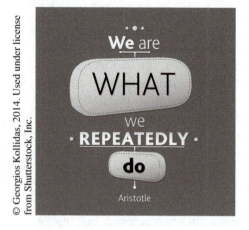

According to Aristotle, it is through the repeated performance of good actions that we become moral and, in turn, happier. He referred to the repeated practice of moral actions as habituation. Practice makes perfect.

Aristotle on learning, "What we have to learn to do, we learn by doing." Aristotle on morals, "The moral virtues, then, are produced in us neither by nature nor against nature. Nature, indeed, prepares in us the ground for their reception, but their complete formation is the product of habit."

Aristotle wrote "virtue discovers the means and deliberately chooses it." By living according to the doctrine of the mean, Aristotle believed that we can find the greatest happiness. Here are some examples of extreme behavior which coincides with the doctrine of the mean, which will be discussed in further detail in chapter 3, the section on ethical theory.

Firefighters arrive on the scene of a structure fire and they don all appropriate safety gear and enter the burning building with a fellow firefighter who has a hose line in place. This is an example of proper virtue of courage. The deficit vice or cowardice example would be that a firefighter is unable to enter the burning building because of fear. The excessive example would be the entering of the burning building without appropriate safety gear, without a hose line, and without firefighter backup. This firefighter is a danger to him or her and others as well. While it would be a great scene in a movie, it makes no sense in real life.

> A police officer arrives at a reported bank robbery and takes all of the appropriate safety precautions, waits for backup, and gathers all of the available intelligence about the situation before entering the bank. This, of course, would be the proper procedure. Another officer sets up a command post four blocks away and therefore is unable to gather any information to guide backup. This, of course, is deficit planning and could likely end up in someone getting injured or worse. It would be irresponsible to just enter the bank with guns blazing. Again, it would be a great scene in the movies, but not realistic.

Aristotle believed that society, friends, and family would be healthier if we were taught the virtues of friendliness, sympathy, compassion, and honesty, for without these we would alienate each other.

Even though Aristotle wrote approximately 2,335 years ago, his thoughts are very timely. What is interesting is that the human race really hasn't progressed in all of this time. If we look at the world in 2014, we have not learned what Aristotle believed we needed in order to survive.

If we just glance at the news on any given day, we can see examples of people, governments, and countries not observing the virtues that Aristotle believed necessary. In Syria, people are fighting and killing each other on a daily basis; in the United States, people of different races and ethnicities are complaining because one group is not appreciative of the other; a surfing contest turns into a riot; and young people are running around a town in Southern California (Huntington Beach), turning over portable toilets and laughing. Politicians are harassing women and others sexually. Anthony Weiner, a former congressman and candidate for mayor of New York City, has a compulsion for showing his "junk" via sexting.* In 2013, the mayor of San Diego, Bob Filner, was asked to resign because numerous women have come forward alleging improprieties. In Iraq, Muslims of different sects are killing each other on a daily basis.

JOHN LOCKE

> The state of nature has a law of nature to govern it . . . that being all equal and independent, no one ought to harm another in his life, health, liberty, or possession . . . And that all men may be restrained from invading others' rights . . .
>
> —John Locke

John Locke was an English philosopher, politician, and educator, born in England in 1632. He died in 1704. Locke was raised in a liberal Puritan family and remained religious throughout his life.[9]

He did not marry or have children, and his lifework pursued equal rights. His writings on religion, education, and civil government were popular. Locke believed the people should resist a government that denies natural rights, and which misuses its power. Government arises from a social contract among the people and that the people have equal rights, also known as "rights ethics." Rights ethics, deontology, and utilitarianism will be discussed further in chapter 3. These natural rights are what we know as democracy. Remember, Locke lived during a time under the king's rule. He also believed that the mind started with a blank piece of paper and said that people are born without natural thoughts and that knowledge is gained only by life's experience, which included education. The events that occurred during Locke's lifetime include the English Restoration, the Great Plague of London, and the Great Fire of London.

Locke's ethics are deeply seated in the politics of the United States. He stated, "The criterion of moral actions is a man's well-being, for experience teaches that man tends to pleasure and flees from pain." His writings influenced early American revolutionaries like Thomas Jefferson and Benjamin Franklin. This influence is reflected in the US Declaration of Independence July 4, 1776. "We hold these truths to be self-evident, that all men are created equal, that they are endowed by their

John Locke (1832–1704) engraving

© icku, 2014. Used under license from Shutterstock, Inc.

*His resignation was in 2011 due to a sexting scandal.

Creator with certain inalienable Rights, that among these are Life, Liberty, and the Pursuit of Happiness."

IMMANUEL KANT

Although we may be entirely within our rights, according to the laws of the land and the rules of our social structure, we may nevertheless be participating in general injustice, and in giving to an unfortunate man we do not give him a gratuity but only help to return him that of which the general injustice of our system has deprived him.

—Immanuel Kant

© rticknor, 2014. Used under license from Shutterstock, Inc.

Immanuel Kant.

Kant was an eighteenth-century German philosopher who was born in Prussia in 1724; he died in 1804. He was one of the last significant philosophers of modern Europe in the traditional progression of the theory of knowledge during the Enlightenment. Kant created a new widespread point of view in philosophy, which is still used today. He came from a large Lutheran family, one of nine children. He had poor health and was five feet tall, which might explain his good humor, playful, and entertaining character. All of this served him well while lecturing at a local university for many years on such topics as physical geography and metaphysics. During his time as a professor, he gained notoriety regarding moral duty. People came from near and far to discuss important issues, including the lawfulness of vaccinations. Sound familiar? His important works on epistemology as well as religion, law, and history are relevant in the twenty-first century. Kant pursued metaphysics, which involves asking questions about the ultimate nature of reality. He suggested that metaphysics can be improved through the study of knowledge. Thereby understanding life's experience of human knowledge, we can ask ourselves questions. He asked, "If an object can be known to have certain properties prior to the experience of that object?" Kant believed in cause and effect. That the mind cannot just store the data/input (life experience) but rather have some interpretation, computation, and arrangement to get data/output.

Good input, good output; bad input, bad output. Like Aristotle, Kant believed that most people already know right from wrong. He believed in moral law, and asked this question, "What gives morality or ought to quality?"[10] The difficulty is doing the right thing all of the time. This was Kant's life's work, discussing in great detail the fundamental principles of the metaphysics of ethics and the foundation of morality.

JEREMY BENTHAM

Nature has placed mankind under the governance of two sovereign masters, pain and pleasure. It is for them alone to point out what we ought to do.
—Jeremy Bentham

Bentham was an English political reformer, jurist, and philosopher. He was born in 1748 and died in 1832. He promoted utilitarianism primarily as a tool of social reform. The eighteenth century had a sudden change in population and growth in Western society. There was a shift from agricultural to commercial and industrial societies. The cities developed into industrial centers, creating many jobs and, for some, not all, a better life. This change also increased the workforce, which led to child labor, and poverty among classes of the working people, as well as the creation of urban slums. Bentham's theory was more about happiness for the working people. He did believe if the people were happy, then the government would be happy and that social ideals grew from the bottom up, and not the other way around. This concept was in response to the start of the industrial revolution and the inequalities that existed as a result of that change. Bentham formulated an ethical theory and the principle of utility as a single simple rule: utilitarianism. "Act so as to produce the greatest good for the greatest number." He also said, "That property in any object whereby it tends to produce pleasure, good or happiness, or to prevent the happening of mischief, pain, evil or unhappiness to the party whose interest is considered." "Mankind," he said, "was governed by two sovereign motives, pain and pleasure; and the principle of utility recognized this state of affairs. The object of all legislation must be the greatest happiness of the greatest number." "All punishment involves pain and is therefore evil." Bentham used utilitarianism to help reform the criminal justice system. He did not agree with the punishment just for the sake of punishment of those incarcerated. For Bentham, the punishment had to have utility. He believed in reform and rehabilitation. His influence shows today in our prison system.[11]

JOHN STUART MILL

Whether happiness be or be not the end to which morality should be referred—that it be referred to as an end of some sort, and not left in the dominion of vague feeling or inexplicable internal convictions, that it be made a matter of reason and calculation, and not merely sentiment, is essential to the very idea of moral philosophy.
—John Stuart Mill

Mill was an English philosopher, a political theorist, a political economist, a civil servant, and a Member of Parliament. John Stuart Mill (1806–1873) was born two years after Kant died. He was influenced by his father, James Mill, and Bentham, who was a close family friend. Aristotle focused on virtue, Kant on duty, and Mill on utility. The scientific method of utilitarianism was his contribution to modern philosophy. In his view, ethical decision making results in the most good or happiness, whereas unethical decisions are not good and do not create happiness. Mill was a liberal thinker of his time whose work on liberty justified freedom of the individual and in opposition to unlimited state control. He wrote . . . the only purpose for which power can be rightfully exercised over any member of a civilized community, against his will, is to prevent harm to others. His own good, either physical or moral, is not a sufficient warrant . . . . Over himself, over his own body and mind, the individual is sovereign.[12]

His education began with the study of Greek at the age of three. He worked for the East India Company for over thirty years as did his father. In 1858, Mill became a Member of Parliament and remained there for ten years. He was an advocate of freedom of thought and expression. Mill believed in women's rights, reform, and free trade. He argued that some pleasures are more desirable than others. Human life is better than nonhuman life. Like Aristotle, he believed that intellectual pleasures, which engaged the mind, are superior to those of any other. Mill said that we seek more pleasure and avoid pain. However, if we only chase happiness as our goal in life, then that pursuit will not make us happy either. Pleasure itself is not the only criterion for judging the morality of an action. The aspect of human life that philosophers associate with human dignity or integrity is morally good, independent of the quantity of pleasure. The freedom to make our own decisions is the basis of happiness. A society that protects people's liberty and self-rule provides the best conditions for happiness to thrive. The best way to ensure happiness is to respect other people's liberty and the right to make their own moral choices. Query: Could adhering to this philosophy be problematic for a society?

John Stuart Mill died in 1873 due to complications from tuberculosis and fever.[13]

ETHICS IN RELIGION

> When I do good, I feel good; when I do bad, I feel bad, and that is my religion.
>
> > —Abraham Lincoln, sixteenth president of the United States.

> Humility: Imitate Jesus and Socrates.
>
> > —Benjamin Franklin

> Man is a religious animal. He is the only religious animal. He is the only animal that has the True Religion—several of them.
>
> > —Mark Twain

Most religions have an ethical or moral component: no killing, no stealing, no lying, no adultery, honor parents, honor a special day, and be kind to others. Moral doctrines have been central to religion. All of the great religions prescribe obedience to the Golden Rule, and all set forth many other instructions about the way people should live and the kinds of characteristics folks should hold. Haven't we all heard "Do unto others as you would have them do unto you"? The Golden Rule or the ethic of reciprocity is found in the scriptures of nearly every religion. It is often regarded as the most concise and general principle of ethics. Here are the world religion examples of the Golden Rule.[14]

- **Buddhism:** Comparing oneself to others in such terms as "Just as I am so are they, just as they are so am I" and "he should neither kill nor cause others to kill."
- **Christianity:** Whatever you wish that men would do to you, do so to them.
- **Confucianism:** Try your best to treat others as you would wish to be treated yourself, and you will find that this is the shortest way to benevolence.

- **Hinduism:** One should not behave toward others in a way that is disagreeable to oneself. This is the essence of morality. All other activities are due to selfish desire.
- **Islam:** Not one of you is a believer until he loves for his brother what he loves for himself.
- **Judaism:** You shall love your neighbor as yourself.

We will investigate a few of the most prevalent world religions and look at their laws. You may be surprised at the similarities and differences and the inclusion of ethics and morals.

Buddhism

It is a man's own mind, not his enemy or foe that lures him to evil ways.

—Buddha

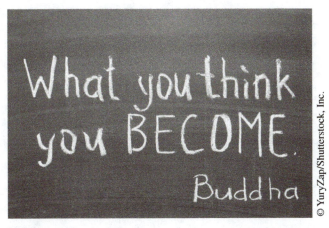

Buddha

Unfortunately, little is known of the life of Gautama Siddhartha, the founder of Buddhism. He was born around 563 BC. Ethics in Buddhism is traditionally based on the enlightened perspective of the Buddha or other enlightened beings who followed him. The *Dhammapada,* a popular ethical text, states, "Abstention from sin, doing good works, and purifying one's mind, this is the teaching of Buddhism," and "One does not repay evil with evil, but one repays evil with good work." The way of Gautama Buddha is called the middle path because it avoids the extremes. For example, Buddhist ethics denounce the extremes of excessive indulgence and self-mortification or self-denial. The fundamental principle of Buddhist ethics is that all men should develop an attitude of compassion, a very esteemed virtue in Buddhism.

According to traditional Buddhism, the foundation of Buddhist ethics is the *Pancasila*: no killing, stealing, lying, sexual misconduct, or intoxicants. In becoming a Buddhist, one is encouraged to vow to abstain from these negative actions. Buddhist monks and nuns take hundreds more such vows. Loving kindness, compassion, sympathetic joy, and equanimity are the four attitudes called the "immeasurable."[15] The Buddhism virtue of ahimsa also calls us to expand the moral community to include respect for all living beings. Buddhists believe practicing good actions is more important than studying theory of good actions.

Christianity

Christian ethical principles are based on the teachings within the Holy Bible. The thought of Christians is fairly unanimous on people's inherent sinfulness. Personal ethics are meant to avoid or correct sin. Specific ethical and

"We only have a few rules around here, but we really enforce them."

© Cartoonresource/Shutterstock, Inc.

moral behaviors originate in the Old Testament's Ten Commandments, teachings in Psalms, and the laws given by God. The Bible is not just one book but an accumulation of many books. It is a recording of biography, drama, history, philosophy, poetry, prophecy, science, and inspirational reading. Christians believe the Bible is the greatest book ever written. In it, God himself speaks to mankind. It is a book of divine instruction. It offers comfort in sorrow, guidance in confusion, advice for our problems, forgiveness for our sins, and daily inspiration for our everyday need. The great theme of the Bible is the Messiah and Lord, Jesus Christ, and his everlasting work for mankind.

The Ten Commandments

1. Trust God only.
2. Worship God only.
3. Use God's name in ways that honor him.
4. Rest on the Sabbath day and think about God.
5. Respect and obey your parents.
6. Protect and respect human life.
7. Be true to your husband or wife.
8. Do not take what belongs to others.
9. Do not lie about others.
10. Be satisfied with what you have.

Matthew 5:43–48
You have heard that it was said, you shall love your neighbor and hate your enemy. But I say to you, love your enemies and bless those who curse you, do good to those who hate you, and pray for those who spitefully use you and persecute you, that you may be sons of your father in heaven; for he makes his sun rise on the evil and on the good, and sends rain on the just and on the unjust. For if you love those who love you what reward have you? Do not even the tax collectors do the same? And yes, if you greet your Brethren only, what do you do more than others? Do not even the tax collectors do so? Therefore you shall be (morally) perfect, just as your father in heaven is perfect.[16]

Confucianism

> To know what is right and not to do it is the worst cowardice.
>
> —Confucius

Said to be the first professional teacher in China, Confucius was mostly self-educated. He was born in 551 BC and died in 470 BC. Because of his outspokenness about the proper conduct of rulers, he had to give up his dream of becoming a government official and settled for being a teacher. In Confucianism, *yi,* or righteousness, demands that we do what is right because it is our moral duty. According to both Confucius and Aristotle, ignorance and malice are always vices, and wisdom is always a virtue. Confucius pointed out that we must start from the nearest point. That point will be different for all. Confucius believed that the ideal ruler "acts like the North Star, staying in place while the other stars orbit around it." He leads by example. Confucianism has been synonymous with learning in China and has been regarded as a religion by some. Every one of the two thousand counties of China built a temple to Confucius, and the Confucian code of conduct was ideally the norm according to which every individual led his life. Confucius stressed such qualities as virtue and righteousness. He said

Confucius statue

© arindambanerjee, 2014. Used under license from Shutterstock, Inc.

the superior man is concerned with virtue; the inferior man is concerned with land. The superior man understands what is right; the inferior man understands what is profitable.

Most virtues entail finding the mean between excess and deficiency. Some people take virtues to an extreme and then they become a vice.

Aristotle and Confucius both believed we can find the greatest happiness and inner harmony. Aristotle's practical advice was "(1) keep away from that extreme which is more opposed to the mean, (2) note the errors into which we personally are most liable to fall, (3) and always be particularly on your guard against pleasure and pleasant things." Aristotle's doctrine of the mean will be discussed more in chapter 3.[17]

Hinduism

Hinduism is proclaimed to be the oldest of all religions and is the third largest in the world. Primarily located in India, Hinduism is not exactly known, and there is no single scripture or prophet. Spiritual leaders are known as gurus or sages, and the purpose of life is to obtain liberation from the cycle of reincarnation. Hindu scriptures refer to celestial entities or the deities as devas (gods) and devis (goddesses). Most Hindus believe that the spirit or soul which is referred to as the "true self" is of every person and is eternal.[18] God in Hinduism is the Supreme Being, which is everywhere and everything and has no form, shape, or gender. The three debts are to gods, gurus/sages, and ancestors. There are three paths to be followed: path of work and action, path of knowledge, and path of devotion to God. There are four stages of life: (1) grow and learn; (2) take care of marriage, family, and career; (3) seek spiritual things; and (4) abandon worldly things. The four purposes of life are (1) fulfilling social, moral, and religious duties; (2) attain financial and worldly success; (3) satisfy desires to God; and (4) attain freedom from rebirth.

The ten basic tenets of Hinduism are:

- *Satya*—follow truth, do not lie.
- *Ahimsa*—follow nonviolence.
- *Brahmacharya*—do not over-indulge.
- *Asteya*—do not steal, do not possess.
- *Aparigraha*—non-corrupt.
- *Shaucha*—be clean.
- *Santosha*—be content
- *Tapas*—be self-disciplined.
- *Svadhyaya*—learn the scriptures.
- Ishvara Pranidhana—surrender to God.

Hinduism believes in karma and the law of cause and effect by which each individual creates his or her own destiny by his or her own thoughts, words, and deeds. Hindus believe that all life is sacred and pure and is to be loved and respected. They believe that the soul reincarnates through many births until it attains moksha, which is the liberation from cycles of birth and rebirth.[19]

Islamic

Founded in Arabia in seventh century AD from the teachings of the Prophet Mohammed, Islam focuses on the rigid monotheism (one God) and strict adherence to certain religious practices. There are many sects and movements however. All followers are bound by a common faith and sense of belonging to a single community; although, in reality, the members of the different sects of Islam kill each other on a regular basis. There is an Arabic term that points to the fundamental religious idea of Islam, namely that the believer, called a Muslim, accepts "surrender" to the will of Allah. Allah is the God, Creator, Sustainer, and Restorer of the world. The Islamic scriptures are in a book called the Qur'an. The Five Pillars are five daily prayers, a welfare tax called the *Zakat,* fasting, pilgrimage to Mecca, and profession of faith. These are to be strictly observed and followed. Allah is one God and unique; he has no partner and no equal. In the Christian belief, God is three entities: Father, Son, and the Holy Spirit. Muslims believe there are no intermediaries between God and the creation that he brought into being by his sheer command. God's presence is everywhere; he is the sole creator and sustainer of the universe. He is just and merciful, his justice ensures order in his creation, and nothing is believed to be out of place and his mercy in unbounded and encompasses everything. God is viewed as being close to man, and whenever a man is in need or distressed, he calls upon him and God responds. Above all, God is guidance to man, and shows everything, particularly the right way, "the straight path." Prophets are men specially elected by God to be his messengers. The Qur'an requires recognition of all prophets as such without discrimination. Abraham, Noah, Moses, Jesus, and Mohammed were such great prophets. These prophets all had missions from God. Abraham was saved from fire, Noah from the great floods, Moses from the Pharaoh, and Jesus from the crucifixion. Mohammed is accepted as the last prophet and its greatest member. For in him, all the messages of the previous prophets were consummated. He had no miracles except the Qur'an, which no human can produce. The Qur'an describes itself as the transcript of a heavenly "mother book" written on a preserved tablet.[20]

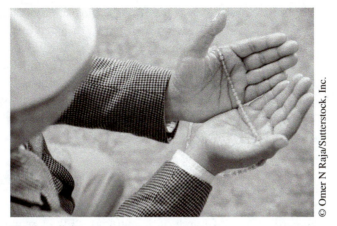

Muslim religion praying

Judaism

Judaism, also referred to as the Jewish religion, is four thousand years old and claims to be the oldest religion. The history of the Hebrews and the Jews has certainly been a challenging one throughout the centuries. The fundamental teachings of the Jewish religion are grouped around the concept of an ethical monotheism, belief in one and only God of Israel. God is all-powerful, all-knowing, and is in all places at all times. The Lord God is also just and merciful. God created man to have freewill and to be responsible for the choices they make. The Prophet Moses accepted the Ten Commandments from God on Mount Sinai, and they are the law, which regulates how man worships God and how they treat each other. The Jewish Ten Commandments are:

Star of David.

1. I am the Lord your God.
2. You shall not recognize the gods of others in my presence.
3. You shall not take the name of the Lord your God in vain.
4. Remember the day of Shabbat to keep it holy.
5. Honor your father and your mother.
6. You shall not murder.
7. You shall not commit adultery.
8. You shall not steal.
9. Do not give false testimony against your neighbor.
10. You shall not covet your fellow's possessions.

The holy book, known as the Torah, is the primary document for Judaism. The title of the book means "teaching" of God's revealed instructions. The Jewish people learn how to act, think, and even feel about life and death. The stories teach about God's relationship with man and contain 613 commandments from God. The Ten Commandments are considered the most important. The Jews believe the Messiah will be a person from the family of King David, who will lead the world to unity and peace. The Jewish religion does not believe that Jesus was the Messiah.[21]

Scientology

> Never regret yesterday. Life is in you today, and you make your tomorrow.
> —L. Ron Hubbard

According to the Church of Scientology, "Ethics may be defined as the actions an individual takes on himself to ensure his continued survival across the dynamics. It is a personal thing. When one is ethical, it is something he does himself by his own choice."[22]

Scientology calls itself the "world's fastest growing religion." The founder of Scientology, L. Ron Hubbard (1911–1986), was raised in rural Montana. He traveled at an early age and loved exploration, and was a well-known author of science fiction stories and books. After the war, he devoted a considerable amount of time to understanding human condition and developed Dianetics, a rudimentary form of Scientology. Dianetics provided practical techniques to free the mind of dysfunctional aberrations. In 1950, his book *Dianetics: The Modern Science of Mental Health* became a best seller.

Unique among religious faiths, Scientology charges for virtually all of its religious services, as opposed to "freewill offerings." This has prompted many to question whether Scientology is a religion or a business.

Many Hollywood stars have publicly identified themselves as Scientologists. These celebrities include John Travolta, Kirstie Alley, Isaac Hayes, Catherine Bell, Chick Corea, Anne Archer, Priscilla Presley, and Jenna Elfman.[23] Probably, the most visible spokesperson is actor Tom Cruise. Cruise has been one of the top box office draws during the 1980s, 1990s, and into the early twenty-first century.

SUMMARY

Because of the advances in technology and science, our lives today are much different than in the past. The way we communicate, travel, work, and recreate has changed and is changing as we speak. Humans, however, have not changed that much. Throughout time, we have been trying to determine whether humans are born with the concept of right and wrong or do we have to learn this behavior. The ethical and moral issues of today and yesteryear are similar and yet different. Everyone has made good and bad decisions. We have to maximize the good ones and minimize the bad ones. We need to find out ways to always do the right thing. The question is how do we do this? Even the forefathers of ethics and morality (Socrates, Plato, and Aristotle) would have difficulties convincing people to do the right thing all of the time. Public safety officers must recognize the pitfalls that exist in their jobs and personal lives. They must learn to be virtuous persons who see the truth in each case. Their jobs, businesses, and religions have ethical and moral components. Remember the Golden Rule, which states, "Do unto others as you would have them do unto you."

NOTES

1. www.dictionary.com (accessed May 28, 2013).
2. Microsoft Encarta Dictionary, English, North American (accessed May 28, 2013).
3. C. C. W. Taylor, R. Hare, and J. Barnes, *Greek Philosophers: Socrates, Plato and Aristotle* (New York: Oxford University Press, 2001).
4. University of Missouri-Kansas City, Law School, "Criminal Procedure in Ancient Greece and the Trial of Socrates." www.law.umkec.edu/faculty/projects/trials/socrates/greekcrimpro.html (accessed October 21, 2009).
5. "Criminal Procedure in Ancient Greece and the Trial of Socrates." (accessed October 21, 2009).
6. Merriam-Webster's Collegiate Dictionary 10th edition. p. 399.
7. Stanford University. "Stanford Encyclopedia of Philosophy." www.stanford.edu (accessed July 8, 2013).
8. University of Tennessee-Martin, "Internet Encyclopedia of Philosophy." www.iep.utm.edu/greekphi (assessed January 24, 2010).
9. J. A. Boss. *Ethics for Life* (New York: McGraw-Hill Companies, Inc., 2004). p.47.
10. Boss, *Ethics for Life*. pp. 305–306.
11. University of Tennessee-Martin, "Internet Encyclopedia of Philosophy" www.iep.utm.edu/bentham (assessed January 24, 2010).
12. John Stuart Mill, *On Liberty* (Indianapolis, IN: Hackett, 1978). p. 5.
13. Boss, *Ethics for life*. pp. 278–279.
14. "World Scripture—The Golden Rule." www.unification.net /ws/theme015.htm (accessed September 6,2013).
15. *Encyclopedia Britannica* (New York: Benton, 1977).
16. *NIV, Life Application Study Bible* (Wheaton, IL: Tyndale House & Zondervan, 1983).
17. *Encyclopedia Britannica*. p. 1091–1092.
18. Buzzle.com, Hinduism Facts about Hindu Religion. www.buzzle.com/articles.hinduism-facts-about-hindu-religion.html (accessed January 30, 2010).
19. Y Go Hinduism, "Hinduism Facts." http://hinduism.ygoy.com/hinduism/facts.php (accessed January 31, 2010).
20. *Encyclopedia Britannica*. pp. 912–914.
21. About.Com, "Basic Beliefs of Judaism." http://judaism.about.com/od/abcsofjudaism/a/beliefsbasis.htm (accessed January 31, 2010).
22. www.scientology.org (accessed February 1, 2010).
23. "Scientology's Inner Self, An Expert's Look at this Little-Understood American Religion," *U.S. News & World Report* (2009). An Interview with J. Gordon Melton. pp. 46–49.

SCENARIO

The Socratic method involves questioning a person about things they thought they already knew. Give an example of something you thought you already knew and later found that, indeed, you did not.

_____

_____

_____

_____

_____

_____

_____

_____

_____

_____

_____

_____

_____

_____

_____

_____

_____

_____

_____

_____

_____

SCENARIO

Aristotle believed that practicing moral virtues and behavior is more important for ethics education than the study of moral theory. How have you practiced moral virtues that have made a difference in your moral development?

SCENARIO

We each have our own path, our own journey to self-awareness and knowledge. What is your path?

_____

_____

_____

_____

_____

_____

_____

_____

_____

_____

_____

_____

_____

_____

_____

_____

_____

_____

_____

_____

SCENARIO

Good ethics and morality can be a way of life, if practiced. Describe how you would incorporate this into your daily life. How can this help you with your pursuit as a public safety officer?

_____

_____

_____

_____

_____

_____

_____

_____

_____

_____

_____

_____

_____

_____

_____

_____

_____

_____

_____

SCENARIO

Give an example of a recent experience that you believed to be unethical. Why do you think the person did not make the best choice?

_____

_____

_____

_____

_____

_____

_____

_____

_____

_____

_____

_____

_____

_____

_____

_____

_____

_____

_____

_____

_____

Why We Study Ethics?

2

CHAPTER OBJECTIVES

1. Understand why ethics are important to public safety officers.
2. Become aware of the expectations of the community.
3. Understand the terms *discretion* and *judgment*
4. Become aware of the ramifications of unethical behavior.

© Aspen Photo, 2014. Used under license from Shutterstock, Inc.

MORGANTOWN, WV Game Officials meet prior to kick off.

Charlotte Bronte wrote in *Jane Eyre:* "Laws and Principles are not for the times when there is no temptation: they are for such moments as this, when body and soul rise in mutiny against their rigor . . . If at my convenience I might break them, what would be their worth?"

What Ms. Bronte says here is profound in that she questions the value of laws and principles if they are not adhered to on a regular basis by everyone, all of the time. Not just when it is beneficial. This quote should always reside in the minds of people who are in positions of trust.

The fact that we are having a conversation about ethics answers the question "Why study ethics?" We need to deal with each other in ways that will be equitable to everyone, and we don't believe that we can do it on our own without rules to ensure compliance. Now this may sound the least bit cynical, but we have laws, rules, contracts, and agreements to regulate most of our behavior. We can't even play games with each other without rules and referees to enforce those rules; if we form a club, we have rules and a sergeant at arms to make sure the members obey the rules. We demand contracts or covenants when entering into business or real estate deals. It seems we need ethics to protect ourselves from us and each other.

Ethics assist us in making decisions about our behavior. We have to learn how to do the right thing. We are always making ethical decisions whether we know it or not, especially in the public safety field. It could be a seemingly very simple thing such as using the police computer to obtain an address of a person for a friend. What's the harm you ask yourself? No one will know, but there is a department rule against using the computer for anything but police business. The whole thing seems harmless enough, but you know of the rule and it would be not only unethical to get the address, but illegal as well. Query: What would you do and what would you tell your friend?

Public safety officers make discretionary calls on a regular basis, and the decisions they make are open to public scrutiny and are many times second-guessed by the people they serve. Police officers, for instance, are bound by the Constitution of the United States to do certain things when questioning suspects or conducting searches to protect the people they interact with. Firefighters are bound by state and local laws when administering fire inspections of commercial and private property.

Ethics are important to public safety officers for numerous reasons.

1. Public safety officers are the people called when there is a problem. It could be a fire, someone is ill, or a crime has been committed. When people need assistance, trust is paramount. They trust you with their fears and disclose personal matters that they may not tell anyone else. An ethical responder will instill that trust.
2. Respect is an attribute that public safety officers need in order to do their job. If the citizenry respects its police and fire departments, they will tend to cooperate with those

agencies and make the job easier. Pragmatically speaking, if the community respects and trusts their public safety officers, it will report crimes, fire hazards, and other problematic situations.

Firefighters fighting fire.

© StockPhotosLV, 2014. Used under license from Shutterstock, Inc.

3. The community has certain expectations of its police and fire departments. It holds the officers and firefighters in higher esteem than it does others, including themselves at times. The community expects its public safety personnel to run toward the trouble while they run the other way. The citizens don't want to confront a group of menacing men standing on a corner, a stranger in our house, a home consumed by flames, or a victim who needs to be resuscitated. The public expects these same officers to be honest and above board and to solve problems in a fair and equitable manner. There have been cases in which convicted felons have complained that an officer was not "behaving like a cop" because he was behaving like a criminal. This illustrates that even criminals expect police officers to behave ethically.

4. Being an ethical public safety officer is "doing the right thing." Officers take an oath to protect life and property, to abide by and uphold the Constitution of the United States, and to serve the people in their jurisdiction. Public safety officers must do the right thing, for altruistic reasons as well as pragmatic reasons.

5. The altruistic rationale should not have to be explained. People should exhibit civility toward each other. Public safety officers should be one of the occupational groups to set the example. They are the professionals and should act accordingly. Others could include those in education and politics, but that is a discussion for another time.

6. A pragmatic reason to be ethical is that public safety officers need to be aware of their surroundings, and the fact that there are people out there who try to bait officers into improper behavior to fulfill an agenda that the officer may not be aware of. An example would be the altercation between Harvard professor Henry Louis Gates Jr. and Sgt. James Crowley of the Cambridge, Massachusetts, Police Department in July 2009. Sergeant Crowley responded to a call from a citizen who reported that two men appeared to be breaking into a house. Upon arrival at the scene, officer Crowley asked Mr. Gates to provide identification to prove he lived in the home. Gates called the sergeant a "rogue" cop and a "racist" and also made derogatory remarks about the officer's mother. President Barack Obama then went on to say that the police "acted stupidly" during the encounter according to the news media. Willie Brown, the former mayor of San Francisco, wrote in his column in the *San Francisco Chronicle* on July 26, 2009, that he knows Gates and that "He's a small person physically, less than 150 pounds, but he is very big when it comes to militancy." In other words, Gates has a hidden, or maybe not so hidden, agenda of race.[1]

Fortunately, Crowley is a principled officer with an excellent reputation. According to Denise Lavoie of the Associated Press, Crowley was handpicked by a black police commissioner to teach recruits about avoiding racial profiling.[2]

A Cambridge police commissioner said that Crowley was a decorated officer who followed procedure. "Sergeant Crowley is a stellar member of this department . . . I don't consider him a rogue cop in any way," Robert C. Haas said. You can see from this case that if you are an ethical officer and behave professionally, you will be protected from individuals who just might be bent on setting up an officer to further their own agenda.

When answering the question "why do we study ethics?" Braswell (1996/2002,8) noted that there are five goals of the study of ethics:

1. Become aware and open to ethical issues.
2. Begin developing critical thinking skills.
3. Become more personally responsible.
4. Understand how the criminal justice system is engaged in a process of coercion.
5. Develop *wholesight,* which roughly means exploring with one's heart as well as one's mind.

Wholesight dictates that we look at things not only cognitively but also emotionally. This means that we think not only about our actions but also how we feel about them. The important thing here is to remember to maintain a balance between thinking and emoting. It appears that whenever a public safety officer's emotions override his or her cognitive processes, he or she gets into trouble. We have to look at situations from a personal, a social, and a criminal justice process point of view in order to make a decision based on *whole sight.*

 ## WHAT THE PUBLIC EXPECTS FROM PUBLIC SAFETY

Public safety officers are public servants; this means that they work for the citizenry of whatever jurisdiction they are employed by. There are basically three levels of jurisdiction: federal, state, and local. There are federal fire and law enforcement agencies as well as the state and local. All of these public safety professionals work for the people; they are all financed by the taxpayers. The public not only pays the bills but also give their public safety officers power and let them use their discretion when doing their jobs. Because of this, the people deserve to have ethical employees doing their bidding. When asked, people say they want their public servants to be honest, to have integrity, to be brave, and to treat people fairly regardless of their financial status or ethnicity. They would like their officers to be polite, friendly, and helpful. They expect professionalism and for the officers to do the right thing. Police and fire departments do all that is possible to ensure that the men and women they hire are dedicated and people who want to provide services to the citizens in their jurisdiction. Most of the recruits for public safety careers are exactly that, but as time goes on, some may forget why they became cops and firefighters. It is important that public safety officers keep focused and remain on task. It is important to remain ethical because of the ramifications not only to individuals but also to our society as a whole. We will look at some specific cases in this chapter that will illustrate what can happen when public safety officers behave unethically.

DISCRETION/CRITICAL THINKING

Discretion is defined by Webster's dictionary as "[f]reedom or power to at or judge on one's own." Another word that is almost parallel to discretion is judgment, which is defined as "the ability to make a decision or form an opinion by discerning and evaluating."

Felkens (1987) wrote that "ethical considerations are central to decisions involving discretion, force, and due process which require people to make enlightened moral judgments." Police officers and firefighters are called upon daily to make decisions that affect peoples' lives; in fact, the lives of the people they work for. As they make these decisions, they make discretionary calls, and, in order to make the right moves, they need to exercise critical thinking. In other words, making ethical decisions and moral judgments requires critical thinking through all of the ramifications of an action.

The police have quite a bit of discretionary power:

1. They can deprive people of their freedom by arresting them.
2. They decide which people to investigate, especially when conducting undercover operations.
3. They determine who to ticket and who to let off with a warning or admonition.

This discretionary power should be wielded judiciously with a focus on a heightened sense of morality. It must be remembered that power requires a deepened sense of responsibility. This power is given to public safety officers by the people they serve to ensure public service and safety. The behavior of one officer can erode to the public's trust in the entire profession.

If police officers, politicians, and other public officials routinely engage in dishonesty, what point are we making on behalf of the general public about the importance of honesty?[3]

In the twenty-first century, we have already seen the problems of credibility as it pertains to politicians. Why? They have purposely deceived the public and, as a result, have lost the trust of many of their constituents. They have forgotten that power and discretion requires responsibility.

There has to be a fundamental procedure for making ethical decisions, and we will cover that topic in chapter 7.

THE RAMIFICATIONS OF UNETHICAL BEHAVIOR

Los Angeles Police Department Rampart Scandal

The ramifications of public safety officers not behaving ethically can be devastating as evidenced by the Los Angeles Police Department (LAPD) Rampart scandal in the late 1990s. As members of the Community Resources Against Street Hoodlums (CRASH) antigang unit, seventy or more officers were accused of misconduct; they were implicated in unprovoked shootings, beatings, planting evidence, stealing, dealing drugs, bank robbery, and perjury among other things.

There were also other incidences of unethical behavior by the officers involved, but as a result of this case, fifty-eight officers were brought before an internal administrative board. As a result, twelve were given suspensions for various times depending on the offense: seven resigned and five were terminated.

Probably the most serious result was that 106 prior convictions were overturned as a result of perjury and falsified evidence, and the city of Los Angeles had to pay out an estimated $125 million in settlements based on 140 lawsuits.

Jaycee Lee Dugard and Phillip Garrido Case

Another case that came to light in August 2009 took place in Antioch, a town in northern California's Bay Area. Jaycee Lee Dugard was abducted some eighteen years ago from South Lake Tahoe and held captive in the backyard of Phillip and Nancy Garrido. Phillip Garrido was a convicted and registered sex offender who was on parole.

Neighbors called local police and reported that there were children living on the property, which is a violation of parole for a convicted sex offender. A deputy was sent to check, but he never went past the front porch. Parole officers who visited his home had no idea that his backyard had a maze of tents and sheds where Dugard and her children lived. Dugard has had two children with Garrido. She was eleven years old when kidnapped; her children are now eleven and fifteen years of age.

According to an article in the *San Diego Union-Tribune,*[4] the Contra Costa County Sheriff's office acknowledged it missed a chance to arrest Garrido in 2006 after the neighbor's complaint about children living in the yard. Contra Costa sheriff Warren E. Rupf said, "I cannot change the course of events, but we are beating ourselves up over this and will continue to do so. We should have been more inquisitive, more curious and turned over a rock or two."

You can empathize with the sheriff, but when public safety officers take an oath to protect the public and then fail to do so, it constitutes unethical behavior. Even though the officers are not taking a bribe or using excessive force, they are being negligent and someone suffers because of it. The deputy didn't think the situation through; he didn't take the time to use critical thinking skills, and as a result, people suffered and the rescue of Dugard and her children was put off for several years.

Parole officers are also public safety officers, and they take an oath to uphold the law. The primary job of a parole officer is to supervise parolees. When a person is on parole, he or she is doing time in the community and needs to be kept track of. Home visits can be made at any time of day or night without prior notification because of the Fourth Waiver. A Fourth Waiver is a condition of parole that stipulates that the inmate gives up his or her Fourth Amendment right against unreasonable searches and seizures. Apparently, in this case, the sheriff's department never notified the parole department of the complaint. However, that does not excuse the parole officer because he or she should have known if Garrido was violating parole.

It appears that the sheriffs' department investigation was less than complete; if they had looked further and enlisted the assistance of state parole, this case might have been solved years ago. This case reinforces some people's erroneous belief that the law enforcement community is not doing its job.

The officers involved in this case probably did not purposely disregard the situation. Many times, there is a lack of personnel to do a proper job, and as a result, they go around putting band-aids on major problems, but public safety officers have to take the time to do a proper job. We know that most officers are dedicated and want to perform to the optimum. This is why it is very important to enlist the assistance of the community. This can be done when the community is included in the public safety process.

Rodney King Case

There was a Los Angeles case in 1991 that involved a man by the name of Rodney King. King was driving down a Los Angeles freeway when two California Highway Patrol (CHP) officers attempted to pull him over for speeding.

Circa 1992-billboard reading "We can get along."

King had been drinking and accelerated to speeds that exceeded 110 miles per hour. The chase ended approximately fifteen minutes later when King's car was cut off. The officers got out of their vehicle with guns drawn and tried to place King under arrest. The LAPD arrived on the scene, and Sgt. Stacy Koon, Officers Lawrence Powell, Theodore Briseno, and Timothy Wind intervened. A citizen, George Holliday, who lived nearby heard the excitement and looked out of his apartment and saw the officers fighting with King; he got out his video camera and filmed the incident.

According to the video, it appeared that the officers hit King numerous times with their batons. Some say over fifty times before finally handcuffing him. Holliday gave his videotape to KTLA, and they took the tape to LAPD headquarters, where it was reviewed by ranking officers. Then KTLA decided to broadcast it on the evening news. CNN obtained a copy as did the networks; viewers were shocked; and the FBI opened an investigation. Los Angeles police chief Daryl Gates held a press conference and announced that the officers would be prosecuted. The district attorney, Karl Reiner, announced that he would seek indictments against the officers. All fifteen officers who were at the scene were suspended. Koon, Powell, Wind, and Briseno were indicted. The Christopher Commission was formed and led by Warren Christopher to evaluate the LAPD. There were charges and incompetence against the LAPD.

After much legal maneuvering, the officers were tried in Simi Valley, which is a community northeast of Los Angeles. On March 2, 1992, a jury was selected and the trial began and ran until April 29, when the jury acquitted Koon, Wind, and Briseno of all charges and were unable to reach a verdict on one charge against Powell. The four officers were later indicted by the federal government for civil rights violations against King. They went to trial in the Los Angeles Federal Court on February 25, 1993. Officers Koon and Powell were found guilty and Officers Wind and Briseno were acquitted.

On the evening of April 29 in Los Angeles, a riot began that ultimately cost the taxpayers of Los Angeles and the state of California more than a billion dollars and left fifty-three people dead. During the course of the riot, over seven thousand people were arrested. Later, King was awarded $3.8 million by the city of Los Angeles. Rodney King died at the age of 47, by accidental drowning in Rialto, California.

San Francisco Firefighters

According to Phillip Matier and Andrew Ross, who write a column for the *San Francisco Chronicle,* an investigation is in progress that involves about thirty San Francisco firefighters who were having a tailgate party outside a soup kitchen run by nuns when an inebriated firefighter might have groped a female kitchen volunteer and then dropped his pants in front of a second volunteer in a bathroom. According to those familiar with the investigation, it all started when the off-duty firefighters were holding a barbecue at an old fire station just down the street from AT&T Park after attending a Giants game. The old building houses both the firefighters' union's Toys for Tots program and a soup kitchen rung by Mother Teresa's Missionaries of Charity.

It has also been reported that there was a fracas either between two firefighters or between firefighters and some homeless who eat at the soup kitchen. Firefighters' union president John Hanley, who was in Boston at the time of the incident, said, "Let's wait until all of the facts are in and we have a thorough investigation before we pass judgment on San Francisco's firefighters. This does not sound like any of the men and women I've worked with." Fire Chief Joanne Hays-White is conducting an investigation. She stated, "The allegations seem to be very serious. If any of the allegations are true, there would be no tolerance. I'm making this a top priority."

However, even if the reports are unfounded, people are quick to criticize. Public safety officers have to be aware of their personal and professional images at all times. They are not allowed to celebrate publicly because of their role as protectors of society. They have to be more discrete than other professions. People have a tendency to generalize and paint members of a specific group with the same brush.

San Francisco Police Scandals

In a 2005 issue of the *San Francisco Chronicle,* staff writers Susan Sward and Bill Wallace wrote an article titled "Scandals Punctuate History of SFPD." It said:

> When Mayor Gavin Newsom last week released police-produced videos he assailed as offensive, he neglected to mention one thing: It was just the latest in a long string of scandals in the San Francisco Police Department.
>
> For decades, the department has been buffeted by controversies and furors. Mayors have wrung their hands and said something must be done. Sometimes, San Franciscans have passed ballot measures aimed at toughening police discipline.
>
> Through it all, though the 2,200 member department has remained a tradition-bound organization where major policies are influenced greatly by the Police Officers Association, and where personal relationships, family connections, and political alliances often interfere with effective administration.

Aware of this history, law enforcement expert have noted that the department operates in an old-fashioned way, trailing other agencies that have adopted modern record keeping and disciplinary standards.

"There have been periodic scandals bringing more pressure for accountability but in the absence of political pressure to adopt reforms in a timely manner, the pace of change slows greatly," said Mark Schlosberg, police practice director of the American Civil Liberties Union's Northern California Chapter.

Some of the scandals have involved allegations of police officer corruption—officers taking bribes, shaking down bar owners, and pimping for a prostitution ring. Others resulted from poor judgment, and some involved fraternity-style activities, like the video skits, that have been offensive to the diverse population the police of San Francisco are sworn to serve and protect.

The department's biggest recent scandal began when three off-duty officers, including the son of the assistant chief, confronted two men outside a Union Street bar in 2002, demanded a bag of fajitas held by one of the men, and engaged in a brawl when the men refused to give up the food. The incident blew up to scandal proportions when critics charged that the department's investigation of the fight was aimed at saving the officers' jobs. The chief and top brass were briefly indicted on charges of conspiracy to cover up the incident before a judge ordered charges dropped.

In the wake of this scandal, several entities, including the city controller's office, issued reports critical of the department, and voters in 2003 adopted reforms strengthening the civilian-run Officer of Citizen Complaints, the police watchdog agency.

When Newsom was running for mayor with backing from the Police Officers Association, the Fajitagate scandal was very much in the news. During his campaign, Newsom opposed the police reform measure, which also cut the number of appointments the mayor could make to the police commission. However, he pledged that finding a new police chief would be his top priority. "I've made a commitment to the people of San Francisco for an order-of-magnitude change in the police department—the command staff level, the chief level," Newsom said in an interview after his election.

To carry out his policy, Newsom selected Heather Fong, a twenty-eight-year veteran who had spent most of her career in administrative jobs. Fong has kept a low profile, launched no major reform drives that might have irritated the Police Officers Association, and has drawn criticism from many rank-and-file officers who consider her to be out of touch with police on the street and a weak voice when it comes to advocating their interests to politicians and the media.

When misconduct allegations against police officers have received considerable publicity such as department charges against Officer Anthony Nelson, who broke the arm of a protester in 2003, Fong has been largely silent. In Nelson's case, she initially asked the police commission to give him a thirty-day suspension, but the commission later fired him for lying about the incident.

However, Fong angrily called the video skits discovery a "dark day in the history of the police department." As of Friday, she had suspended twenty-four officers allegedly involved in production of the videos. Experts contacted by *The Chronicle* after the release of the video skits, which Newsom characterized as sexist, racist, and homophobic, view their production as a reflection of how poorly the department is managed.

"This video says something about the culture of this department, it is fraternity house behavior, and you have to be really stupid to not know this is offensive," said Samuel Walker, a University of Nebraska at Omaha professor, who is one of the nation's top experts on police discipline.

"The fact that officers were in uniform and used department facilities and cars in the video reflects a failure of leadership over a period of many years," Walker said. At his City Hall news conference Wednesday night, Newsom said the videos were the tipping point that would lead him to take steps that would change the culture of the police department. He left unsaid that the incident was only the most recent in a long series of episodes to tarnish the department's reputation.

Back in 1937, Edwin Atherton, a former FBI agent hired by the city to look into police graft and corruption, found so much of it that hundreds of officers were reassigned and more than a dozen were fired or resigned.

When George Moscone was elected mayor in 1975, he selected Charles Gain, Oakland's police chief, to run the department. After Gain began implementing reforms, the Police Officers Association held a no-confidence vote on him. After Moscone was assassinated in 1978, the union was influential in engineering Gain's replacement.

In May 1984, Mayor Dianne Feinstein was infuriated by the revelation that two vice officers had hired a prostitute to perform oral sex on a handcuffed rookie policeman at the Rathskeller bar before an audience of off-duty police officers. With Feinstein demanding action, five officers were fired. Only four months after the Rathskeller episode, the police descended on Lord Jim's, an upscale bar at the corner of Broadway and Polk, looking for drugs the owner allegedly had. They held sixty patrons—including doctors and lawyers—for more than an hour, prompting lawsuits that cost many thousands of dollars. Police Chief Con Murphy reorganized the department again, transferring some of the involved officers to other assignments.

In the 1980s and the 1990s, controversies erupted periodically. During the 1984 Democratic National Convention in San Francisco, a group of officers was spotted holding up rating cards ranking the attractiveness of female passersby. In 1992, Police Chief Richard Hongisto was fired after it was disclosed that he had made comments critical of a weekly magazine's portrayal of him, allegedly prompting three officers to seize more than 2,000 copies of the magazine. One of those three officers, Gary Delagnes, is now president of the Police Officers Association.

As far as Delagnes is concerned, the uproar over the video has gotten completely out of hand. "Compared to other departments across the country, I believe the San Francisco Police Department has fewer problems and less serious problems," Delagnes said. "When mayors and other officials say there is a culture in the San Francisco department that needs to be changed, I don't have a clue what they are talking about."

Another observer watching the department's latest turmoil has been former San Francisco Police Chief Gain, who left in 1980.

> Gain, noting he struggled with a department badly needing reform, said, "In a professional department where there is an understanding there will be appropriate conduct adhering to rules and regulations, conduct of this nature—producing a video ridiculing people because of their race or because they were gay or homeless—simply would not occur. If officers felt they could get by with this, what is wrong with the top management that word has not gotten down to the street?"

This article listed five incidents of police misbehavior going back to 1937. It also mentioned officers taking bribes, pimping, and shaking down bar owners but failed to cite any specific cases. The authors have no doubt that some of this probably happened, but without evidence, it is a little nebulous.

The rationale for presenting this article in its entirety is to make the reader aware of how closely public safety officers' behavior is scrutinized. Newspapers and other media have an agenda and that is to sell newspapers and TV commercial time. Firefighters and police officers have to realize this and behave accordingly. Remember: *It is always news when public safety officers get in trouble.*

Porn Star Ball

In July 2004, a group of Sacramento firefighters from station 20 attended the "Porn Star Ball" with a fire engine and were reported to have given women rides on the unit and even took some back to the station. As a result of this, there was an internal investigation and one firefighter resigned.

Firefighter Hooman Ghazanfari, the group's spokesman, said, "We work hard . . . we put our lives on the line. We want the community to remember that . . . that we do that for them every day."

The firefighter said they've been jeered in public since the scandal, often asked "where's the party," and even called rapists. Ghazanfari said he understands the public's frustration. "They have a right to be upset. It's an unfortunate thing that happened. They see the engine, uniform, and badge . . . they feel like they have to vent," he said.

The firefighter who resigned was a ten-year veteran facing allegations of sexual assault, but the district attorney said that no charges would be filed.

Ghazanfari said that the firefighter who resigned was an asset to the department and will be missed.

"He organized toy drives, and food drives where we've fed homeless people," Ghazanfari said.

We can see here what a tragedy a lapse in judgment can cause. One ten-year veteran lost his career, and the others have been ridiculed by the people in the community. And now, other public safety officers are looked upon with suspicion.

These firefighters are probably dedicated people who do their jobs every day and love it. They go to an event that looks as if it would be fun, and they suffer the ridicule of the people they work to help every day.

Public safety officers are held to a higher standard than the rest of the population. They are role models for children; parents point them out to their kids when they are seen on the street; they are heroes, and they need to remember that and behave accordingly.

Mafia Cops

On April 6, 2006, Louis Eppolito and Stephen Caracappa were convicted of racketeering, obstruction of justice, extortion, and eight counts of murder and conspiracy and sentenced to life terms in federal prison.

The investigation went back to cases that occurred in the 1980s and the early 1990s in New York and in the early 2000s in Las Vegas.

Eppolito was born in New York City in 1948, and some members of his family were alleged to have been connected to organized crime. Eppolito claimed he had avoided the Mafia lifestyle and became a New York City police officer in 1969 and became the eleventh most decorated officer in New York Police Department (NYPD) history. He was made detective in 1979 and in 1983 was suspected of passing NYPD intelligence reports on to Rosario Gambino, a distant relative of Carlo Gambino and Paul Castellano, past bosses of the Gambino crime family. He was ultimately cleared of that charge. Eppolito retired in 1990 and wrote a book titled *The Story of an Honest Cop Whose Family Was the Mob.* In his book, he said he retired because of the damage to his reputation as a result of the Gambino case.

Caracappa was born in Brooklyn, New York, in 1942. He also joined the NYPD in 1969 and was appointed detective in 1979. He was assigned to the Organized Crime Homicide Unit, which is in the Major Case Squad based in Brooklyn. Apparently, after hooking up with Eppolito, they began accepting bribes from various mobsters for services performed.

Anthony "Gaspipe" Casso, the underboss of the Lucchese crime family, testified while applying for the Witness Protection Program in 1994 that since 1985 he and his boss Vittoria "Vic" Amuso had paid the two detectives $375,000 in bribes for murder "contracts." Among other things, Casso shared that in 1986, on the orders of Amuso and himself, Eppolito and Caracappa kidnapped and turned over an associate of the Gambino crime family named James Hydell to be murdered in retaliation for an attempt on Casso's life. Eppolito and Caracappa also apparently killed Lucchese mob member Bruno Facciolo with the help of Louis Daidone on Casso's orders because they believed he was an informant for law enforcement.

In April 1991, Detectives Eppolito and Caracappa were implicated in the murder of Gambino soldier and John Gotti (head of the Gambino crime family) friend Bartholomew "Bobby" Boriello. They apparently supplied information that led to his murder. Frank "Big Frank" Lastorino, a captain in the Lucchese family, reportedly ordered the two detectives to kill Patrick Testa, a former Gambino mobster and current Lucchese member, and to make it look as if the Gambinos were responsible in an attempt to start a war with the Luccheses.

In the mid-1990s, indictments were issued against just about every New York crime family. Detectives Eppolito and Caracappa retired from the police department and moved to Las Vegas, Nevada. Casso said that the detectives were still very much in business while living in Las Vegas and

© Skovoroda/Shutterstock, Inc.

Mafia

were contacted by Frank Lastorino regarding some murder contracts on current mobsters in New York.

On June 30, 2006, a judge threw out a murder conviction because it was a federal case and the statute of limitations had run out. On September 17, 2008, the two detectives' racketeering convictions were ordered and reinstated by a federal appeals court.[5]

On March 6, 2009, Eppolito was sentenced to life in prison plus hundred years. Caracappa received life plus eighty years. Each was fined more than $4 million.[6-7]

This case is definitely a particularly egregious one, the height of not only unethical behavior but immoral and illegal as well. Imagine the damage done to the reputation of all detectives and police officers everywhere. These two detectives let everyone down: the public and the police department. In fact, all police departments, their families, and themselves. Now these men are probably going to spend the rest of their lives in prison.

What caused this to happen? Was it greed or excitement? Were these men criminals before becoming police officers or did their attitudes change as a result of the job? Did seeing "even the best people at their worst" cause them to think that it was okay to engage in taking bribes and killing mobsters? Did they believe that nobody cared because they weren't hurting "good" people?

Maybe they thought that they were above the law or that they were so smart that they wouldn't get caught, and even if they did, who would believe the criminals who would be testifying against them, they were cops after all.

Knapp Commission

In April 1970, the Knapp Commission was formed in New York City as the result of publicity and revelations about police corruption in the city. The main whistleblowers were Officer Frank Serpico and Sergeant David Durk.

This commission coined the phrases *Grass Eaters* and *Meat Eaters* to describe levels of police corruption.

The term *Grass Eaters* is used to describe police officers who "accept gratuities and solicit five-, ten-, twenty-dollar payments from contractors, tow-truck operators, gamblers, and the like but do not pursue corruption payments." Grass eating is something that a significant number of officers are guilty of but which they learned to do from other officers or from imitating the miscreants they deal with on a daily basis. The commission concluded that "grass eating" was used by cops in New York to prove their loyalty to the brotherhood. One way of preventing cops from becoming corrupt is to knock out this step by removing the more seasoned officers who do this. Then without any experienced cops to learn this from, rookies might never decide to do "eat grass."

The *Meat Eaters* are cops who actively search out situations that they can use for monetary gain. The previously mentioned Rampart scandal in the LAPD and NYPD case of detectives Eppolito and Caracappa are excellent examples of Meat Eaters.[8]

Another investigative body formed in 1993 was called the Mollen Commission. They found that the Meat Eaters were now not only just cooperating with criminals but were actively engaging in criminal acts such as selling drugs, robbing drug dealers, and operating burglary rings.[9]

John Leonard Orr—Serial Arsonist

John Leonard Orr is a former fire captain and arson investigator for the Glendale, California Fire Department, who was convicted of arson and murder and is currently serving life in prison. Orr wanted to be a police officer but failed the examination, so he became a firefighter. During the 1980s and 1990s, the Los Angeles area was experiencing a lot of fires that cost millions of dollars in damages and claimed four lives. Orr was found to be responsible in most of those fires.[10]

On July 31, 1992, a federal court jury convicted Orr of three counts of arson in a five-count indictment, and the judge in that case sentenced Orr to three consecutive terms of ten years in prison.[11]

On June 25, 1998, a Californian jury found Orr guilty of four counts of first-degree murder with special circumstances for a 1984 hardware store fire.[12] The prosecutor sought the death penalty, but the jury locked 8–4 in favor of execution, so the judge sentenced Orr to life plus twenty years in prison without the possibility of parole. Orr is serving his term with the California Department of Corrections and Rehabilitation.

Orr has been called one of the worst serial arsonists of the twentieth century by some law enforcement officers. Alcohol, Tobacco, and Fire Arms (ATF) agent Mike Matassa believes that Orr set nearly two thousand fires between 1984 and 1991.[13]

Joseph Wambaugh has written a book recounting Orr's story titled *Fire Lover.* Actor Ray Liotta played Orr in the HBO film *Points of Origin,* and Orr authored a book by the same name

Orr maintains his innocence and says that the book he wrote is a composite of all the arsonists he arrested.

This case is another heinous abridgment of trust by a public safety officer. How must the public feel when the very person they hire to protect against the dangers of fire is setting them. This behavior undermines all of the men and women who are in the fire service, even when we know that most are professional and dedicated to their careers.

The Bowling Cops

Steve Andrews of News Channel 8 broke a story regarding the Polk County Sheriff's Office in Florida. Sheriff's deputies entered the home of convicted drug dealer Michael Difalco in March 2009 to conduct a search for drugs. Apparently during the operation, some of the officers found a Wii video bowling game and began bowling frame after frame. While some of the detectives were removing evidence, such as flat-screen televisions and shotguns, others threw strikes, gutter balls, and worked on picking up spares. One Polk County detective repeatedly put down her work, which was cataloging evidence, and picked up a Wii remote to bowl. When she hit two strikes in a row, she raised her hands and started jumping and kicking. There were other departments involved in the search, and their officers also participated in the game playing. What the officers didn't know there was a wireless security camera connected to a computer inside Difalco's home, and it recorded their activity. Now there are questions on how the extemporaneous bowling tournament might affect the case against Difalco.

Sheriff Grady Judd said that the behavior was inappropriate, and the officers showed a lapse in judgment, but the bowling should not affect the outcome of the search or the admissibility in court.

Sheriff Judd and Police Chiefs E. C. Waters and Roger Boatner are conducting internal investigations to see if any inappropriate behavior took place and will take action if that is the case.

"Obviously, this is not the kind of behavior we condone," Lakeland Police Chief Boatner said. "There was a lot of down time, but that does not excuse the fact that we should act as the consummate professionals."

"Certainly this was a case of bad judgment," Auburndale Police Chief Nolan McLeod said. "We will handle it appropriately."

Court records show that Difalco was placed under task surveillance in December 2008. He was reported to have had weapons in the house as well other contraband. According to documents filed in March 2009, the detectives found methamphetamine, marijuana, drug paraphernalia, weapons, and more than thirty thousand dollars in stolen property. There are eleven charges against Difalco, and they include trafficking in methamphetamine, possession of a firearm by a convicted felon, and operating a chop shop. The search took about nine hours and cost the taxpayers about four thousand dollars.

Defense attorney Rick Escobar thinks that not only is the playing of the games bad judgment or inappropriate but also could have turned the search into an illegal search. He believes that as soon as they turned on the video game and started playing the game, they seized it and therefore made a legal search illegal.

"I've never seen anything like this," Escobar said after he viewed some of the video. Escobar has no direct interest in the case because he does not represent Difalco.

"All the citizens are thinking; wait a minute, we are paying these people to go out and protect us and here they are playing bowling on our time," he said.

"The real question here is have they seized property that wasn't described in the search warrant?" Escobar asked. "Clearly if they're using it, they've seized it and for totally improper purposes, because it's for entertainment. Investigations are not for entertainment."

A spokesperson for the Polk County State Attorney declined to comment on the video or the validity of the search warrant. He said, "That's a discussion that will occur in court." If these cops hadn't screwed up, this case would probably have never gone to court. The case would have been plea bargained because of the quantity and quality of the evidence. Now there will be a court trial, and it will cost taxpayers a lot of money all because of a lack or lapse of judgment.

Did the cops do anything illegal or immoral? No. But public safety officers have to remember that while they are on duty, they must pay attention to the job at hand; there is no room for error because, especially in the case of the police, some defense attorney is waiting to pounce on some minor transgression to make them look as if they are vulnerable to having normal feelings and behaving in a way that most human beings would. In many cases, a defense attorney cannot go into court and claim his or her client is not guilty because that wouldn't be the truth, so they have to look for some minor transgression of the police during the investigation. This is called a technicality, and it is used by the defense to get the defendant off.

Activists shouting and yelling in Toronto.

Abner Louima

On the evening of August 9, 1997, a Haitian immigrant by the name of Abner Louima was out for the evening at a nightclub in East Flatbush called Club Rendez-Vous. Apparently, there was an altercation between two women that resulted in a physical confrontation, and Louima along with some other celebrants were trying to break it up. The police were called and the officers proceeded to break up the fight; during the melee, one of the responding officers Justin Volpe was blindsided by a punch. Volpe thought that Louima was responsible, so he placed him under arrest for disorderly conduct, obstructing justice, and resisting arrest.

During the ride to the precinct, the officers beat Abner Louima with their fists, nightsticks, and handheld radios.[14] Once at the station, Louima was strip-searched and placed in a temporary holding cell. Louima still handcuffed was then taken from the cell by officer Volpe and taken into the station men's room where Volpe attacked Louima by kicking and grabbing his testicles, and then jamming a toilet plunger up his rectum and then forcing it into Louima's mouth. Volpe then walked through the station showing the plunger to those present. Volpe denied ever boasted about torturing Louima.[15]

Edwin J. Delattre wrote, "I do not know whether Justin Volpe's fellow officers could have deterred him by preventive moral reproach from his assault on Abner Louima, or whether they were in a position to prevent him physically from isolating Louima in the restroom."[16]

The very least that should have been done by someone in that station house is to have made sure of the safety of the suspect. This is the same phenomenon that happened in the Rodney King case, with pretty much the same result. A detainee has been injured, officer's careers are ruined, and the reputation of good police officers and departments everywhere has been diminished.

This case ended with Officer Justin Volpe getting thirty years in prison. Officer Charles Schwarz was initially sentenced to fifteen years in prison, but the case was overturned on appeal. But he was sentenced to five years in prison for perjury. Abner Louima received a settlement of approximately $8 million dollars from the taxpayers of New York.

Displaying Human Emotions

People who work in public safety must remember they cannot express or display human emotions and behavior while working. In other words, they are not allowed human emotions during the work day: no fear, no anger, no frustration, no boredom, no humor, no recreation, no happiness, and no sadness because citizens expect them to be on alert and ready to take care of business whenever they are called upon.

As we have seen from reading some of the above cases, police officers get into trouble when they emote rather than think. It is very important that public safety officers stay aware of who and where they are. They have responsibilities that very few people in other professions have; they are responsible for the safety of people they come into contact with and always keep that premise at the forefront of their behavior.

Deindividuation

The previous cases bring to mind Gustave Le Bon (1841–1931), a French social scientist who developed and wrote a theory about crowd behavior.

The theory was called "deindividuation." The theory maintains:

1. in crowds or groups many people lose their sense of individuality and
2. remove self-imposed controls and internalized moral restraints over behavior.

Deindividuation is often used to try and explain various expressions of collective behavior, such as violent crowds, mindless thugs, and gangs.

Public safety officers sometimes work in groups and engage in groupthink and maybe do things that would be better left undone. Public safety officers must not lose their sense of individuality and remember their self-imposed controls and internalized moral restraints.

CAN ETHICS BE LEARNED AND WHY ARE THEY IMPORTANT?

Our hope is that ethics can be learned, or we are wasting our time and effort writing books and studying the topic. Because we learn most of what we know and much of our knowledge is not innate, the assumption is that it is learned. We do (at least some of us) learn right from wrong. Most of us know what "doing the right thing" is. So let's go with the premise that ethics can be learned.

Socrates said, "Ethics consists of knowing what we ought to do, and such knowledge can be taught." He also believed that a person who knows what is right will act rightly. It appears that the best way to learn ethics is to be practicing. If we do the right thing often enough, we will become better at it.

Ethical behavior requires a mind-set in which the person goes through a check-list every time he or she makes a decision that requires an ethical decision. We will discuss this further in chapter 7.

Ethics are important for public safety officers because of many of the things we have already discussed in this chapter. Police officers and firefighters are public employees, and the community depends on them for their safety. It is imperative that the public trust their safety employees.

Samuel Adams said, "Private and public vices are in reality connected. Nothing is more essential to the establishment of manners in a state than that all persons employed in places of power and trust be men of exceptional character. The public cannot be too curious concerning the characters of public men."

What Adams is alluding to is the citizens' right to know and trust the men and women they hire to protect. Their right to go to bed every night with the knowledge that they are as safe as they can possibly be and that the guardians are on duty and behaving in an ethical and professional way.

The political entities who hire the officers take a multitude of precautions: they conduct background investigations and give myriad examinations and tests to ensure that only the best applicants are hired.

After the people are hired, they go through training at fire and police academies, and upon graduation from the training programs, they serve a probationary period before they are fully certified for duty.

So what happens? Why do we have safety officers behaving unethically?

In the case of the public safety officer, he or she sees even the "best people at the worst." They respond to child and spousal abuse cases, fires, neighborhood fights, murders, rapes, riots, frauds, medical emergencies, floods, earthquakes, and auto accidents. They also have to deal with the victims and perpetrators of these incidents.

Officers can become overly cynical, and frustration can set in because they don't seem to be making any progress in their endeavor to make the world a better place. They are now part of a group that sees the same things they do, day in and day out. Not only do these folks work together but they socialize together because their work schedules are different from the rest of the world. During social functions, the discussions turn to "the job" and they begin to look at the world as "us versus them." Pretty soon, the "ends justify the means," and the officers are behaving unethically. They are engaging in groupthink, which will be discussed more fully in another chapter. This by no means an excuse for inappropriate behavior. It is meant as an explanation as to what can happen if the officer is not thinking and paying attention to his or her thoughts and feelings about his or her work milieu.

California Highway Patrol

According to an editorial in the *San Diego Union-Tribune* on October 5, 2009, the CHP, the State Attorney General and Governor Arnold Schwarzenegger were refusing to investigate possible wrongdoing by the highway patrol. The article stated that court documents brought to light by the *Ventura County Star* showed strong evidence that members of the CHP thwarted a hate crimes investigation of Officer Seth Taylor in 2007, shortly after an incident in an Oxnard Hotel that was hosting an unofficial CHP party. The editorial goes on to say that the CHP refused to provide the Ventura County District Attorney's Office with important evidence until ordered by a Superior Court judge. This is on top of another scandal called "Chief's Disease," in which it is alleged that 80 percent of top CHP officials used the ruse of claiming enigmatic work-related injuries in their final years on the job to spike their pensions.

There were other transgressions in recent years: the apparent preferential treatment given a state senator caught operating a motor vehicle while under the influence of prescription drugs, iniquity regarding promotions and contract bidding, sordid person misconduct by an official in the CHP's Inland division, gross abuse of overtime pay, and so on.[17]

The editorial goes on to say that Governor Schwarzenegger thinks the no investigation is warranted and that the CHP is "one of the top law enforcement agencies in the world."

To have an ethical public safety agency in a democracy, there needs to be transparency. If the perception is that an investigation is needed, then it is paramount that one should be conducted to maintain the reputation of the department and the trust of the community that it is sworn to protect. If the CHP is in fact one of the top law enforcement agencies in the world, then you would think it would demand an investigation of any alleged unethical behavior.

Sweeping wrongdoing under the rug does no good for the agency. It reinforces the negative feelings people may have regarding public safety and other governmental agencies. They can say "see told you so," when the situation does come to light. Public safety agencies need to be proactive when it comes to investigating themselves in affairs such as these.

SUMMARY

In this chapter, we have examined some of the cases in which police officers and firefighters have behaved unethically. In some cases, these behaviors were particularly egregious, and others were a lapse or mistake in judgment. But they all contribute to the public's perception and opinion of public safety officers.

We have probed the financial costs of unethical behavior: the lawsuits and overturned cases that have resulted because of bad judgment and criminal behavior perpetrated by the public servants who were hired to protect their constituents. For example, the city of Los Angeles paid Rodney King almost $4 million as the result of a lawsuit filed in his behalf for a beating at the hands of police officers. The Rampart scandal cost Los Angeles $125 million, just in lawsuits, and that doesn't take into account other costs such as court trials and the money lost because the officers involved were sent to prison and lost their jobs. We have to remember it is expensive to train and equip public safety officers, and that even after training, it is years before they reach the level of expertise needed to effectively perform their jobs. So corruption and unethical behavior is costly in terms of money, human suffering, and quality of life.

We talked about trust and credibility and how important these are to people who are charged with keeping the public safe. For our society to survive, we must have complete confidence in our public servants.

As Homer Simpson said, "I don't mind being called a liar when I am lying, when I am about to lie or just finished lying . . . but not when I am telling the truth."[18]

NOTES

1. Willie Brown's column, *San Francisco Chronicle,* page A8 July 26, 2009.
2. "Officer Taught Others How To Avoid Profiling," *Reno Gazette* 7/24/2009. P.3C.
3. See, e.g. Erich Fromm, "The State as Educator: On the Psychology of Criminal Justice." In Kevin Anderson and Richard Quinney (Eds.), *Erich Fromm and Critical Criminology: Beyond the punitive society.* (Urbana, IL: University of Illinois Press, 2000).

4. *San Diego Union-Tribune,* July 30, 2009.

5. *New York Times,* "Convictions Reinstated in Mob Case." www.nytimes.com/2008/08/18/nyregion/18cops.html (accessed 2/12/2010).

6. Mafia Cops Louis Eppolito and Steven Caracappa sentenced to life in prison," *New York Daily News,* March 6, 2009.

7. *Wikipedia,* "Louis Eppolito and Steven Caracappa" http://en.wikipedia.org/wiki/knappcommission (accessed 2/13/2010).

8. Wikipedia, "Knapp Commission." http://en.wikipedia.org/wiki/ (accessed 2/14/2010).

9. Pollock, Joycelyn M. (2007). *Ethical Dilemmas and Decisions in Criminal Justice.* Fifth Edition (Thomson/Wadsworth) p. 235.

10. Wayne Petherick, *Serial Crime: Theoretical and Practical Issues in Behavioral Profiling* (New York: Academic Press, 2006) p. 256.

11. Wambaugh, Joseph. *Fire Lover* (New York: Aron Books, 2003).

12. *Firehouse Magazine,* September 1998.

13. "Arson: The Scorched Earth Obsession," *Newsweek,* November 5, 2008.

14. Chandler, D.L. *Abner Louima was Savagely Beaten by NYPD 15 years Ago Today (8/9/2012) http://newsone.com/2029939/abner-louima-case/* (Retrieved 11/19/2013).

15. Tom Hayes, "Volpe: I'm the Real Victim," Associated Press, 1999, accessed at www.abcnews.go.com/sections/us/dailynews/volpe991101.html.

16. Delattre, Edwin J., *Character and Cops: Ethics in Policing, Sixth Edition* (Washington, DC: The AEI Press, 2011) p. 363.

17. "CHP Running Wild." Editorial, *San Diego Union-Tribune,* p. B6, October 5, 2009.

18. A quote by cartoon character Homer Simpson. www.hotinnorthcounty.com

DILEMMA

You are a police officer working in the traffic division of a large police department. You observe a motorist make an illegal left-hand turn. You stop the person, and she begins yelling at you and is rude, so you give her a citation.

The next person you pull over for the same violation is smiling, polite, friendly, is not rude, and acknowledges his mistake; so you let him off with a warning.

Is this ethical?

What are your thought processes?

Should you have treated both people alike?

Why or why not?

_____

_____

_____

_____

_____

_____

_____

_____

_____

_____

_____

_____

_____

_____

_____

_____

_____

_____

DILEMMA

You are a firefighter, and you and your family are going to a Saturday matinee at the local theater. Your daughter is wearing a tee shirt with "My mom's a firefighter" emblazoned across the front. The person in the box office asks if you're a firefighter, and you reply in the affirmative. She says that because you are a firefighter, you and your family get free admission to the theater.

What do you do?

Is this any different than doing the same thing for a member of the armed forces? Why/Why not?

_____

_____

_____

_____

_____

_____

_____

_____

_____

_____

_____

_____

_____

_____

_____

_____

_____

_____

DILEMMA

You're working the graveyard shift, and you and your partner are checking businesses for unlocked doors and possible burglaries. You find the back door to a delicatessen unlocked. You and your partner enter the store and search the premises; everything appears to be in order. After notifying the owner and while waiting for him to respond, your partner goes into the refrigerator and takes out two soft drinks and then takes a couple of bags of potato chips from the shelf. He gives you the drink and a bag of chips and begins to eat and drink his.

Is this okay? What do you do? What is your rationale for your actions?

_____

_____

_____

_____

_____

_____

_____

_____

_____

_____

_____

_____

_____

_____

_____

_____

_____

_____

_____

DILEMMA

You are working vice and enforcing prostitution violations. When arresting one of the women, she tells you of an officer who is getting favors from the prostitutes by trading free for sex.

    What are your options?

    What are you going to do?

_____

_____

_____

_____

_____

_____

_____

_____

_____

_____

_____

_____

_____

_____

_____

_____

_____

_____

DILEMMA

As a fire inspector, your job is to ensure that buildings' capacities are not exceeded. You enter a concert hall and see that the auditorium is definitely overcrowded. The manager offers you several hundred dollars to overlook the situation.

Ethically, what are your choices?

_____

_____

_____

_____

_____

_____

_____

_____

_____

_____

_____

_____

_____

_____

_____

_____

_____

_____

_____

Ethical Theories

3

CHAPTER OBJECTIVES

1. Identify various ethical theories.
2. Compare and contrast the theories.
3. Understand the rationale for the various theories.
4. Utilize the theories in solving ethical dilemmas.

Webster dictionary defines theory as "{s}ystematically organized knowledge applicable in a relatively wide variety of circumstances, especially a system of assumptions, accepted principles, and rules of procedure devised to analyze, predict, or otherwise explain the nature or behavior of a specified set of phenomenon."

In this chapter, we are going to examine some ethical theories that may assist in leading us to the most ethically correct resolutions of our ethical dilemmas. Most transactions or behaviors involve ethics, and it is difficult to identify neutral behavior, that is, behavior that has no moral or ethical content. Most of our behavior affects other people, so we must look at what we do in that context, especially if we are public safety officers.

VIRTUE ETHICS

Waste no more time arguing about what a good man should be. Be one
— Marcus Aurelius

© stefanel, 2014. Used under license from Shutterstock, Inc.

Socrates in front of the National Academy in Athens, Greece

A brief definition of Virtue Ethics "Is a classification within Normative Ethics that attempts to discover and classify what might be deemed of moral character, and to apply the moral character as a base for one's ethics and actions."[1] Instead of asking "What is a good action" the Ethics of virtue ask "What is a good person?"[2]

Socrates (469–399 BC), Plato, and Aristotle are credited with the development of virtue ethics.

Socrates spent his time roaming the streets of Athens asking questions of the people he met. The inquiries involved the meanings of virtue, life, and knowledge. He challenged his followers by continually asking questions in a way that compelled them to come to their own conclusions.

Socrates was put to death in 399 BC for corrupting the minds of the youth. He could have escaped, but he had agreed to live under the city's laws, so he implicitly subjected himself to the possibility of being accused of crimes by its citizens and found guilty by a jury. To run away would have violated his social contract with the state and would be an act contrary to Socratic principle.[3]

As you can see, Socrates was a very moral and ethical person. He drank his judgment to die. In today's language, we would say, "He not only talked the talk, he walked the walk." As far as Socrates was concerned, no man could suffer a greater loss than his personal integrity.

Plato

Socrates never wrote down any of his thoughts, but his loyal student Plato did. When Plato was twenty years old, he became disenchanted with the corruption of Greek politics and became a follower of Socrates.

Moral Character

Plato had a proposal for an ideal city in which there were few laws because the people who resided there had a highly developed moral character. Plato said, "If you want justice, you must be moral." He saw a link between individual moral conduct and the ideal society.[4] If you think about this statement, it really makes sense. If everyone acted morally, the society would be ideal. Even though that most likely will never happen, people who work in a profession that serves the public should be the first to adhere to the concept of presenting a strong moral character. Subconsciously the public expects civic employees and leaders to display a strong moral character. That is why we are so surprised and outraged when a public official displays a moral weakness.

For public safety officers, this concept is extremely important in that their moral conduct can lead us in the direction of an ideal society because the people will trust the system and the laws. If the officers are immoral or corrupt, the people of the society will lose faith in the system and the society will be less than ideal and could possibly collapse.

Reputation

Plato also wrote, "In dealings with the state and one's fellow citizens, the best man by far is the one who, rather than win a prize at Olympia or any of the other contests in war and peace, would prefer to beat everyone by his reputation for serving the laws of his country—a reputation for having devoted a lifetime of service to them with more distinction than anyone else."[5]

In public safety, as in other aspects of our lives, reputation is important. Many say that, "perception is reality"; if this is true, the way people see their employees is significant.

Public safety in most cases is a government responsibility and as a result gets its funding from the taxpayers. When the citizens go to the polls, one of the things they consider is the reputation of the agencies they are voting to fund. Among the questions the voters ask are, do the police and fire departments need or deserve a raise, better benefits, new equipment, and so on?

The police and fire departments depend on the cooperation of the public for information to do their jobs. If the citizenry think that the police are corrupt, brutal, and uncaring, they could say, "Oh the hell with it, they won't do anything anyway." You can see that reputation is important.

Bribes

Plato also examined public officials and bribes. He wrote, "Members of the public service should perform

PLATO, The famous Greek philosopher bust kept in the Louvre.

© Antonio Abrignani, 2014. Used under license from Shutterstock, Inc.

their duties without taking bribes. Such a practice must never be extenuated by an approving reference to maxims like 'One good turn deserves another'. It is not easy for an official to reach his decisions impartially and stick to them, and the safest thing he can do is to listen to the law and obey its command to take no gifts for his services."[6]

Plato prescribed the death penalty for taking a bribe. Although that may be a tad draconian, the taking of bribes is a serious offense for public safety officers and must never be taken or solicited under any circumstances.

Personal Morality

"A man who commits no crime is to be honored; yet the man who will not even allow the wicked to do wrong deserves more than twice as much respect. The former has the value of a single individual, but the latter, who reveals the wickedness of another to the authorities, is worth a legion.[7] Plato thought that a moral person should not only not do anything wrong but should also not allow anyone else to do wrong. The responsibility of all moral people is to support others in doing right. If a person does this, he or she will have made the world a better place.

This thought of Plato's is especially important for public safety officers because of the nature of the work. If an officer sees his or her workmates behaving unethically, it would be advantageous for all concerned if he or she intervened and didn't allow the behavior. Query: Why would it be advantageous?

Aristotle

Aristotle joined the Academy of Plato in 367 BC and stayed for twenty years. I guess you could have called him a research student who later became a graduate assistant. The death of Plato in 347 BC had a profound effect on Aristotle's life. He left Athens mainly because the person chosen to lead the academy after Plato's death was not acceptable to Aristotle and his colleagues. He settled in Assus and started the "colonial" academy, also called the Lyceum, with friends.

Aristotle asked the question. "How ought people live their lives?" He wrote a book titled *Nicomadhean Ethics*. Aristotle thought all human endeavors should be focused on some good, but some goods are more important than other goods. That is, there is a hierarchy of goods.

> To judge from the lives that men lead, most men of the most vulgar type, seem (not without some ground) to identify the good, or happiness, with pleasure; which is the reason why they love the life of enjoyment.[8]

Aristotle believed that the ultimate goal was happiness. He said that those living the political life seek happiness through honor, which he believed to be superficial because it focused more on those conveying the happiness than the person receiving it.[9] Query: Can you identify an instance where the former could be applied to modern politics?

Making money is important to some people, and they think they will be happy if they are wealthy, but money does not guarantee happiness. Pleasure and happiness are often used interchangeably and they shouldn't be. People can achieve pleasure by making money, but they won't necessarily be happy. Aristotle said that happiness usually involves other people and is therefore good because helping others is the ultimate good.

Virtue

Aristotle wrote, "And justice is perfect virtue because it is the practice of perfect virtue; and perfect in a special degree because its possessor can practice his virtue towards others and not merely by himself; for there are many who can practice virtue in their own private affairs but cannot do so in their relations with another. That is why we approve the saying of Bias, 'Office will show a man'; for in office one is brought into relation with others and becomes a member of a community."[10]

This passage is important when thinking about your position as a professional public safety officer. As such, you are a member of a community not only of your fellow workers but also of the people you serve, and how you behave toward them is critical for their safety and the efficiency of your work.

According to Aristotle, moral virtue is a mean. Table 3.1 is a summary of those means.

TABLE 3.1

Excess	Mean	Deficiency
Foolhardiness	Courage	Cowardice
Extravagance	Generosity	Stinginess
Vanity	High-Mindedness	Small-mindedness
Boastfulness	Truthfulness	Self-depreciation
Obsequiousness	Friendliness	Grouchiness
Bashfulness	Modesty	Shamelessness

What is moral virtue?

- It is a mean.
- A mean between two vices, one marked by excess and the other by deficiency.
- A mean in the sense that it aims at the middle point in emotions and actions.[11]

FORMALISM

Duty and obligation was central to the ethics of Immanuel Kant (1724–1804). He argued that ethical conduct should be the result of reason drawn from elementary inflexible rational premises. He believed that a person should always do his/her duty regardless of what might happen. Consequences were not important to Kant. According to Kant, a person ought to do what he ought to do.

When considering ethical formalism, consequences do not enter into the mix; it is the motive of the actor that is important. If you stop to assist someone, and it turns out you actually do the person harm, but if you are acting in good faith, the act will be moral.

Sometimes people in public safety have to do things that are not pleasant, fun, or even popular. They have to do their duty regardless of the consequences.

Russia, Kaliningrad tomb of famous philosopher Immanuel Kant.

We saw this on 9/11—firefighters and police officers going into the smoke and flames to see if they could be of aid to the victims. They did this without thinking of the dangers; they did it because it was their duty.

Kant regarded the categorical imperative as the philosophical basis of the famous golden rule that we should do as we would be done by.[12] He thought that the only thing that is fundamentally good is a goodwill.

Some of the common intuitions explained by Kant's theory are[13]:

1. The content of morality: Common morality commands respect for others and us. It regards all people equal before the moral law. You respect the rights of others. It forbids certain acts such as murder, rape, theft, fraud, and dishonesty.

2. The force of morality: Kant says the motive of morality rules us absolutely and we feel its power even when we are defying it. This is what is meant by conscience.

3. The goodwill: Moral judgment is directed, not to the effects of an action but to the good or bad intention that it shows. As Kant said, "nothing can possibly be conceived in the world, or even out of it, which can be called good without qualification, except good will."

4. The moral agent: Makes decisions for the future; sometimes resists and subdues desires. His or her actions have causes and reasons; he or she is both passive and active and stands as the controller of his or her emotions.

5. The role of law: A person may act as a good person, but it is his or her motive that counts. If a person does something for self-interest, it is of no credit to the person.

6. Reason and the passions: Sometimes there is a conflict between duty and desire, and that is where conscience comes in as an independent motive to legislate among desires and either forbid or permit them.

Application of Formalism to Public Safety

As we investigate Kant's ideas about morality and ethics, we can see that they can be of value to public safety officers in that our professional expectations of behavior are stated in more or less precise terms when it comes to our relationships with the public. We are duty bound to behave in certain ways by laws and the constitution. So we could possibly use some of what Kant says.

However, the weakness we see here is the rigidity of Kant's theory. When discussing "lying," for instance, he maintains that a person should never lie under any circumstances. But in law enforcement, when an officer takes on an undercover assignment, he or she will have to lie to function in that position. However, Kant did say that it is permissible to lie if someone is trying to harm you. We may be able to broaden Kant's theory to include lying in undercover work because if the criminals do find out you are not who or what you say you are, you could get hurt or worse.

He also stated that potential outcomes should not be considered when lying, but what if you are a firefighter and you are tending a severely burned victim who you know is going to succumb to his or her injuries. Do you tell the truth if asked, or do you tell the person something to comfort him or her during their last few moments? Under Kant's thinking, you should never take a life to save a life of someone else because that would violate categorical imperative. As a result, it would make a bad universal rule and would be using another as a means to an end and therefore break the practical imperative. Police officers are mandated by law and by oath to protect themselves and others; this rule could be problematic for public safety officers.

UTILITARIANISM

Although David Hume (1716–1776) and Jeremy Bentham (1784–1832) had written works that contained elements of utilitarianism thought, the idea was passed on by Bentham to James Mill, the father of John Stuart Mill, who incorporated the theory into the education of his son. Today, John Stuart Mill's essay on "Utilitarianism" is the most widely read piece on the topic.

In Mill's theory, consequences are the important consideration, not motives; the goodness of an act is determined by the consequences of an action.[15]

Mill wrote, "Society between equals can only exist on the understanding that the interests of all are to be regarded equally."[16] This has important ramifications for public safety in that we have to make sure of this to maintain a lawful society. If people perceived themselves as being treated unfairly, they could rebel against the laws that hold our society together.

Mill goes on to say, "And since in all states of civilization, every person. Except an absolute monarch has equals, everyone is obliged to live on these terms and with somebody; and in every age some advance is made toward a state in which it will be impossible to live permanently on other terms with anybody."[17] People have to consider others to have a civilization. It is impossible to live with each other and not behave ethically toward one another, at least peaceably. Mill doesn't care what the motive is for people behaving well toward each other, just that they do. The motive could be practical, self-serving, or altruistic, it doesn't matter. It is important that the greatest amount of good be realized by the largest number of people. Bentham theorized that the morality of an act should be established by how much it benefited the majority. If all of the foregoing takes place, goodness and pleasure will prevail to the detriment of pain; this is a hedonistic ethical theory.

Jay Albanese opined, "For utilitarianism to work properly, individuals making decision must weigh the consequences toward themselves and toward others equally and impartially".[19]

Mill Wrote:

"The utilitarian doctrine is that happiness is desirable, and the only thing desirable as an end; all other things being only desirable as means to that end. What ought to be required of this doctrine—what conditions is it requisite that the doctrine should fulfill—to make good its claim to be believed? The only proof capable of being given that an object is visible is that people actually see it. The only proof that a sound is audible, is that people hear it, and so of the other sources of our experience. In like manner, I apprehend, the sole evidence it is possible to produce that anything is desirable, is that people do actually desire it."[20]

Mill also said that people desire virtue, but desire it for itself. In other words, it is an end. It may be felt, a good in itself, and desired as such with as great intensity as any other good.[21]

Mill said it is related in that he thought virtue, although not originally desired except for its conduciveness to pleasure, and especially to protection from pain through association, became a good in itself, and desired with as great intensity as any other good.[22]

According to the utilitarian tenet, public safety officers should always behave in a way that will provide the most amount of good to the greatest number of people. So to summarize, consequences are more important than motives and determines whether or not an act was ethical. The group is more important than the individual; the behavior must contribute to the health of the community.

OTHER WAYS TO MAKE ETHICAL DECISIONS
Natural Law

The natural law ethical system maintains that there is a universal array of rights and wrongs that is similar to many religious beliefs, but it is connected to a God or heavenly figure. This system believes it is a given that what is good is what is natural and what in natural is what is good. They believe that morality is part of the natural order of the universe and is the same across time and civilizations. These laws exist apart from religion because they are universally determined moral laws. Religions such as Christianity, Judaism, or Islam merely included God or Allah as the origin of law.

There seems to be a focus on duty attached to the natural law theory much like formalism. Thomas Hobbs and John Locke changed the original natural law theory that stressed duties of humans in the natural order to one that stressed natural human rights.[23]

The natural rights theory historically balanced rights and duties. Rights and obligations go hand in hand. The scales of justice shows blindfolded dame justice balancing the scales, which depicts the rights of individual and the rights of society. This has been called the "Social Contract Theory," which dictates that one gives up some freedoms to be safe.

Blaise Pascal, a French philosopher born in June of 1623, also wrote about the natural law. He was a very religious person and most of his ideas have to be digested with this in mind. He had a negative opinion of human nature.

> "Human beings, by their own nature, always have the power to sin and to resist grace, and since the time of their corruption they always have an unfortunate depth of concupiscence which infinitely increases this this power of resistance."[24]

Pascal also stated, "Being unable to cure death, wretchedness, and ignorance men (and women) have decided to in order to be happy, not think about such things."

It appears that Pascal, because of his religiousness, believed that people were predestined to behave ethically by God. In other words, He decides who will behave with grace and therefore experience salvation. Some others are also given this grace but some will resist the chance of salvation.

It appears that Pascal, although he wrote and spoke about free will, believed that God determined will, not the individual.

Egoism

Egoism puts the individual first. It declares that the individual comes first; whatever is good for one's own survival and happiness is moral. Many philosophers dismiss the theory because it disregards the basic canons of an ethical system. Ethical systems address our behavior toward others and ourselves; we need to consider other people when living in a society. Each person cannot do his or her own thing because we would, in many cases, intrude on others' rights. John Rawls, a twentieth-century philosopher, said that each person is free and worthy of respect and liberty is restricted only out of respect for the liberty of others.

I guess we could look at egoism in a little broader light and make it a little more palatable. I have always had the idea that if you take care of number one first, you will then be able to take care of the people who depend on you.

In public safety, our reason for being dictates that we take care of others in their time of need. They are sick, injured, have lost loved ones and property, have been victims of rape, fire, accidents, assault, robbery, or murder. Public safety officers see people in trouble. This can be stressful for people who work in public safety, and they need to deal with that stress so that they can take care of the people and do it ethically. In other words, they need to put themselves first in order to function at their jobs. This includes physically, morally, and ethically.

We could call the former what Ayn Rand (1905–1982), a philosopher and novelist, labeled *ethical egoism,* which means humans should be self-interested. Rand also promoted the idea of *psychological egoism,* which states that humans are naturally selfish. We see and experience psychological egoism every day. We buy things at the lowest prices we can find, while others try to sell goods at a higher price. We try to get higher wages for our endeavors and our employers try to get away with paying as little as possible.

That being said, we can see that psychological egoism does have some relevance in natural law because self-preservation and utilitarianism are natural because hedonism is a natural tendency.

There is evidence that people are selfish and self-serving, but there is also evidence to the contrary. We have seen evidence of both tendencies. I guess the question is what is the true nature of humankind?

Relativism

Ethical relativism dictates there are no universal prohibitions or laws; it all depends on who you are with and what you are doing.

A police officer related a story to the authors that took place in the 1960s that best illustrates the problem we could have with this theory. The officer was on patrol in Marin County in California. He was in plain clothes and an unmarked car. He saw a "hippie" siphoning gas from a Volkswagen bus and watched awhile as the guy stuck a small hard rubber hose down the gas nozzle and sucked on the hose until gas began to flow. The hippie filled a one-gallon can with gas and began to walk away when the officer approached him and asked if the VW was his? He said,

"No it wasn't." And he didn't know who it belonged to. The cop asked if he had permission to take the gas. The hippie answered "no", but he didn't need it because was a natural resource that came from fossil remains and therefore belonged to everyone. The officer said, "Yes," and then asked, "but what about the person who owned the VW, didn't he have the right to the gas since he paid for it?" The guy repeated that no, the gas was a natural resource and he was just doing his thing as everyone should do. The cop said "OK, you're under arrest." The hippie recoiled with his hands in front of him saying, "Hey man, don't do your thing."

If we are to live in a civilization, we can't all "do our own thing" because we will eventually violate someone else's rights.

Although cultural relativism accepts the fact that different communities may have different moral standards, it also demands that individuals within a culture conform to the principles of their culture. Relativism is flawed in that there are no absolutes; what might be right in one area may be wrong in another; it is logically inconsistent.[25]

Situational Ethics

Situational ethics and relativism are sometimes considered the same. There is a difference in that there are no laws according to relativism, and situational ethics recognizes absolute laws.

Joseph Fletcher an Episcopal priest, a member of Euthanasia Educational Counsel, and a supporter of Planned Parenthood, was the father of situational ethics. He called his ethical theory a "method" of decision making instead of a "system." The rationale for this, according to Fletcher, was that systems lack life, freedom, and variety; "methods" can have all of these.

Fletcher cited a conversation that a friend of his had with a St. Louis cab driver at the end of a presidential campaign. The cab driver initiated the dialogue by saying "I and my father and grandfather before me, and their fathers, have always been straight ticket Republicans." "Ah," said Fletcher's friend, who is himself a Republican. "I take it that means you will vote for senator So-and-so." "No," said the cab driver, "There are times when a man has to push his principles aside and do the right thing."[26]

© alexmillos, 2014. Used under license from Shutterstock, Inc.

do the right thing.

Sometimes a situation may come along in which you must behave in a way that is contrary to your ethical stance. An example could be an officer working undercover trying to infiltrate a pedophile ring. The situation would require him or her to communicate with others on the computer regarding his or her sexual exploits with children and to exchange pictures as well. This will be repugnant to the officer but he or she needs to lie and fabricate stories to successfully complete the assignment. The officer will have to organize his or her thoughts in order to make the proper decision.

Most of us have learned that it is good to be generous and to help our fellow citizen when able. But whether an act is beneficial or not depends on the situation.

Are we being generous if a friend with a gambling problem wants to borrow some money to go to the track, or are we contributing to his difficulty? On the other hand, if the same friend needs money to buy food for his family, aiding him would be the right thing to do. In the one case, it is a bad idea to lend the money, but in the other situation, you are helping feed a family.

Fletcher indicated "Four Factors" that could be considered when attempting to make a decision about a certain situation.

1. The end: What is the object or result desired?
2. The means: How am I going to do it?
3. The motive: Why am I doing this?
4. The consequences: What could be the direct or indirect results of the action"[27]

If we examine the four factors mentioned, we are more likely to make a knowledgeable decision based on a thorough investigation of all of the elements of the situation.

In this chapter, we have explored some of the many theories and theorists and attempted to make sense of the various approaches to doing the right thing. One thinker believes that in order for an act to be ethical, the consequences of the act have to be considered, while another said that motive is the distinguishing factor that makes an act ethical. Relativism says there are no universal laws, while natural law maintains there is a natural law ethical system. Later in the book, we will investigate various processes of decision making, and in doing this, we will attempt to determine the most efficient method for arriving at a resolution to the question of "how to do the right thing?"

NOTES

1. Virtue Ethics-Windows Internet Explorer. http://www.ethicsmorals.com/ethicsvirtue.html Retrieved 11/25/2013.
2. Jocelyn M. Pollock, *Ethical Dilemmas and Decisions in Criminal Justice* 5th edition (Thomson-Wadsworth, 2007.) p. 47.
3. Plato, *Last days of Socrates* (New York: Penguin Classics, 1993).
4. Plato, *The Republic,* Book II (Oxford University Press, 1994).
5. Plato, *The Laws.* (Baltimore: Penguin, 1970, p. 193.
6. Plato, *The Laws.* p. 507.
7. Plato, *The Laws.* P. 194.
8. Jay Albanese, *Professional Ethics in Criminal Justice: Being Ethical When No One Is Looking.* 2nd Ed. (Boston: Allyn-Bacon, 2008) p. 32.
9. Albanese, *Professional Ethics,* P. 16.
10. Aristotle, *Nicomachean Ethics* (Cambridge, MA. Harvard University Press, 1926, p. 259.
11. R. Milch & C. H. Patterson, *Cliffs Notes on Aristotle's Ethics* (Lincoln, NE: Cliff's notes, Inc. 1992.
12. R. Scroton, P. Singer, Y.C. Janawa, and M. Tanner, *German Philosophers: Kant, Hegel, Schopenhauer, & Nietzsche* (New York: Oxford University Press, 1997).
13. Scroton, et al., *German Philosophers,* pp. 79–81.
14. Albanese, *Professional Ethics.* p. 34.

15. John Stuart Mill, *Utilitarianism* (Cambridge, MA: Hackett Publishing, 1979) p. vii.

16. Mill, *Utilitarianism.* (New York: Prometheus Books, 1993/1863), p. 16.

17. Mill, *Utilitarianism.* (1979), p. 31.

18. Albanese, *Professional Ethics,* p. 31.

19. Albanese, *Professional Ethics,* p.48.

20. John Stuart Mill, *Utilitarianism, Liberty, & Representative Government* (London: J.M. Dent & Sons, 1910, p. 3.

21. Mill, *Utilitarianism, Liberty, & Representative Government.* p. 35.

22. Mill, *Utilitarianism, Liberty, & Representative Government.* p. 35.

23. J.M. Pollock, *Ethical Dilemmas and Decisions in Criminal Justice, 5th ed.* (Belmont, CA: Wadsworth, 2007) p. 46.

24. Desmond Clarke, *Blaise Pascal.* Stanford Encyclopedia of Philosophy. http://plato.stanford .edu/entries/pascal/ Retrieved 12/13/2013.

25. Pollock, *Ethical Dilemmas,* p. 59.

26. Fletcher, Joseph, *Situation Ethics* (Philadelphia: The Westminster Press, 1966).

27. Fletcher, *Situation Ethics,* pp. 127–8.

DILEMMA

You are assigned to drive the sergeant around the district for the entire watch. The sergeant directs you to drive over to a bar and to park the car in the back lot. You do this, and then you and the sergeant enter the bar and the bartender says "Hi Sarge how's it going?" The sergeant says, "I'm good." "Give me a Jack Daniels and water." He asks you, "What're you having it's on the house?" What are your options? What are you going to do? Why?

_____

_____

_____

_____

_____

_____

_____

_____

_____

_____

_____

_____

_____

_____

_____

_____

_____

_____

_____

DILEMMA

You are called to the home of a person who has passed away. You enter the house and confirm that the person is indeed dead, and as stated in the rules and regulations, call your supervisor. He responds and takes charge of the scene in the house. You observed him searching the house and taking things from drawers and putting them in his brief case.

What are you going to do? Discuss various options.

_____

_____

_____

_____

_____

_____

_____

_____

_____

_____

_____

_____

_____

_____

_____

_____

_____

_____

_____

DILEMMA

There is a fire alarm at a bar; it was 3:30 a.m., and the fireplace was left on, which inadvertently started the fire. About three fire units and a police unit respond. After the fire has been put out, you see other firefighters and a police officer taking bottles of liquor out of the bar and stashing them in various places on the units and in their personal gear.

What are your options? What are you going to do? Why?

DILEMMA

You and your partner are on patrol when you receive a radio call to meet another officer to join in a search for a suspect in a local park. By the time you arrive, the suspect has been apprehended and handcuffed. As you approach the others, the suspect makes a remark and one of the officers hits him in the face with a heavy steel flashlight. Your partner says, "Let's go." And turn to leave.

Was it okay for the officer to hit the suspect? If not, what should you do? What are your options?

_____

_____

_____

_____

_____

_____

_____

_____

_____

_____

_____

_____

_____

_____

_____

_____

_____

DILEMMA

You are a firefighter in charge of a junior firefighter program. The focus of the program is to provide education and training to young people who are interested in firefighting. You see another firefighter who assists you in the program coming out of a movie with one of the young ladies in the program. She is a senior at the local high school and is 17 years of age.

Is this a potential problem? What are your options? Ethically, what should you do?

How Ethical Are You?

CHAPTER OBJECTIVES

1. Recognize types of ethics
2. What do we expect of ourselves?
3. How do you ensure ethical behavior?
4. What does ethics mean to you as a public safety officer?

4

TYPES OF ETHICS

Ethics exists in different shapes and sizes in today's society. There is business ethics, computer ethics, corporate ethics, education ethics, EMS ethics, end-of-life ethics, environmental ethics, firefighter ethics, government ethics, Internet ethics, police ethics, and workplace ethics. For a good example; Lockheed Martin has an ethics program that is considered a good corporate model. They have mandatory ethics awareness training for all of their 100,000 employees each year. They state that ethics is the essence of their business, do what's right, respect others, and perform with excellence. They believe that setting the standard is expected of all employees, directors, and consultants to participate in this ethics awareness training. Interesting to note, it is also a condition of continued employment with Lockheed Martin. For a bad example; Royal Caribbean Cruises has claimed that it's an environmentally responsible company. However, their actual conduct couldn't be further from the truth. The company was fined $18 million in fines and assessed an additional $9 million for dumping wastewater and hazardous chemicals at sea and in ports. Their motto was "Save the Waves" during the same timeframe of the illegal dumping.

Michael D Brown/Shutterstock.com

How do you interpret ethical? Gaming such as casinos or even games that we play at home such as Monopoly, include rules and ethics.

Let's discuss medical ethics. Medical ethics is primarily the study of moral values and judgments as they apply to medicine. In 2004, the State of California passed a controversial bond measure (Proposition 71) that authorizes the state to sell $3 billion in bonds and then dispense nearly $300 million a year for ten years to researchers for human embryonic stem-cell experiments, including cloning projects intended solely for research purposes. It bans the funding of cloning to create babies. This measure pitted scientists, sympathetic patients who could benefit from stem cells, and biotechnology interests against the Roman Catholic Church and conservatives opposed to the research because it involves destroying days-old embryos and cloning. Many scientists believe stem cells hold vast promise for treating an array of diseases from diabetes to Parkinson's and Alzheimer's.[1] There are public health policy ethics that includes pandemic influenza. In 2004, the Centers for Disease Control and Prevention (CDC) created a panel of ethicists for the first time in history to help it deal with the life and death questions of who should receive flu vaccine after a major shortage of the vaccine occurred.[2] Then, five years later the CDC's Advisory Committee on Immunization Practices (ACIP) met on July 29, 2009, to consider who should receive 2009 H1N1 vaccine. The CDC was concerned that the new

H1N1 virus could result in a particular severe 2009–2010 flu season. The recommendation considered several factors including current disease pattern and populations most at risk for severe illness based on current trends in illness. In order, the groups recommended were: pregnant women; caregivers for children younger than 6 months of age; healthcare and emergency medical services personnel; children from 6 months through 18 years of age; young adults 19 through 24 years or age; and persons aged 25 through 64 years who have health conditions associated with higher risk of medical complications from influenza.[3]

On October 29, 2009, the government website (www.flu.gov) stated that "More than half of the hospitalizations from 2009 H1N1 flu reported by twenty-seven states from September 1st and October 10th were people age twenty-four and younger. About 23 percent of the deaths reported from twenty-eight states during this period were in this age group. In addition, about 90 percent of the hospitalizations and deaths from the 2009 H1N1 flu are in people age sixty-four and younger. "As of October 14, 2009, 5,885,900 doses of H1N1 vaccine doses were shipped; 836,900 doses were shipped to California."[4] The *Science Daily* from October 4, 2009, reported the release of nine papers from the University of Toronto Joint Centre for Bioethics for public discussion involving the anticipated onset of a second wave of the H1N1 influenza pandemic. Topics included duty of healthcare workers to work during a serious flu pandemic, how to allocate limited medical resources, and the obligation of rich countries to share such resources with those less fortunate. "Now is the time to think through the serious ethical challenges societies may confront, not in the midst of crisis with line-ups at hospital doors. These issues and concerns, drawn largely from a Canadian point of view, have relevance to countries everywhere."[5] The Joint Centre for Bioethics papers stated a major pandemic will demand difficult ethical choices related to ventilators, vaccines, antiviral, and other resources. For example, who should get the first vaccine? Who should receive the last vaccine? Which patient will receive the last ventilator?

In 2009, President Barack Obama declared the H1N1 outbreak a national emergency. This enabled his health chief to move emergency departments offsite to speed treatment and protect patients who were not infected. At this time, forty-six states reported having widespread flu activity.

Some hospitals opened drive-thrus and drive-up tent clinics to screen, treat, or vaccinate H1N1 patients.[6] The goal was to keep infected people out of regular emergency departments and away from other sick patients. Other people waited in line for hours throughout the country to receive the vaccination.

There are other medical ethical situations as well. Difficult ethical dilemmas exist in the case of assisted suicide. In the 1990s, Dr. Jack Kevorkian claimed to have provided lethal drugs to 130 terminally ill patients. Many people call his work "murder" or "assisted suicide." On the other hand, many people believe that these drugs allow for "death with dignity."[7] Our society allows for the legal euthanasia of our pets when they are terminally ill or severely injured. *Webster' New World Dictionary* defines euthanasia as a "painless death to end suffering." Some people feel that Kevorkian was "playing God." After a televised assisted suicide in 1999, Kevorkian was convicted of second-degree murder and sentenced to ten to twenty-five years in prison. According to Kevorkian, "Planned death is a rational system that honors self-determination and extracts from a purposeful, unavoidable death the maximum benefit for the subject, the subject's next of kin, and for all of human-ity."[8] Medicide: The Goodness of Planned Death," Free Inquiry (Fall 1991), p. 15

The World Wide Web has embraced Internet ethics, or the lack of. In Chapter 8, we will discuss computer ethics and technology that has affected us in ways that you might not have thought about.

WHAT DO WE EXPECT OF OURSELVES?

Many of our ethical and moral dilemmas are "every day" decisions, which, by the way, start when you wake up in the morning. For example, you're standing in line at your favorite coffee house before work. The person in front of you reaches into their pocket and pulls out some money. A minute later you notice a bill on the floor. So, you pick it up and notice it's a twenty-dollar bill. What would you do? I believe most people would ask that person in line if they dropped this money. They would return the money no matter what denomination it is. But there are those that would say, "easy come, easy go," as the saying goes. There would be some sort of justifi-cation in their mind that they did not see the money fall from the person's pocket and you really don't know who it belongs to. Another example, you're now in your car driving to work and it took longer to get that coffee. You're late and running into some additional traffic and red lights. The clock is ticking and the boss, again, will not be happy if you're late. Light turns yellow, you accelerate to move through the traffic light, which by the way turns red before you enter the intersection. You guessed it, there is an accident and you have just hit someone. You know you are in the wrong by running a red light, that's against the law. But did you do anything wrong according to ethical and moral principles? Is it only when we hurt someone that makes it a bad ethical decision? It was only a fender bender; no one was hurt and then perhaps it was only bad luck. I didn't get away with it this time. Most of us, as in the preceding examples, have run through a yellow light and even perhaps a red light. The critical thinking process of ethical and moral principles would then teach us to know in advance the probability of getting into an accident. The rami-fications of that one-second decision, the chance that it's only a fender bender, or more seriously the possibility of a deadly accident, should be considered well in advance. Ethics takes critical thinking to the next step by examining our behavior and taking responsibility for our actions.

We could also ask ourselves about drinking and driving under the influence. Public safety officers see firsthand the end result of this serious problem. This process of critical thinking of ethical and moral principles is not something we do consciously on a regular basis, or is it? Can we learn and train ourselves to critique our situations in advance? Many primary schools today do not teach this thought process of critical thinking. However, you can take a class today in college on critical thinking for English, how to read between the lines. In today's society and media, ethical and moral principles can get lost easily. Pick your favorite mov-ies; they depict those public safety officers acting and behaving as heroes or then again maybe not. Firefighters running into burning buildings without full protec-tive equipment and turnouts not secured. Police officers racing into a bank robbery with guns drawn and firing away as if they were in the old West. We as firefighters and police officers enjoy the entertainment, but we also must remember the public watching this movie really believes that this is our daily routine. The public does not know about our daily, and sometimes mundane, routines. Their only perception about public safety officers and their jobs could very well be associated with movies and TV shows.

So I ask, what do we expect of ourselves? As a public safety officer we should know better than to take such a chance and risk an injury or accident. Remember, safety, safety, safety.

HOW DO YOU ENSURE ETHICAL BEHAVIOR

According to the report, January 24, 2010 officers arrived to the scene at around 1:15 A.M., twelve minutes after the reporting party called 911 saying, "I set the house on fire with the thing from my nose." The 74-year-old gave her address and the line went dead. Her reference was to an oxygen machine she used when she slept. This was used to help with her chronic obstructed pulmonary disease (COPD). Fire officers reported they found no signs of a fire when they first arrived. They drove around the cul-de-sac, slowly, but no one exited the engine or walked up the driveway to investigate further. Two firefighters, however, did get out of the apparatus to help spot while backing. Five hours later, after a neighbor called 911, firefighters returned and the home was completely engulfed in flames. The body of the victim, seventy-four, was discovered in the garage of her burned-out home. Multiple firefighters have been placed on leave in connection with this deadly house fire. Dunwoody, Georgia, is a northern suburb of Atlanta and incorporated as a city December 1, 2008. In the report, DeKalb officials said "The officers on the scene did not establish command and they didn't follow department policy."[9]

The Dunwoody police have opened a criminal investigation into the fatal fire, with the help of the DeKalb county district attorney's office. The victim's family believes she would still be alive had firefighters done their job and they also would like individual apologies from the firefighters involved.[10]

Here is a sad example of public safety officers not doing their job.[11] If only one firefighter or police officer had knocked on the door to talk to the reporting party, this fatal fire may not have happened. One apparatus operator, two Captains, and two Battalion Chiefs were terminated after the investigation. Reason, officers on the scene did not establish command and follow department policy. There was a higher court ruling on January 9, 2012; the Georgia Supreme Court ruled to reinstate one of the Captains. There are serious ramifications, legally, that affect our job as public safety officers. If we do not do our job someone may get hurt, or worse, may die.[12]

One daydream most all of us have had is to be a hero of some sort. We have many pretenses of who a hero is. We think of many popular images, such as a comic book hero like Superman, Spiderman, perhaps a firefighter, a policeman, a soldier, or an astronaut. But is there more to heroes than that?

The definition of a hero according to *Encarta Dictionary* is a main character in a fictional plot; man with super human powers; somebody admired; and a remarkably brave person.[13]

Most of us remember or have read about the explosion of the space shuttle *Challenger*. On January 28, 1986, at 11:38:00 A.M. EST, the *Challenger* lifted off.

An explosion seventy-three seconds after liftoff claimed the entire crew and shuttle. The cause of the explosion was determined to be an o-ring failure in the right solid rocket booster. Cold weather was determined to be a contributing factor.[14]

On that day in 1986, President Ronald Reagan had planned to report on the state of the Union but he said the

> events of earlier today have led me to change those plans. Today is a day for mourning and remembering. . . . And I want to say something to the schoolchildren of America who were watching the live coverage of the shuttle's takeoff. I know it is hard to understand, but sometimes painful things happen like this. It's all part of the process of exploration and discovery. It's all part of taking a chance and expanding man's horizons. The future doesn't belong to the fainthearted; it belongs to the brave. The *Challenger* crew was pulling us into the future, and we'll continue to follow them.

President Reagan went on to say that "the crew of the space shuttle *Challenger* honored us by the manner in which they lived their lives. We will never forget them, nor the last time we saw them, this morning, as they prepared for their journey and waved goodbye and 'slipped the surly bonds of earth' to touch the face of God".[15] Many people believe the *Challenger* crew were heroes.

Are heroes born or do they have a choice? If heroes are not born, who or what makes them? Some heroes are fictional and some are real life. Surely Mother Teresa and Mahatma Ghandi would be regarded as heroes. Most people agree that a hero displays emotional and physical courage or behave in an ethical and moral way. Celebrities are different than heroes. A celebrity is a celebrity because he or she is famous for being well known.

Many people dream of being a firefighter or a police officer. Children dress up in costume as firefighters and police officers. Many people feel firefighters and police officers are heroes. Especially after the tragic events at the Twin Towers on 9/11, most people believed firefighters, police officers, and EMS were heroes because they gave their lives protecting the public and those in need. They are exposed to events and situations far beyond the average person's experience on a daily basis. But aren't firefighters, for instance, supposed to rush into burning buildings? Isn't that their job? Is it not the job of the police officer to draw his weapon and shoot at the bad guys to protect the innocent? What about the "ordinary" mother who, without thinking, rushes back into a smoke-filled apartment in an attempt to save a child? Isn't she a hero as well? The ability to leap tall buildings in a single bound or to run faster than a speeding bullet is the definition of Superman, or a TV show with the title *Heroes*. Is that what the public thinks about public safety officers? Is that what public safety officers think of themselves? I certainly hope not on either account. I believe that firefighters, police officers and EMT/paramedics choose this profession because they truly want to help. They like the idea of making a contribution to society in a positive way to help their fellow man. They like the idea of a dynamic workplace, challenging, always different, and ever-changing.

From the website, www.imahero.com, you can see how people vote for their favorite heroes.

Timothy: A firefighter and loving brother.

My Aunt: She fights in the Navy.

My parents: Because they are loving and caring. They keep a roof over my head and food in my stomach. They're my heroes!!

My Mom: She is my hero because she never gives up on me.

Do you have a hero? If so, who is your hero, and why? Who do you think is deserving of the title, hero?

The public often thinks of firefighters and police officers as heroes. The 2001 annual CNN/*USA Today*/Gallup Poll ranking of the honesty and ethics of professions reflects this respect; firefighters rank first among people of different professions for their honesty and integrity, with 90 percent of Americans rating them "high" or "very high" on these characteristics. Following the 9/11 terrorist attacks in the United States, firefighters and other rescue personnel have been widely praised for their heroics as they risked their lives to save others. Nurses and the U.S. military rated close behind in the ratings. This is the only year firefighters were included in this Gallup Poll.

The police experienced an improvement in their ratings. In 1995, the year of the O. J. Simpson trial, only 41 percent gave the police a high rating. In 2001, 68 percent of Americans gave the police high ratings on their honesty and ethics. The lowest rating at the end of the scale was given to car salesmen.[16]

November 26–27, 2001

Please tell me how you would rate the honesty and ethical standards of people in these different fields: very high, high, average, low or very low?

	Percentage Saying "Very High" or "High"
Firefighters	90
Nurses	84
U.S. military	81
Policemen	68
Pharmacists	68
Medical doctors	66
Clergy	64
Engineers	60
College teachers	58
Dentists	56
Accountants	41
Bankers	34
Journalists	29
Congressmen	25
Business executives	25
Senators	25
Auto mechanics	22

Stockbrokers	19
Lawyers	18
Labor union leaders	17
Insurance salesmen	13
Advertising practitioners	11
Car salesmen	8

WHAT THE PUBLIC THINKS OF PUBLIC SAFETY OFFICERS

We all remember what we were doing on 9/11. Hundreds of firefighters, emergency medical personnel, and police rushed into the World Trade Center on that day to never to be seen alive again. These men and women were not forced to put their lives at risk; they were practicing what they had been trained to do as professionals. And in doing so they reminded us of the most distinguishing feature of the professions, namely altruism, the commitment to put the well-being of others ahead of their own.

So it should not come as a surprise that when firefighters and police behave in an unethical way that the public is then sometimes quick to judge because they are disappointed. Public safety officers are not supposed to do bad things. We trust them, as the public would say. What happened to their hero? What happened to those we trust—those who save us, help us, and protect us? Public safety is public service. You are on stage, on the job and off, publicly, and in your private life. Your neighbor knows who you are and what you do. The public is paying our salaries. They, at times, believe we get paid too much, especially for making bad ethical decisions.

In response to the alleged "using the Internet to exchange child pornography" charges against a thirty-year veteran fire captain, his department said in a news statement that they were "deeply saddened" that one of their employees had been arrested. This thirty-year veteran of the fire department was placed on administrative leave and subsequently retired when police started their child sexual exploitation investigation.[17]

Then, the youngest firefighter ever to be promoted to captain in his department, recipient of the medal of valor, and 9/11 rescuer, is one who we would never expect to plead guilty to possessing images of minors engaged in sexually explicit conduct. His attorney stated that "9/11 had such a traumatic experience on him that experts believe it created a circumstance that these events happened when he had too much to drink." He has accepted responsibility and has paid a heavy price."[18] Unfortunately, emergency work can take a tragic toll on first responders. In New York, three firefighters who helped rescue 9/11 victims killed themselves within a year. In Oklahoma City, a police sergeant, who rescued victims at the federal building bombing, committed suicide.

There have been other such situations that have profound and lasting impact. In 1987, Baby Jessica became wedged in a pipe twenty-two feet down and eight to fourteen inches wide. Rescuers piped fresh air and heat down to her while they labored to rescue her. Scores of rescuers drilled a parallel tunnel and connecting shaft through solid rock to rescue her. A vital part of the rescue was the use of the then relatively new technology of waterjet cutting. When she was finally pulled out, she was filthy but alert, wrapped in gauze, and strapped to a backboard. Rescuers cheered and there was even a White House Reception with President George H. W. Bush and First Lady Barbara Bush. She had become "Everybody's Baby," the title of an ABC TV movie about her rescue. The photograph of her being rescued taken by Scott Shaw of the *Odessa American* won the 1988 Pulitzer Prize for spot news photography. The footage of Jessica being rescued is shown in Michael Jackson's music video *Man in the Mirror*.

Ten years later, a Pew Research Center project showed that only the death of Princess Diana drew more worldwide media coverage than Jessica's rescue. In May 2007, the staff of *USA Today* placed Jessica twenty-second on a list of the twenty-five people who have had the most impact on our lives during the past quarter century. During that time the only other media coverage that drew more interest was the coverage of Rodney King, the crash of TWA Flight 800, the Columbine High School shootings, and the end of the first Gulf War.[19]

Donations for her poured in after her rescue. The money, estimated at the time to be between $700,000 and $1 million dollars, was put into a trust fund that she will be able to access when she is twenty-five. She said she intends to sign the fund over to her son, Simon. Jessica has a visible diagonal scar on her forehead. It marks where her forehead had been rubbed raw against the well casing during the almost three days she was trapped. She endured fifteen surgeries in the years after the incident to repair injuries she suffered. Her small toe and part of her right foot had to be removed because gangrene had set in where circulation had been cut off. She has scars on her thighs from where skin was harvested for grafts. In high school, she was diagnosed with juvenile rheumatoid arthritis. In March of 2011, Baby Jessica turned twenty-five and gained access to her trust fund which was valued around $800,000. She is now a contented stay-at-home mother of two and lives less than two miles from the site of the 1987 rescue. According to her father, she has no memory of being wedged in the pipe or the fifteen operations that followed.

In 1995, a paramedic and rescuer, who squeezed into the passageway and slathered a frightened Baby Jessica in petroleum jelly before sliding her out into the bright TV lights, shot and killed himself at his parents' ranch outside Midland. His brother said his life "fell apart" because of the stress of the rescue, the attention it created, and the anticlimactic return to everyday life.

In 2004, a former Midland police officer who helped in the rescue was sentenced to fifteen years in federal prison on charges of sexual exploitation of a child and improper storage of explosives. A year later, he was sentenced to twenty years on two state charges of sexual assault.[20]

The police officer, firefighter, and EMT/paramedic are expected to perform under these situations of putting a complete stranger's well-being first. This is our job, our training, and our expectations, both of ourselves and the public's.

According to an October 16, 2009, article in the *Sacramento Bee*, a retired Sacramento County veteran lieutenant pled guilty to possession of hundreds of images of child pornography found on his home computer. He was charged with possession of items depicting minors engaged in sexually explicit conduct and entered a plea agreement in which he agreed to plead guilty, court documents state. Agents found more than six hundred images on computer hard drives.[21]

The ethical behavior of public officials is critical to the performance of public agencies. Police officers, regularly and without warning, confront important value choices. The demands of the job may be in itself too much for some officers. Facing danger constantly, having unusual hours and sleep habits, and being continually surrounded by criminals may be too much stress, particularly when experienced over a period of several years.[22] Firefighters and EMT/paramedics are exposed to the same situations. They work twenty-four to ninety-six hours straight before they can go home to their families. The stresses of the public safety officers are a constant reminder of the daily job.

Police officers and firefighters have a higher divorce rate than the national average. According to Police-Dynamics.com, studies consistently show that the police profession has a divorce rate 60 to 70 percent higher than the national average; the alcoholism rate is two times the national average; the domestic violence rate is among the highest of all professions; and the suicide rate is three times the national average.[23] As discussed previously, they are facing danger, are under stress, and have unusual sleep habits.

In 2008, Sherwood Baptist Church in Albany, Georgia, produced the movie *Fireproof*. The film has both a marriage-saving message and a Christian message. In the movie, firefighter Caleb Holt lives by the firefighter's credo: "Never leave your partner behind." He saves a victim from a burning building, and he states "I am a hero to everybody—except my wife." Because firefighters divorce at a rate of 70 percent, firemen and spouses were invited by churches to come see the movie for free. *Fireproof* was more than a movie. It is being used to strengthen marriages. To help save a marriage, go to www.fireproofthemovie.com.[24]

After digesting all of that, you may be asking, why would I put myself and my family through all of that negative stuff? To expose myself to the public safety officer's stresses and adrenalin rushes; to be held to higher standards than other professions; and to fall farther than other professions when we make a mistake or when we make poor ethical and moral decisions. We believe that most, if not all, public safety officers feel that it is a privilege to serve the public and to be held accountable for their actions. We are compelled and driven to do good work. The competition is challenging and tough. For every one person hired, there may have been one hundred qualified applicants. To finally be able to submit a resume that represents the high level of standards required to get the job takes many years of education, volunteer work, community service, and experience. I ask my students every semester: Who do you want to respond to a call for your loved ones? A 911 call from your parents or grandparents who expect only the best to show up and perform their job and to possibly save a life. It really does not matter whether it's for a heart attack, a fire, or a burglary. The public expects only the best to arrive, make appropriate, quick, and ethical decisions. To protect us, to save us, and to be their hero for that few moments in time.

WHEN PUBLIC SAFETY OFFICERS ADVERSELY DISAGREE IN PUBLIC

On the evening of February 5, 2014, Chula Vista firefighters responded to an unfortunate rollover accident on Interstate 805 in Chula Vista, California. During patient care, a CHP Officer instructed a fire engineer to move the fire engine from the center divider (where it was protecting the ambulance, firefighters and patients). There were conflicting reports, however, the end result was that a fire engineer on scene while providing patient care was arrested and placed in the back of a CHP vehicle for a reported 30 minutes.

Many videos and news articles appeared in different places with lots of photos and lots of opinions of what happened at the crash site with this 12 ½-year fire service veteran.

The following are just some of the headlines that followed (even internationally):

- Firefighter Responding to Crash Victims, Handcuffed by California Highway Patrol
- Must see: Firefighter Handcuffed at Crash Scene by California Highway Patrol
- Firefighter Arrested by CHP Officer During Rescue: Move Your Truck From Accident, Said Cop
- Fire, Police Chiefs Meet After Firefighter's Arrest
- CHP Calls Chula Vista Firefighter's Arrest At Crash Scene 'Unfortunate Incident'

Meetings took place between the CHP and the Fire Department all in an effort to join in training so this situation wouldn't happen again. Statements were released by the Chula Vista Fire Department stating they were proud of how the firefighters handled the situation and treating and transporting the victims to the hospital. During the initial few days after this detainment the CHP had no comment. In most instances, both fire and police are able to perform their jobs professionally with the safety and best interest for the public. This particular night the public did not see that fire and police were working together for public safety.

To no surprise, some of the public's general comments included statements that a lot of people were thinking:

> How do they act when there isn't a camera filming? Could they both be right and wrong and acted out of ego? Isn't saving a life a priority? The cop handled this one poorly! No winners here! This cop needs some time off to think about what is truly important. Poorly trained cops! If the police treat firefighters like this, just imagine what goes on with the police and public when there are no cameras. Why don't you arrogant firemen take off those stupid fire hat stickers and license plates off your vehicles and quit driving like jerks? 25 tons of fire truck works better at protecting emergency responders than flares do. Settle your differences off the scene. They should have decided to have the pissing contest after the emergency was over. Aren't public safety servants required to be professional at all times? This guy could have died and the CHP officer is still thinking about traffic laws.[25]

As you can plainly read here, the public is very confused, perplexed and just does not understand how firefighters and police officers can't do their jobs professionally. If there was a disagreement on scene, there are much better ways to handle this.

A few weeks after this incident, the fire engineer filed a lawsuit against the CHP. His intent is making policy change and he is not looking for compensation.[26]

It is clear there is "No Winner". Whatever happened that evening in the middle of a freeway rescue will not be remembered for the rescue, but for the handcuffed fire engineer. This is a very poor judgment call during an emergency which has lasting ramifications. That is, we as public safety officers must remember who we work for . . . the public. When the taxpayers have negative thoughts about our professions, there is a price to pay somewhere. Like building new police and fire stations, or hiring new public safety officers. When we choose to be professionals, and resolve these differences back at the station, there would be no reason to have a black eye in the public's eye. There have been other such instances across the country where law enforcement and firefighters adversely disagree, where a firefighter was arrested on scene. All public safety must take a hard look at the total long-term outcomes of such near-sighted actions.

NYPD vs. FDNY Annual Charity Hockey Match Turns In to a Brawl

Many of you have heard "New York's Finest" and "New York's Bravest". What happened on Sunday, April 6, 2014 when police and firefighters played a charity hockey match and an unbelievable brawl took the stage was not the best example of our Finest and Bravest.[27] It's sad to say no one will remember the names of the charities for which these New York Departments played for, but rather the brawl that took center ice. The ice fight sent social media into hyper speed with photos and videos of the violence. Some of the videos had disclaimers because the video contained Adult Language. This all took place at Nassau Coliseum on Long Island, home of the New York Islanders NHL team and turned into a full-out fight. The only difference was the players were professional firefighters and police officers.[28]

The game was delayed for 25 minutes as gloves; sticks and other equipment were picked up off the ice. Several players were ejected from the game. Despite numerous black eyes and bruises, no players appeared to be seriously injured. The score was tied, 3-3. The NYPD team went on to win the game, 8-5 for their first victory over the FDNY in six years. The game benefited various charities, including the New York Police and Fire Widows' and Children's Benefit Fund. Both departments declined to comment after the event.[29]

Is there a moral to the story? How can two professional organizations act like hockey players out of control? Come on, when you call 911, who do you want to arrive on scene? Many of the spectators stated they thought they were rolling back the years in the 70's and 80's when bench clearing occurred at every game. The only two not fighting were clearly the goalies standing mid-ice together watching.[30]

This is another example of being in the public's eye… these are our heroes, as the public often refers! There have been many comments made of this charity game, and to no surprise, certainly not favorable ones. Some say this has gone on for 40 plus years, between New York Police and Fire, boys will be boys. After all, it's just hockey. While others say, this is a poor example of our public servants. They should lead by example, they are not professional hockey players; they are professional firefighters and police officers. We are held to a higher standard, we are in the public's eye every day, on and off duty. The judgment public safety officers receive from the public is expected. We are sworn to duty, to protect life and property, all the time.

Speaking of black eye, here are some general thoughts about this charity hockey match between fire and police from the public: Aren't they supposed to be lead by example? Wild animals in different uniforms. One side the "bravest", the other the "finest". Collectively, they're both the stupidest. If I was playing a game, and someone punched me, would it not be a crime? Not acceptable.

WHAT DOES ETHICS MEAN TO YOU?

Sociologist Raymond Baumhart asked business people, "What does ethics mean to you?" Some replies were:

> "Ethics has to do with what my feelings tell me is right or wrong."
> "Ethics has to do with my religious beliefs."
> "Being ethical is doing what the law requires."
> "Ethics consists of the standards of behavior our society accepts."
> "I don't' know what the word means."[31]

Being ethical is also *not* following your feelings or following the law. Do you think that being ethical is doing what is acceptable to society? What are some examples of laws that have deviated from what is ethical? Unfortunately, we can look to our own history in the United States or Nazi Germany of World War II to find unethical and immoral practices.

Now, let's take a look at the Boy Scouts and Girl Scouts. The Scouts teach at an early age about high moral standards, community involvement, and good citizenship.

In 2008, a tornado hit an Iowa Boy Scout camp, killing four Scouts and injuring dozens. There were many stories of heroism, describing how older boys shielded younger ones with their bodies and, remembering their motto when it counted most and using their training to save lives. There were ninety-three Scouts, ages thirteen to eighteen at the remote camp, which was out of cell phone range. The tornado warnings issued twelve minutes previously did not reach many of the Scouts. The tornado destroyed cabins, burying boys under the rubble. Iowa Governor Chet Culver confirmed that "All four of the young men who were killed are Scouts, . . . they responded as quickly as they could. Think lives were saved. They were the real heroes of this story."[32] The Scouts were personally challenged, and they performed admirably.

Both the Boy Scouts and Girl Scouts teach at an early age to be true at all times, to have a high morale code of virtues, ideals, standard of behavior, and to be a good citizen. These are all a way of life.

A police officer that knows a fellow officer has engaged in wrongdoing must choose between the values of friendship and loyalty to the organization and society. Whistle-blowers are not disgruntled employees. Whistle-blowers are normal people who have a strong conscience, are high performers committed to the formal goals of their organization, and have a strong sense of professional responsibility."[33]

Police tend to find themselves in a fish bowl, or on videotape, and then have to defend actions they thought were noble or at least appropriate at the time. Most police are visible in their uniforms and in their vehicles, making their actions—both good and bad—more noticeable to the public. Police officers are exposed to temptations not often found in other vocations.[34]

The overall results of law enforcement organizations lacking ethical behaviors are mistrust and the loss of support. As governmental organizations, law enforcement agencies must demonstrate their ability to retain the trust of the citizens they protect. Gaining public trust requires the process of an organization and public administrators to possess trustworthy behaviors. Ethical behaviors that lead to public trust include integrity, openness, loyalty, ethical competence, and consistency. The more ethical a government is, the more public trust it gains.[35] Length of service has some impact on officer attitudes and behavior. New officers with less than one year of service have high ethical awareness and standards but are reluctant to report misconduct. This is understandable considering new recruits are on probation and may not be familiar with what happens to officers who report misconduct.[36]

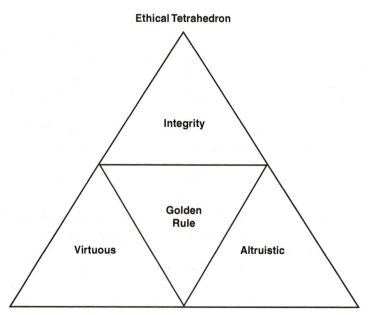

integrity: noun
quality of being honest, strong principles, uprightness, honesty, good character, righteousness, fairness, truthfulness, trustworthiness

altruistic: adjective
unselfish, selfless, compassionate, kind, public spirited, humanitarian, charitable

virtuous: adjective
righteous, good, pure, high morals, upstanding, high minded, reputable, noble,

golden rule: noun
the rule of conduct that one should behave toward others as one would have others behave toward themselves

Just as police officers, firefighters, and other emergency responders drive police vehicles, fire trucks, fire engines, and ambulances; it is not easy to blend into the public eye. After all, they're not intended to "blend in." They are designed to represent public safety. In Chapter 2, the Sacramento City firefighters who attended the "Porn Star Ball" with a fire engine, likewise, did not blend in. The public, rightfully so, was outraged that public funds were being spent at an event of this nature and not for an emergency call. The public asked the question, "Do these firefighters have this much time on their hands? Shouldn't they be saving lives and fighting fires?"

JUSTIFICATION?

Some may say, it doesn't hurt anyone; I'm just fighting fire with fire; it's all for a good cause; everyone's doing it, it's okay if I don't' gain personally; I've got it coming. People who feel overworked or are underpaid rationalize that minor "perks" are nothing more than fair compensation for services rendered. This is also an excuse to abuse sick time, insurance claims, overtime, personal phone calls, and personal use of office supplies.

Is the action that I am considering legal? Does it violate any rules, laws, or policies? Is the action balanced? Is it fair for all concerned in the short term and in the long term? Is anyone being exploited or harmed? How will the action make me feel about myself? How would I feel if this action were made public? If it were in tomorrow's paper? On the news? If my family found out? Can I explain it to others?[37]

It is important to recognize that the greater the potential consequences, the greater the need for careful decision making.

1. Could you or someone else suffer physical harm?
2. Could you or someone else suffer serious emotional pain?
3. Could the decision hurt your reputation, undermine your credibility, or damage important relationships?
4. Could the decision impede the achievement of any important goal?[38]

SUMMARY

Consider the following: to do my best, serve God and Country, help others at all times, morally straight, honest and fair, helpful, caring, courageous and strong, respect others and authority, make the world a better place. All are excellent attributes for everyone to follow, especially for public safety officers. We are in the spotlight every day, on every call, whether we are on duty or off duty. Ask yourself this question, would I or someone I love be embarrassed about this decision? Would I be proud or would I be embarrassed to see this on the front page news in the paper? We should constantly be aware of our responsibility to ourselves, our families, to our department, and to the public for whom we serve, and we should be honored to have this opportunity.

NOTES

1. MSNBC, "California Gives Go-Ahead to Stem-Cell Research" www.msnbc.com/id/6384390 (accessed October 18, 2009).

2. Jay Albanese, *Professional Ethics in Criminal Justice* (Boston: Pearson Allyn and Bacon, 2006).

3. Centers for Disease Control and Prevention. "2009 H1N1 Vaccination Recommendations." www.cdc.gov/h1n1flu/vaccination/acip.htm (accessed October 18, 2009).

4. Centers for Disease Control and Prevention. "2009 H1N1 Flu Continues to Impact Young People." www.flu.gov/news/blogs/youngpeople.html (accessed October 21, 2009).

5. Science Daily, "Medical Ethics Experts Identify, Address Key Issues in H1N1 Pandemic." www.sciencedaily.com/releases/2009/09/090923132958.htm (accessed October 18, 2009).

6. P. Elliott, "Obama: H1N1 an emergency." *North County Times.* October 25, 2009. p. A1.

7. Albanese, *Professional Ethics in Criminal Justice.* p. 128.

8. Jack Kavorkian, *Medicide: The Goodness of Planned Death*, Free Inquiry (Fall 1991), p. 15.

9. CBS Atlanta, "Fifth DeKalb Firefighter Fired after Deadly Blaze." www.cbsatlanta.com/news/22367003/detail.html (accessed February 8, 2010).

10. Atlanta Journal Constitution, "DeKalb Firefighters Fired, Criminal Probe under Way." www.ajc.com/news/dekalb/dekalb-firefighters-fired-criminal-286964.html?cxntlid=daylf_artr (accessed February 8, 2010).

11. www.wsbtv.com (accessed April 3, 2014).

12. www.firehouse.com (accessed April 3, 2014).

13. Microsoft Encarta Dictionary, English, North American (accessed 10/21/10).

14. National Aeronautics and Space Administration, "Mission Archives STS-51L." www.nasa.gov/mission_pages/shuttle/shuttlemissions/archives/sts-51L.html (accessed January 27, 2010).

15. National Aeronautics and Space Administration, "Explosion of the Space Shuttle Challenger Address to the Nation, January 28, 1986 by President Ronald W. Reagan." http://history.nasa.gov/reagan12886.html (accessed January 27, 2010).

16. D. Moore, "Firefighters Top Gallup's "Honesty and Ethics" List."www.gallup.com/poll/5095/Firefighters-Top-Gallups-Honesty-Ethics-List.aspx (accessed February 15, 2010).

17. KCRA, "Man Arrested at Home Wednesday." http://www.kcra.com (accessed February 15, 2010).

18. J. Jimenez, "Ex-fire captain pleads guilty to child porn charges." www.3signonsandiego.com/stories/2009/oct22/bn22porn-fire-captain (accessed October 22, 2009).

19. M. Celizic, "Baby Jessica 20 years later." www.today.msnbc.com/id/19165433/ (accessed February 3, 2010).

20. B. Blaney, "20 Years Later, 'Baby Jessica' Will Collect $1 Million." www.katu.com/news/national/10625457.html (accessed February 3, 2010).

21. S. Stanton, "Sacramento County Sheriff's Veteran Pleads Guilty to Child Porn Charges." www.sacbee.com (accessed October 16, 2009).

22. J. Raines, *Ethics in Policing Misconduct and Integrity* (Sudbury, MA: Jones and Bartlett Publishers, 2010). p. 5.

23. Police-Dynamics, "Highest Rates of Divorce, Alcoholism, Domestic Violence and Suicides." www.police-dynamics.com/divorce.html (accessed October 22, 2009).

24. M. McManus, "Ethics and Religion." www.ethicsandreligion.com/redesignedcolumns/C1413.htm (accessed September 17, 2009).

25. http://www.cbs8.com/story/24637357/firefighter-detained-by-chp-after-dispute-at-crash-site (accessed February 23, 2014).

26. http://www.utsandiego.com/news/2014/mar/25/firefighter-gregoire-chp-arrest-handcuff/ (accessed March 26, 2014).

27. http://www.huffingtonpost.com/2014/04/07/nypd-fdny-brawl_n_5103022.html?utm_hp_ref=charity (accessed April 9, 2014).

28. http://www.foxnews.com/us/2014/04/07/bench-clearing-brawl-breaks-out-during-charity-hockey-game-between-nypd-and/ (accessed April 9, 2014).

29. http://newyork.cbslocal.com/2014/04/06/charity-brawl-nypd-fdny-engage-in-wild-fisticuffs-at-nassau-coliseum/ (accessed April 9, 2014).

30. http://www.nydailynews.com/new-york/cops-firefighters-fight-charity-hockey-game-article-1.1747865 (accessed April 9, 2014).

31. M. Velasquez, C. Andre, S. J. Shanks, and M. Meyer, "What Is Ethics?" www.scu.edu/ethics/practicing/decision/whatisethics.html (accessed September 17, 2009).

32. M. Celizic, "Boy Scouts Describe Heroism Amid Tornado Terror." http://today.msnbc.com/id/25113624/ (accessed January 30, 2010).

33. Raines, *Ethics in Policing Misconduct and Integrity*. p. 3.

34. M. Braswell, L. Miller, and J. Pollock, *Case Studies in Criminal Justice Ethics* (Long Grove, IL: Waveland Press, Inc., 2006). p. 9.

35. Raines, *Ethics in Policing Misconduct and Integrity*. p. 175.

36. Raines, *Ethics in Policing Misconduct and Integrity*. p. 210.

37. California Commission on Peace Officer Standards and Training, "Ethical Decision-Making Tools for California Law Enforcement." p. 20.

38. California Commission on Peace Officer Standards and Training, "Ethical Decision-Making Tools for California Law Enforcement." p. 20.

DILEMMA

List four ethical or moral situations that you have recently experienced. Then, answer the following questions:

Dilemma #1 _____

_____

_____

_____

_____

_____

_____

_____

_____

_____

1. Did this decision affect someone else in a negative way?
2. Did you have an opportunity to give input for a different outcome?
3. Was the outcome the best choice?
4. Would you change anything about that outcome?

Dilemma #2 _____

_____

_____

_____

_____

_____

_____

_____

_____

_____

1 Did this decision affect someone else in a negative way?
2. Did you have an opportunity to give input for a different outcome?
3. Was the outcome the best choice?
4. Would you change anything about the outcome?

Dilemma #3 _____

_____

_____

_____

_____

_____

_____

_____

_____

_____

_____

_____

1. Did this decision affect someone else in a negative way?
2. Did you have an opportunity to give input for a different outcome?
3. Was the outcome the best choice?
4. Would you change anything about that outcome?

Dilemma #4 _____

_____

_____

_____

_____

_____

_____

_____

_____

_____

_____

1. Did this decision affect someone else in a negative way?
2. Did you have an opportunity to give input for a different outcome?
3. Was the outcome the best choice?
4. Would you change anything about that outcome?

Ethics for Public Safety

5

CHAPTER OBJECTIVES

1. Understand the history of law enforcement ethics.
2. Comprehend the importance of ethical behavior.
3. Understand the importance of obtaining the cooperation of the public.
4. Compare and contrast the Police Code of Ethics to Peel's Sets of Principles.

Courtesy of the author.

A code of ethics is an external control on people's behavior, where ethics have to come from the moral beliefs of the individual. Many professions have codes of ethics that endeavor to ensure that the people practicing in that particular field serve their clients to the best of their ability. The legal profession has a code of ethics and the Hippocratic Oath seeks to regulate the professional behavior of physicians. While these oaths are definitely beneficial to the people who practice these professions, it is the moral fabric of the individual that dictates whether or not a person behaves ethically.

The reality is that while codes of ethics are important and should be adhered to, they are very difficult to enforce. For example, most of the public safety officers behave in an ethical manner, but they are reluctant to snitch on an officer who is misbehaving and then to testify in a formal hearing against that colleague. The "Blue Wall of Silence" that is often referred to when discussing the unwillingness of police officers to testify against other officers is an example of this. This is especially true when the violation is a minor one.

Morality is not simply about *what* we do, but more importantly, it is about *why* we do what we do.[1] Officers need to do the right thing because it is the appropriate response to a situation, not because the code of ethics says they should. Codes of ethics cannot possibly take into consideration all of the various scenarios that can take place during the course of doing police work. There are many temptations that can arise on any given day and there is many times no official supervision to indicate the right course of action. So the officer has to use his or her discretion (judgment) and his or her moral compass.

An article written by Eric Tucker for the Associated Press on January 24, 2014, states that Washington D.C. officer Marc Washington was charged with taking seminude pictures, while on duty, of a teenage runaway who had returned home. He said he wanted to photograph the girl's injuries so he asked her to disrobe. Shortly after his arrest, the officer was found dead; it is alleged that he took his own life.

Another case in the District of Columbia alleged that Officer Linwood Barnhill Jr., who had been in the police department for twenty-four years, harbored a sixteen-year-old girl, who had been reported missing, in his apartment and had offered her money to have sex with other men.[2]

These are two cases where the moral compass malfunctioned. Why do things such as these happen?

Are they planned or are they the results of opportunity?

The Chief of the Washington D.C. department Cathy Lanier said that many of the arrests of D.C. officers happened while they were off duty. It doesn't matter whether the problems are off or on duty because the code of ethics states, "I will keep my private life unsullied as an example to all." It is imperative that officers behave ethically at all times.

British Police Helmet.

EARLY ATTEMPTS AT POLICING

When the settlers first came to this country, they established a night watch. These folks were responsible for the safety of the community. To supplement the night watch, there were also sheriffs and constables. In the southern colonies, the people organized slave patrols, whose task was to apprehend, control, punish, and return the slaves. In 1837, Charleston South Carolina had a one-hundred-member slave patrol. This patrol was larger than any northern city police force at the time.[3] Policing formally began in 1829. Prior to that, crime in England was judged to be pretty much out of control. People had to deal with crime on their own because there was no strong central government. So as a result, criminal activity was left unchecked and allowed to thrive. Because crime was so prevalent, the death penalty was imposed quite frequently. It is said that between the years of 1509 and 1547, seventy-two thousand criminals were executed by hanging.[4]

Kin policing was an early attempt at law enforcement. Basically, it entailed the victim's family being involved in the solving of the crime. The family was actually responsible for apprehending and bringing the criminal to justice. This was an informal system that was more like common law and was not based on any precept of law.

According to the Metropolitan Police Archives, the word *police* means, generally, the arrangements made in all civilized countries to ensure that the inhabitants keep the peace and obey the law. The word also denotes the force of peace officers employed for this purpose.[5]

In 1829, Sir Richard Moore wrote:

The primary object of an efficient police is the prevention of crime; the next that of detection and punishment of offenders if crime is committed. To these ends all the efforts of police must be directed. The protection of life and property, the preservation of public tranquility, and the absence of crime, will alone prove whether those efforts have been successful and whether the objects for which the police were appointed have been attained.[6]

To do much of what is mentioned previously, the police need the approval and cooperation of the citizens. The amount of approval and cooperation is usually determined by the level of esteem and respect in which the police are held.

It is interesting that we are still discussing concerns that were prevalent in the nineteenth century. Respect can be achieved simply by doing the job ethically. Which it seems is not that easy, based on the history of law enforcement.

London's first police officers were called the "Bow Street Runners" and were formed around 1750 by Henry Fielding, who, in addition to being a well-known author (*Tom Jones*), was a justice of the peace for Westminster and Middlesex and crusaded against corruption in legal issues. The Bow Street Runners didn't patrol as officers do today, but traveled around the country serving warrants, doing

Robert Peel (1788–1850). Engraved by J. Cochran and published in the letters of Queen Victoria 1844–1853, United Kingdom, 1907.

detective work, and arresting criminals. The Bow Street Runners wore red waist coats and were sometimes referred to as the "Robin Red Breasts."

The Runners were initially financed by the government who gave Fielding £200 to pay them, but after that money ran out they survived mainly on rewards and payments from victims who would pay them. Fielding would advertise in newspapers informing victims of crimes about the existence of the Bow Street Runners.

After Fielding retired, his brother John Fielding took his place and improved the group and made it the first effective police department in London. He hired more officers and later created a horse patrol.

This was the beginning of formal policing; a move toward the professionalization of the occupation of law enforcement was continued by Sir Robert Peel.

Sir Robert Peel

Sir Robert Peel (1788–1850) is known as the father of modern policing. He was the oldest son of a wealthy cotton manufacturer. He was educated at Harrow and Oxford in England. At one time, he was the prime minister of the United Kingdom. In 1829, Peel established the London Metropolitan Police, which is housed at Scotland Yard. He developed a set of principles to define an ethical police department, and actually there are a few sets of principles that are attributed to Peel.

The original Peelian Principles were:

1. Every officer should be issued a badge number, to assure accountability for his actions.
2. Whether the police are effective is not measured on the number of arrests, but on the lack of crime.
3. Above all else, an effective authority figure knows trust and accountability are paramount.[7]

Peel said:

> The police are the public and the public are the police; the police being only members of the public who are paid to give full time attention to duties which are incumbent on every citizen in the interests of community welfare existence.

This statement says quite a bit; in a democratic society, the police are not apart from society, they are a part of society. The police are hired and controlled by the citizens of whatever jurisdiction that employs them. Officers take an oath of office that states they will uphold the Constitution of the United States and whatever state, city, or other political subdivision the officers are working in, and that they will uphold the constitutional rights of the citizens of that jurisdiction.

Peel also said that all citizens are responsible for the community welfare. This means that all citizens need to cooperate with the police and report crimes that they witness and also help people who become victims of crimes.

The New Westminster Police Service in Canada listed nine principles of policing that are accreted to Peel. They are:

1. The basic mission for which the police exist is to prevent crime and disorder.
2. The ability of the police to perform their duties is dependent upon the public approval of police actions.
3. Police must secure the willing cooperation of the public in voluntary observation of the law to be able to secure and maintain the respect of the public.
4. The degree of cooperation of the public that can be secured diminishes proportionately to the necessity of the use of physical force.
5. Police seek and preserve public favor not by catering to public opinion, but by constantly demonstrating absolute impartial service to the law.
6. Police use of physical force to the extent necessary is to secure observance of the law or to restore order only when the exercise of persuasion, advice, and warning is found to be insufficient.
7. Police, at all times, should maintain a relationship with the public that gives reality to the historic tradition that the police are the public and the public are the police; the police only being members of the public who are paid to give full-time attention to duties which are incumbent upon every citizen in the interests of community welfare and existence.
8. Police should always direct their action strictly towards their functions, and never appear to usurp the powers of the judiciary.
9. The test of police efficiency is the absence of crime and disorder, not the visible evidence of police action in dealing with it.[8]

German, Day, and Gallati listed twelve more principles by Peel:

1. The police must be stable, efficient, and organized along military lines.
2. The police must be under government control.
3. The absence of crime will best prove the efficiency of police.
4. The distribution of crime news is essential.
5. The deployment of police strength, both by tie and area, is essential.
6. No quality is more indispensable to a policeman than a perfect command of temper; a quiet, determined manner has more effect than violent action.
7. Good appearance commands respect.
8. The securing and training of proper personnel is at the root of efficiency.
9. Public security demands that every police officer be given a number.
10. Police headquarters should be centrally located and easily accessible to the people.
11. Policemen should be hired on a probationary period.
12. Police records are necessary to the correct distribution of police strength.

As you can see after reviewing the principles attributed to Peel, they are as relevant today as they were back in the nineteenth century. In fact, the community policing of the twenty-first century is based on the principles of Peel. For community policing to succeed, the police need the cooperation and respect of the public.

To get this assistance from the public, the police need to be transparent, ethical, and in tune with the wants and needs of the public.

Because the police are professionals at dealing with crime and public safety, they need to take the initiative in establishing mutual trust and respect within the community. They need to understand all of the various cultures and subcultures that are present in the population and to be able to relate to them on a daily basis. The police have to adhere to the principles put forth by Peel.

As we digest the preceding principles, we realize the importance they hold for the ethical behavior of the police. For instance, the fact that police officers should be identifiable by a badge and a number is important in establishing trust. The officer is not anonymous.

Another important idea of Peel is that the use, or lack of use, of force affects the degree of cooperation of the people. If the police are seen as brutal or as armies of occupation, it will preclude the citizenry from coming forward to report crimes or identify suspects. The other consideration put forth by Peel was that force is used as a last resort; after all, attempts at persuasion and warning are unsuccessful.

Peel also stressed the importance of demeanor and appearance of police officers. He stated that officers should be able to control their tempers and have an aura of quiet determination and maintain a good professional appearance. Peel also placed an emphasis on training and the existence of a probationary period for new officers.

Another focal point for Peel was the location of police stations. He believed that they should be strategically located so the people would be able to access them whenever needed. He also thought that the dispersal of crime news was essential. These two beliefs align with Peel's idea that policing is a community undertaking and so the public should have easy entrée to the police and should be aware of the criminal activity within the area.

Police efficiency was important to Peel as well, and he said the test of that efficiency was not the visible evidence of police activity but the absence of crime and disorder. In other words, arrests were not necessarily the best indicator of good work. If the police were successful at what they did, there would be less crime. It may mean that the people are voluntarily obeying the law or that the criminal justice system is conducting business in such a way that the citizens are agreeing with the premise of the law.

POLICING IN THE UNITED STATES

In this section, we are going to explore the beginnings of modern policing in the United States in order to give us a better perspective on our history and our future. Policing has changed dramatically since the nineteenth century and continues to change almost daily. Court decisions, technology, and the demographics, among a myriad of other occurrences dictate the direction of law enforcement.

The Political Era of Policing

The "Political Era" (1840–1930) of policing was characterized by officers catering to the needs of politicians and generally doing whatever they wanted done.

During the late nineteenth century, the United States was going through the Industrial Revolution and people were moving from the farms and ranches into the cities. With the migration came the increase in crime, and as a result, city administrators were realizing a need for law and order. There was also immigration from Europe and that was increasing the population in the large cities on the East Coast.

In 1845, New York created the first police department in the United States, and it was modeled after the London Metropolitan Police. Chicago followed suit in 1851 and then Boston and Philadelphia started their departments in 1854. There were many problems with professional and ethical shortcomings in these law enforcement organizations.

In the book *A Pickpockets Tale* by Timothy J. Gilfoyle, there is a passage that states, "Certain police captains received regular bribes from operatives in return for protection sometimes as much a 50 percent of all the profits."[10] It goes without saying that this was unethical at the least, and criminal as well. But unfortunately, this was not an isolated case.

There was a police officer by the name of Alexander "Clubber" Williams who started out as a ships carpenter around the docks in New York City. On the weekends, he would get drunk and get into fights, and sometimes the police would be his victims. In 1866, he became a cop in New York, and on his first night on duty, he allegedly got into an altercation with two of the toughest guys on his beat and clubbed them into submission. Many of their friends tried to intervene and met the same fate. Williams is quoted as saying "There is more power in the end of a policeman's stick than in all of the US Supreme Court." He is said to have had 358 charges filed for misbehavior of which 224 were upheld, but he was never suspended or fired. Williams was eventually transferred to the Manhattan precinct, which was a much more lucrative beat and had more opportunity to make money. Clubber said upon being reassigned, "All my life I've never had anything but chuck steak; now I'm going to get me some tenderloin," and as result, the district became known as the "Tenderloin." Williams became even more corrupt, and at the end of his career he retired with a personal fortune of over $300,000 (approximately six million dollars in today's dollars), which included a mansion and a yacht. He died a millionaire.[11]

One of the biggest problems of the late nineteenth century attributed to the police was corruption. Officers were hired not to provide public safety and arrest criminals but to provide political safety for the elected officials of the reigning political party. Police officer positions were political appointments, and, as a result, officers were more beholden to the politicians than to the people of the community.[12]

The politicians controlled the police and this local control created unethical police behavior. In the United States today, our police departments are controlled by the municipal government. There are state police departments, but most of the departments are city and county. The founders of this country did not want a federal police department because of their distrust of government; they wanted local control.

As if the local corruption wasn't bad enough, the corruption by politicians and police administrators was as bad and probably worse. Because the post of police officer or police administrator was a political appointment, there was also a pay-off to obtain the position in most cities. In New York, for instance, it cost $300 to get the police officer job, $1600 to become a sergeant, and between $12,000 and $15,000 to make captain.[13]

In Chicago, police officers were expected to contribute to the political party that was in office by giving part of their salaries to the campaign of the incumbents. They hung posters, sold raffle tickets, and worked the precincts during elections. This all points to the fact that during this time in history, police departments were corrupt and they reflected the society at large.

The political era was characterized by what is called street justice. The police exercised their discretion in dealing with miscreants and criminal activity. There was brutality and bribery. Corruption was rampant and much of it was institutionalized in that everyone participated in the taking of money. The payoffs went from the top to the bottom and sometimes the other way around.[14]

Lexow Committee

The Lexow Committee was a New York state Senate committee that was set up to investigate corruption in the New York City Police Department in 1894. The committee was made up of seven state senators and the group's chairman was Clarence Lexow. Throughout the duration of the hearings which lasted from March to December, the committee summoned 678 witnesses and assembled more than 5,700 pages of testimony and documentary evidence entailing election fraud, blackmail, and extortion. The depth of political and police malfeasance extended beyond simple toleration of saloons, brothels, and gambling dens; police officials extorted payments from steamboat operators, produce merchants, sail makers, bootblacks, pushcart peddlers, and numerous other small merchants. By 1896, even police officials admitted that the police department was "honeycombed with corruption."[15]

Theodore Roosevelt Island Statue

© Zack Frank, 2014. Used under license from Shutterstock, Inc.

The committee was able to show that many officers, such as Williams, were selectively enforcing vice crimes such as prostitution, illegal sales of alcohol, and gambling, and becoming wealthy as a result. Because these crimes are known as "victimless crimes," there was a dearth of victims and witnesses to come forth to testify. (The reason these crime are called victimless is that all of the participants are committing crimes. As a result, there are no victims.) A further problem in the investigation was that all ranks of the department were involved in the corruption. The precinct captains would specify the amount of money needed for the bribe, and bagmen would go around and collect. Bagmen were usually patrolman or detectives who would be transferred whenever the captain was moved.

Because of the committees' investigation, a new mayor was elected and he appointed Theodore Roosevelt as the police commissioner. Corruption was by this time institutionalized in New York and Commissioner Roosevelt was not successful in stemming the tide of corruption.

At this time in US history, the corruption benefited most of those around. The public was content because the crime was contained in certain areas of the city. They also were aware that if they did commit a small infraction of the law it could be made right by greasing someone's palm. The officers, their supervisors, and the criminals all benefitted from the unlawful practices.

The Twentieth Century

The Eighteenth Amendment to the Constitution of the United States ushered in prohibition. This amendment mandated that no alcohol would be produced, possessed, or consumed in the country. Alcohol was outlawed in the United States. The rationale for this prohibition was that it would help alleviate poverty and vice, and people would be able to realize their full potential. What happened instead was that gangsters had a new avenue to riches. Illegal booze was being manufactured in clandestine stills, and also being smuggled into the country from Canada and Europe.

Speakeasies, which were illegal drinking establishments, proliferated. In New York alone, by the close of the 1920s, there were approximately 32,000 speakeasies; Detroit had 15,000. Some stores sold alcohol surreptitiously. In the rural areas, the people made "White Lightning" or "Moonshine." It has been said that more people drank during prohibition than before. These activities all went on under the police department's nose and many times with their blessings.

As a result of the Volstead Act (the originator was named Andrew J. Volstead), crime increased and opportunities for corruption and bribery compounded. There were hijackings and robberies of liquor trucks. Because people could use alcohol for medicinal purposes, doctors were issuing bogus prescriptions. Federal agents and local police officers were being arrested for bribery. One in every twelve federal alcohol agents was dismissed for dishonesty. There was one case in which the US Coast Guard was paid to deliver a load of alcohol. In Philadelphia, the grand jury found that numerous high ranking police officials had bank accounts of $250,000 or more. The jury also found 138 officers unfit for duty.

Prohibition opened up myriad opportunities for organized crime, also known as the Mafia. One of the most notorious bootleggers was Alphonse ("Scarface") Capone, a Chicago mobster who made most of his money on the profits of alcohol during prohibition.

Arabic business man.

© Boris Franz, 2014. Used under license from Shutterstock, Inc.

Capone was born in New York and dropped out of school at a young age and became a gangster. He belonged to many gangs as a kid and ended up working for a guy named Frankie Yale in the Five Points Gang. Capone got into trouble in New York and was sent to Chicago until things quieted down. In Chicago, he went to work for John Torrio who was Yale's mentor. Soon he was helping to run the bootlegging operation and was Torrio's number two man.

When Torrio was gunned down by rival gang members, Capone took over. It has been reported that Capone's income was about $100 million per year. He had to leave Chicago because the mayor William Hals Thompson (who had been in Capone's pocket) hired a new police chief to run him out of town. Capone was convicted of income tax evasion and did time in Alcatraz and Atlanta. He was eventually released and died at home of syphilitic dementia.

Capone was successful in Chicago because he was able to bribe the police and the local politicians. Organized crime cannot exist unless they have the government under their control, and in most cases that means the police.

There was a defense lawyer and bootlegger named George Remus who lived in Cincinnati and was reported to have bribed hundreds of police and government employees, including a US Attorney General to whom he gave $500,000.[16]

During this time, the reputation of the police reached an all-time low; there was a huge amount of police corruption and the police were not held accountable. Taking bribes and looking the other way when crimes were committed became standard operation procedure.

© ducu59us, 2014. Used under license from Shutterstock, Inc.

Part of the reason there was so much corruption at that time was because the law was unpopular with the public. People wanted to drink and didn't care how they obtained the alcohol. There were millions of lawbreakers, who for the most part were law-abiding citizens. They also weren't concerned with their police taking bribes and engaging in other criminal activity.

As far as the enforcement of the liquor laws went, federal, state, and local authorities paid them little attention. Some cities such as San Francisco, Chicago, and New York didn't even bother enforcing them. And as mentioned previously, just about everyone in the criminal justice system was on the take. By 1927, only eighteen of the forty-eight states were spending any money on the enforcement of prohibition.[17]

Prohibition seemed to be a failure; it didn't accomplish what it set out to do. The administration of Herbert Hoover (1928–1932) tried to put some teeth into the enforcement of prohibition, but there was little enthusiasm for his effort, and in 1932, Franklin D. Roosevelt ran against Hoover and won the presidency while calling for the repeal of prohibition. On December 5, 1933, the last state voted for the Twenty-First Amendment to the constitution and prohibition was over.[18]

Professionalization

The 1930s signaled the beginning of professional policing in the United States. August Vollmer is considered by many as the "father of modern law enforcement." He was the first police chief of Berkeley, California, appointed in 1909, and was elected as president of the California Association of Police Chiefs. During his tenure as chief, Vollmer reorganized the Berkeley Police Department by starting a bicycle patrol and a call box system to keep the officers in touch with headquarters. He also used the polygraph in questioning of suspects and in the screening of applicants for the position of police officer. Vollmer also initiated the idea of a centralized recording system for policing, which helped in the investigations of crimes. He also had officers riding motorcycles and patrolling in cars.

A book written by August Vollmer in 1936 titled, *The Police and Modern Society,* was considered one of the seminal works in the discipline of police administration. He also required his officers to have a bachelors' degree and was responsible for the implementation of the criminology program at the University of California in Berkeley. Vollmer became head of the department and taught another famous criminologist and professor named O. W. Wilson who went on to encourage the professionalization of policing.

Education and Training

Some say the first police academy was started in 1923 in San Francisco, California. Another account states that the first formal police training took place in Berkeley in 1908. The point is that training was becoming popular among police professionals in the early part of the twentieth century. Raymond D. Fosdick's 1915 book, *European Police Systems,* promoted the emphasis on police education and training as did Wilson's 1943 book, *Police Administration.*

Wilson has a long list of accomplishments in the field of policing. He was a professor at the University of California at Berkeley; a professor at Harvard University in the 1930s; and the Chief of Police at Fullerton, California; the Chief of Police at Wichita, Kansas; investigator for Pacific Finance Corporation; and Superintendent of Police of the Chicago Police Department.

In his book, he stressed rapid response to calls and preventive patrol. He felt that this would create an illusion of the police being everywhere and knowing everything. His ideas were widely used among police departments in the United States.

Wilson thought that police corruption was the result of actions by society. He thought that the people, by offering small gratuities to the police, were opening the door for criminals to do the same with large gratuities. Another similar idea is that when officers come to realize that other parts of the system are corrupt, for instance if they observe a politician or judge take a bribe, they think it's okay for them to do the same.

Police training was coming of age in the 1930s. New York, Michigan, Connecticut, Oregon, New Jersey, Texas, and Washington all started state police training centers.[19] San Jose State College in California and Michigan State College started their first Police Science programs, which led to bachelor's degrees.[20]

In the late 1930s and the 1940s, interest in the police seemed to take a back seat because of World War II. Many of the men were getting drafted and going off to war and as a result, many departments were undermanned. Many departments relied on reserve officers and other volunteers. The police department in Washington, D.C., lost over 341 officers to the armed forces. The Federal Bureau of Investigation (FBI) was, of course, busy with investigations that were related to sabotage and espionage, so many of their criminal investigations other than the ones connected to the war effort were suspended.

During the late 1950s and into the 1960s, police viewed themselves as crime fighters who opposed prying from the public. The premise was that the police were the experts on fighting crime, so let them do their job. I remember hearing a police officer in San Francisco telling a citizen, "This is police business sir; it is none of your concern."[21] Of course, this attitude only increased the isolation of the police.

With the advent of the civil rights and the anti-Vietnam war movements in the 1960s, police conduct, as well as misconduct, became more public. The riots during the 1968 Democratic National Convention in Chicago were characterized as a "Police Riot" and showed the police in a bad light, even though the police were not totally at fault. The government, of course, formed several commissions to deal with the perceived problem of police misconduct. There is no doubt that police misconduct existed, as anyone remotely aware of the justice system knew. The point here is that the days of police autonomy were over, and the federal government would intercede when it deemed necessary.

One arena of federal involvement was the funding for police-related programs. Two important pieces of legislation that resulted were the "Safe Streets Act of 1968" and the Law Enforcement Assistance Administration (LEAA). These programs stressed education for police officers among other things.

One such program was the Law Enforcement Education Program (LEEP). The program provided funds in certain disciplines (e.g., administration of justice, psychology, sociology, and public administration) so that working police officers could attain an advanced education. A federal grant was provided and it would be funded for every year of police work completed. This program enabled many police officers to obtain bachelors, masters, and doctorate degrees. The idea was that the police should be at least as educated as the people they police.

The Twenty-First Century

During the nineteenth century and well into the late twentieth century, the United States was populated with people who had left their countries of origin and came to the United States in search of a better life. European immigrants seemed to have come here with the idea of becoming an American. This is not to say that the Europeans sought to divest themselves of their native cultures but they wanted to assimilate. As a result of this, they incorporated American values into their cultures. These folks from foreign lands became for the most part very patriotic to the United States. At this time in history, this country was known as a melting pot.

As a result, the folks who lived in the country seldom questioned the behavior of the police; they could operate with impunity. Even with the many different nationalities and races that resided here, the desire to belong to the majority dictated an acceptance of the status quo. The police more or less ran the cities in which they operated.

An example of the general attitude of the citizenry at the time, the first police chief of San Francisco, a man by the name of Malachi Fallon said in 1849, "San Francisco's population was then made up of rough young men with adventurous spirits, excited by the discovery of gold. They needed a strong experienced hand to keep them in control. Many of them were of the cowboy class, while the worst were deserting whalemen coming from all parts of the world. They were not men of evil principles but they felt the excitement of the time and enjoyed the lack of restraint in a town where there was no social organization of adequate legal control. Outside of this looseness or moral force at the time, they were good fellows."[22]

That strong experienced hand was provided by the cops and they usually were heavy with the club back in the day; it was referred to as street justice. Earlier in the chapter, we looked at the history of Alexander "Clubber" Williams an officer who would not survive in this century; but he not only survived during his time but also was very successful.

When police departments were first organized, it was difficult to get officers. The Irish were discriminated against in the United States during the nineteenth century and there were signs announcing employment that read "Irish need not apply." So one of the jobs left was that of police officer. In your large cities throughout the nation, the majority of cops were of Irish descent. Police departments were homogenous organizations, members were of like mind and culture. No one would question their actions or behaviors. Even during most of the last century, many police officers were still Irish-American. This started to change around the middle of the twentieth century and the police departments began to be integrated. People from other ethnic groups and lifestyles were being actively recruited and attitudes started to change as a result. In the late 1960s and early 1970s, women were entering the police service in larger numbers and the demographics of police departments started to change. The civil rights movement was also in full bloom during the 1960s and 1970s, as a result people began to question the authority of the police and the government. In the 1980s and 1990s, police departments were becoming professional and were stressing on honesty and transparency.

The police are protective of their own, partially because they are an identifiable minority and if you look at people who are considered minorities in this country, they are also protective of their own members. There is no doubt that cops are reluctant to turn in their fellow officers for misbehavior, especially relatively minor violations of rules. However, I don't feel many cops would refrain from turning in an officer who was committing a felony.

That being said, officers in the twenty-first century are under constant scrutiny and must behave accordingly. People today want to know what their public safety officers are up to and with the technology available, it is very easy to monitor people's behavior. Some police departments are issuing personal cameras to their officers to wear on their uniforms. Others install GPS on police cars. Just about every citizen has a phone that can take pictures. In short, officers have to be aware of their behavior as it can be documented in myriad ways.

In March of 2014, San Diego, California, appointed a new police chief. Her name is Shelley Zimmerman and one of the first things she did after being sworn in was to start a "Professional Standards Unit." This unit is staffed by undercover detectives who investigate misbehavior by officers. The new chief also announced that she has a zero tolerance policy towards misbehavior and she also handed out copies of the Law Enforcement Code of Ethics.

San Diego has gone through a period of alleged police misconduct, with officers being accused of various acts of abuse of power and the chief is attempting to bring the department under control and reestablish the trust of the public.[23]

THE LAW ENFORCEMENT CODE OF ETHICS

- As a Law Enforcement Officers, my fundamental duty is to serve mankind; to safeguard lives and property; to protect the innocent against deception, the weak against oppression or intimidation, and the peaceful against violence or disorder; and to respect Constitutional rights of all men to liberty, equality and justice.
- I will keep my private life unsullied as an example to all, maintain courageous calm in the face of danger, scorn, or ridicule; develop self-restraint; and be constantly mindful of the welfare of others. Honest in thought and deed in both my personal and official life. I will be exemplary in obeying the laws of the land and the regulations of my department.
- Whatever I see or hear of a confidential nature or that is confided to me in my official capacity will be kept ever secret unless revelation is necessary in the performance of my duty.
- I will never act officiously or permit personal feelings, prejudices, animosities or friendships to influence my decisions. With no compromise for crime and with relentless prosecution of criminals. I will enforce the law courteously and appropriately without fear or favor, malice or ill will, never employing unnecessary force or violence, and never accepting gratuities.
- I recognize the badge of my office as a symbol of public faith, and I accept it as a public trust to be held so long as I am true to the ethics of the police service. I will constantly strive to achieve these objectives and ideals, dedicating myself before God to my chosen profession . . . law enforcement.[24]

From *Law Enforcement Code of Ethics* by International Association of Chiefs of Police. Copyright © International Association of Chiefs of Police. Reprinted by permission.

SUMMARY

This chapter has taken us through some of the history of western policing, and we've seen that the individuals who are passionate about law and justice are also zealous about "doing the right thing." Law and order mean nothing in a democratic society unless the practitioners involved in the process pay attention to the rules of the community otherwise known as the law.

We have also read about some of the characters who misbehaved under the color of authority and how this behavior undermines the work of the men and women who behave ethically. With these opposing sides in mind, we will continue in our work and in chapter 7 to look at the process of ethical decision making.

We will dissect the "Law Enforcement Code of Ethics" and other guides to ethical decision making to facilitate the making of the right choices in our chosen profession.

NOTES

1. Christopher R. Williams & Bruce A. Arrigo, *Ethics, Crime, and Criminal Justice, 2nd Ed.* Pearson (2012) p.20.
2. Eric Tucker. *DC Police Facing Scrutiny Over Arrested Officers.* Associated January 1, 2014.
3. *Police: History-Early Policing in Colonial America.* Grantham University. http://law.jrank .org/pages/1640/police-history-early-policing-in-colonial-America.html>Police:History— Early Policing In Colonial America Retrieved 2/13/2014.
4. V.E. Kappeler, R.D. Sluder, and A.P. Alpert, *Forces of Deviance: Understanding the Dark Side of Policing* (Prospect Heights, IL., Waveland Press, 1994)
5. The Metropolitan Police Archives, www.met.police.uk/history/archives.htm (acce. Retrieved 2/13/2014
6. The Metropolitan Police Archives.
7. Susan A. Lentz and Robert H. Chaires "The invention of Peel's Principles: A study of policing history." *Justice of Criminal Justice* 35 (2007) 69–79.
8. New Westminster Police Service; Sir Robert Peel's Nine Principles.
9. A.C. German, Frank D. Day, and R.J. Gallati, *Introduction to Law Enforcement and Criminal Justice* (Springfield, IL: Charles C. Thomas, 1970), p.54.
10. Timothy J. Gilfoyle, *A Pickpockets Tale: The underworld of the Nineteenth Century New York.* (New York: Norton 2006), p.214.
11. T. Repetto, *The Blue Parade* (New York: Free Press, 1978); T. Repetto, and J. Lardner, *NYPD A City and Its Police* (New York: Henry Holt, 2000).
12. C.D. Uchida, "The Development of American Police: An Historical Overview." IN Criticall Issues of Policing: Contemporary Readings B.G. Dunham & G.A. Alpert (ed.) Waveland Press. Pp. 18–35.
13. Kappeler, Sluder, and Alpert, *Forces of Deviance.* P. 193.
14. Peterson, Morgan, *Enforcement Psychology: Coping with the rigors of policing.* Kendall Hunt (2013) p. 180.
15. New York City, *Report of the Police Department for 1896* (New York City. 1897).
16. Thomas M. Coffey, *The Long Thirst: Prohibition in America* (New York: W.W. Norton & Co., 1975).
17. Willard M. Oliver and James F. Hilgenberg, Jr., *A history of Crime and Criminal Justice in America* (Boston: Pearson, 2006). p.246.
18. Oliver and Hilgenberg, *A history of Crime and Criminal Justice in America* (Boston: Pearson, 2006) p. 247.
19. W.J. Bopp, and D.O. Schultz, *A Short History of American Law Enforcement* (Springfield, IL: Charles C. Thomas, 1972).
20. J. Foote, *Two Hundred Years of American Criminal Justice* (Washington. DC: U.S. Government Printing Office, 1976).
21. Morgan Peterson, "*A Christmas Story.*" Unpublished.
22. Mullen, Kevin J., *The Toughest Gang in Town: Police Stories From Old San Francisco.* Noir Publications, Novato, CA. 2005. P.26.
23. Kristina Davis. *S.D. Police Chief Hits the Ground Running.* San Diego Union Tribune. 3/8/2014 p B-1.
24. International Association of Chiefs of Police. www.theicap.org.

DILEMMA

You are a police officer in a large East Coast department and the police officer's union has voted to go on strike. Will you go out? What are your feelings about police officers going out on strike? In your opinion is it ethical? Why/Why not?

_____

_____

_____

_____

_____

_____

_____

_____

_____

_____

_____

_____

_____

_____

_____

_____

_____

_____

_____

DILEMMA

You are a rookie police officer and you get a call dispatching you to a possible dead body in a private residence. You respond and the ambulance is already there and the EMT has pronounced the individual dead. You notify the coroner and call your sergeant as the rules of your department dictate. The sergeant responds and instructs you go outside and await the arrival of the coroner. The coroner arrives and you direct her to the body. The sergeant comes outside and offers you a hundred dollar bill, saying, "This is your share of what I found in the house." List your options. Which one do you follow through with?

_____

_____

_____

_____

_____

_____

_____

_____

_____

_____

_____

_____

_____

_____

_____

_____

_____

DILEMMA

You are a young officer in a West Coast city and you are working the swing shift when the sergeant calls you in and instructs you to pick up the night supervising captain and chauffeur him for the evening. During the course of the evening, you visit numerous precincts and officers. Later that night, the captain asks you to stop at a bar. You and he enter the bar and the bartender says "Good evening, Captain." The captain orders an alcoholic drink and asks you what you'll have? What is your response? What do you do? Is it ethical to drink on duty?

_____

_____

_____

_____

_____

_____

_____

_____

_____

_____

_____

_____

_____

_____

_____

_____

_____

_____

DILEMMA

You're working an undercover pickpocket detail and you meet colleagues for lunch at a local grill. You are dressed in jeans, sweatshirt, and are wearing a beard. Your partners are dressed alike and have various facial hair and different hair styles. No one would ever make this group as a bunch of cops. You order your meal and while eating, the other guys start up a conversation with some females and ask them to join your table. One thing leads to another, and pretty soon drinks are being ordered, and there is talk of continuing this party at another place. What do you do? Is this proper? Is there a case where it could ever be OK to engage in this type of behavior while on duty?

_____

_____

_____

_____

_____

_____

_____

_____

_____

_____

_____

_____

_____

_____

_____

_____

_____

DILEMMA

Your partner has an avocation of carpet laying and works the job during his off-duty time. One day as you are on patrol your partner says, "I have a job on 19th avenue, and it will only take an hour to do. Why don't you drop me off and pick me up in an hour. Okay?" Is this okay? If it isn't, why isn't it? What is your response? What should you do?

_____

_____

_____

_____

_____

_____

_____

_____

_____

_____

_____

_____

_____

_____

_____

_____

_____

_____

Firefighters and Emergency Medical Services: Code of Ethics

6

CHAPTER OBJECTIVES

1. Define *code of ethics* and *core values*.
2. Explain the significance of the code of ethics and core values.
3. Describe who is responsible for your poor decisions.
4. Recognize your role and responsibility as a firefighter or EMT/ paramedic.

Courtesy of the author

BENJAMIN FRANKLIN'S WISDOM

When we think of Benjamin Franklin, one of our founding fathers, many things come to mind. The *Declaration of Independence* and the U.S. Constitution are at the top of the list. He was well known for his best seller, *Poor Richard's Almanack*. According to Franklin himself, many of the proverbs and aphorisms found in *Poor Richard's* were from the "wisdom of the ages and nations." Many of his sayings are still heard today: "Well done is better than well said"; "No gains without pains"; "Haste makes waste"; "God helps them that help themselves"; and in his humorous way "Fish and visitors smell in three days." Then, he was also a scientist. He was always inquisitive and performing electrical tests. Many terms that he described during his experiments we still use today such as: battery, positive, negative, charge, neutral, condense, and conductor. Franklin captured and stored electric charges in a capacitor called a Leyden jar, named after the town where it was invented. He proved that by flying a kite that lightning was electricity; hence came his invention of the lightning rod. This was at a time when many felt lightning was a message from the heavens. He devised bifocal glasses. Using his knowledge of convection and heat transfer, he invented the Pennsylvania Fireplace that he said minimized cold drafts and kept smoke from being forced back into the room. The governor of Pennsylvania offered Franklin a patent, but Franklin noted in his autobiography "As we enjoy great advantages from the inventions of others, we should be glad of an opportunity to serve others by any invention of ours, and this we should do freely and generously."[1] Franklin felt the best way to serve God was doing good for others. Franklin also invented the first urinary catheter to be used in the United States. His brother became gravely ill and Franklin designed the catheter to help him urinate.

He also felt that the common cold "may possibly be spread by contagion" because he never caught a cold even in freezing temperatures. "People often catch cold from one another when shut up together in close rooms, coaches, etc., and when sitting near and conversing so as to breathe in each other's transpiration."[2]

One of Franklin's famous (and controversial) comments was about the United States's values and the national bird:

> I wish the bald eagle had not been chosen as the representative of our country; he is a bird of bad moral character, he does not get his living honestly; you may have seen him perched on some dead tree, near the river where, too lazy to fish for himself, he watches the labors of the fishing-hawk. . . . The turkey is, in comparison, a much more respectable bird, and a true original native of America . . . he is (though a little vain and silly, it is true, but not the worse emblem for that) a bird of courage, and would not hesitate to attack a grenadier of the British guards.[3]

When Franklin was seventy-nine years old he wrote about his project he launched to attain "moral perfection." He made a list of twelve virtues that he thought were a desirable way to live:

Temperance: Be not to dullness; drink not to elevation.

Silence: Speak not but what may benefit others or yourself; avoid trifling conversation.

Order: Let all your things have their places; let each part of your business have its time.

Resolution: Resolve to perform what you ought; perform without fail what you resolve.

Frugality: Make no expense but to do good to others or yourself; (i.e., waste nothing).

Industry: Lose no time; be always employed in something useful; cut off all unnecessary actions.

Sincerity: Use no hurtful deceit; think innocently and justly, and, if you speak, speak accordingly.

Justice: Wrong none by doing injuries, or omitting the benefits that are your duty.

Moderation: Avoid extremes; forbear resenting injuries so much as you think they deserve.

Cleanliness: Tolerate no uncleanliness in body, clothes, or habitation.

Tranquility: Be not disturbed at trifles, or at accidents common or unavoidable.

Chastity: Rarely use venery but for health or for offspring, never to dullness, weakness, or the injury of your own or another's peace or reputation.

Humility: Imitate Jesus and Socrates.

Franklin added the thirteenth virtue "humility," after a discussion with a friend.[4]

Franklin believed these virtues to be not spiritual but worthy traits to live by in this world and to use these traits to be a good citizen and make the appropriate contributions to society. He made a chart with columns for the seven days of the week that were labeled with these thirteen virtues. He used this chart to keep on track and to practice these virtues in his daily life. Interesting to note, his most difficult virtue was order because he was an untidy man. He was pragmatic and scientific about his beliefs and focused on understanding these virtues rather than religious beliefs.

Last, but definitely not least, Franklin launched many public service ideas, including a library, college, law enforcement, and a volunteer fire brigade. Franklin sought to raise public awareness about the city's need to improve firefighting techniques. Franklin wrote a description of the "brave men" who volunteer to fight fires using a pseudonym for his paper, and suggested that those who didn't join them should help bear the expense of ladders, buckets, and pumps. For the February 4, 1735, issue of the *Pennsylvania Gazette*, Franklin sent an anonymous letter to his own newspaper titled "Protection of Towns from Fire," writing as an old citizen who declared "an ounce of prevention is worth a pound of cure."[5]

He noted that the Philadelphia volunteers lacked order and method. He outlined what duties the volunteers should have and he said there should be wardens, who carry a "red staff" of five feet," as well as axmen and hookmen and other specialties. He further urged that chimney sweeps should be licensed by the city and held responsible for their work. Franklin organized the Union Fire Company, which was incorporated on December 7, 1736. A group of thirty men came together to form the Fire Company. Their equipment included "leather buckets, with strong bags and baskets (for packing and transporting goods) which were to be brought to every fire."[6] He detailed the rules and fines that would be levied for infractions. Homeowners were mandated to have leather firefighting buckets in their homes. They also met once a month for dinner to discuss the subject of fire prevention and firefighting methods. He remained actively involved in the Union Fire Company for years, and Philadelphia became one of the safest cities in the world in terms of fire damage.

Perhaps we can also credit Benjamin Franklin for not only the first fire department in Philadelphia but also the first firefighter *Code of Ethics*. He brought the community and volunteers together with their respective jobs of keeping the city safe. Not only did the volunteers have their part, but the homeowners and businesses were also required to participate in fire prevention. Now, almost 275 years later, we are asking for the same cooperation and leadership to keep our communities, businesses, homes, and citizens safe. Consider the recent firestorms in southern California in 2003 and 2007, a joint effort not only between the fire departments and government but also the citizens that own homes and businesses need to participate in the prevention of these conflagrations. These firestorms in southern California happen mostly in the fall months between September and November due to the intense nature of the Fohen winds, otherwise known as the Santa Ana winds.

CODE OF ETHICS AND CORE VALUES

In Chapter 4, we discussed the ethical standards of what the public expects from their public safety team. Most people trust their fire department more than any other organization. Ethics play a central part in all fire departments, from the top five bugle chief to the company officer, to the firefighter, and all department employees for that matter. Remember, we are held to a much higher standard than most other professions. When someone calls 911, they expect a fast response, professional attitude, service, and a trust that we will do the right thing—always. That is a big boot to fill! We believe that trust is well earned and should not be taken for granted. We must always remember who we are serving; the public is our client. That client, as with any other business, pays our salaries and benefits. The client deserves respect and a high level of service. It is our job, our way of life, our obligation, and our oath.

Most departments have rules that cover expectations about behavior, personal beliefs, values, honesty, integrity, accountability, fairness, respect, truthfulness, and dependability. The department also expects neutrality, dignity, confidence, a positive attitude, professionalism, effective communication and a high level of standards and skill. And, the list goes on, you get the idea. We are presumed innocent until proven guilty, as our Constitution states. However, public opinion can quickly change and condemn a person or group right away. We all have formed an opinion in one way or another before we've had all the facts. Our job does not fit into a neat and tidy tool box. It is too diverse, too dynamic, and does not always play fairly. Every call is different; it may be a medical aid, auto extrication, or a fire that does not always present itself in the same manner. The people, the vehicle, the house, the location, the time of day, the weather, and a crew that you are working with are all different. And that just may be the reason why you want to become a public safety officer, a firefighter or EMT/paramedic. When a bombshell occurs it may be immediate and obvious, be sneaky and complicated, or just plain awkward. Let's now take a look at those codes and core values as stated by departments and organizations. Think about these as you read them. They are the core values, the ethics and morality we live by as public safety officers, as EMT/paramedics and as firefighters.

FIRE DEPARTMENT CORE VALUES

The City of San Marcos Fire Department in North San Diego County, California has a simple mission statement and core values. Simple in this case means "easy to remember," and yet this is full of accountability, high ethical and high core values to work and live by. From their city website:

Mission Statement/Core Values

Mission Statement
The mission of the San Marcos Fire Department is to provide the highest level of customer service by protecting life, property and the environment, through the delivery of innovative, fiscally responsible and ethical emergency services in our community.

Core Values
Leadership
- We value the development and application of all personnel's leadership skills.
- We believe that leadership occurs at all levels of the organization and is everyone's responsibility.

Integrity

- We do the right thing, ethically, honestly and with integrity—always.
- We treat each other and the public with respect based on mutual trust and open communication.

Safety

- We recognize San Marcos Fire Department employees as our most valuable resource.
- We believe our health and safety are essential to fulfilling the department's mission.

Competency

- We embrace accountability for the quality of services that the department provides to the community.
- We take responsibility for developing and training each other and ourselves.

Customer service

- We treat all customers with respect, dignity, fairness, and compassion.
- We are responsive to the changing needs of our community.[7]

This document was a joint endeavor between the firefighters and administration. This Mission Statement and Core Values came from the floor, from the firefighters. All employees are held to this high ethical standard.

FIRE DEPARTMENT POLICY AND PROCEDURES

The next department is also from North San Diego County in California. The North County Fire Protection District covers the communities of Fallbrook, the avocado capital of the world, and Bonsall. Their Code of Ethics and Values is found in their *Policy and Procedure Manual*, and it states:

1.0.   Background Information:

1.1.   North County Fire Protection District designed its Code of Ethics & Values to provide clear, positive statements of ethical behavior reflecting the core values of the District and the communities it serves. The Code includes practical strategies for addressing ethical questions and a useful framework for decision-making and handling the day-to-day operations of the District. The Code is developed to reflect the issues and concerns of today's complex and diverse society.

2.0.   The Goals of the Code of Ethics & Values:

2.1.   To make North County fire protection District a better District, built on mutual respect and trust.

2.2.   To promote and maintain the highest standards of personal and professional conduct among all involved in the District government, district staff, volunteers and members of the District's Board. All elected officials, officers, employees, members of advisory committees, explorers and volunteers of the District, herein called officials for the purpose of this policy.

2.3.   The Code of Ethics & Values is a touchstone for members of the District Board and Staff in fulfilling their roles and responsibilities.

3.0.   Preamble:

3.1.   The proper operation of democratic government requires that decision-makers be independent, impartial and accountable to the people they serve. The North County Fire Protection District has adopted this Code of Ethics & Values to promote and maintain the highest standards of the personal and professional conduct in the District's government.

3.2.   All elected and appointed officials, District employees, volunteers and others who participate in the District's government are required to subscribe to this Code, understand how it applies to their specific responsibilities and practice its eight core values in their work. Because we seek public confidence in the District's services and public trust of its decision-makers, our decisions and our work must meet the most demanding ethical standards and demonstrate the highest levels of achievement in following this Code.

4.0.   Applicability:

4.1.   This Code of Ethics and Values shall apply to all District officials as defined in 2.2.

5.0.   <u>Core Values:</u>

5.1.   As participatory officials in the District's government, we subscribe to the following Core Values:

5.2.   **<u>As a Representative of North County Fire Protection District, I will BE ETHICAL.</u>**

5.2.1.   <u>In practice, this value looks like:</u>

5.2.1.1. I am trustworthy, acting with the utmost integrity and moral courage.

5.2.1.2. I am truthful. I do what I say I will do. I am dependable.

5.2.1.3. I make impartial decisions, free of bribes, unlawful gifts, narrow political interests, financial and other personal interests that impair my independence of judgment or action.

5.2.1.4. I am fair, distributing and benefits and burdens according to the consistent and equitable criteria.

5.2.1.5. I extend equal opportunities and due process to all parties in matters under consideration. If I engage in unilateral meetings and discussions, I do so without making voting decisions.

5.2.1.6. I show respect for persons, confidences and information designated as "confidential."

5.2.1.7. I use my title(s) only when conducting official District business, for information purposes or as an indication of background and expertise, carefully considering whether I am exceeding or appearing to exceed my authority.

5.2.1.8 I will avoid actions that might cause the public or others to question my independent judgment.

5.3.   <u>As a Representative of North County Fire Protection District, I will BE PROFESSIONAL.</u>

5.3.1.   <u>In practice, this value looks like:</u>

5.3.1.1 I apply my knowledge and expertise to my assigned activities and to the interpersonal relationships that are part of my job in a consistent, confident, competent and productive manner.

5.3.1.2. I approach my job and work-related relationships with a positive, collaborative attitude.

5.3.1.3. I keep my professional education, knowledge and skills current and growing.

5.4.   <u>As a Representative of North County Fire Protection District, I will BE SERVICE-ORIENTED.</u>

5.4.1.   <u>In practice this value looks like:</u>

5.4.1.1. I provide friendly, receptive, courteous service to everyone.

5.4.1.2 I attune to and care about the needs and issues of citizens, public officials and District workers.

5.4.1.3. In my interactions with constituents, I am interested, engaged and responsive.

5.5   <u>As a Representative of North County Fire Protection District, I will BE FISCALLY RESPONSIBLE.</u>

5.5.1.   <u>In practice this value looks like:</u>

5.5.1.1 I make decisions after prudent consideration of their financial impact, taking into account the long-term financial needs of the District, especially its financial stability.

5.5.1.2 I demonstrate concern for the proper use of District assets (e.g., personnel, time, property, equipment, funds) and follow established procedures.

5.5.1.3. I make good financial decisions that seek to preserve programs and services for District residents.

5.5.1.4. I have knowledge of and adhere to the district's <u>Purchasing and Contracting and Allocation of Funds Policies.</u>

5.6.   <u>As a Representative of North County Fire Protection District, I will BE ORGANIZED.</u>

5.6.1.   <u>In practice this value looks like</u>:

5.6.1.1. I act in an efficient manner, making decisions and recommendations based upon research and facts, taking into consideration short and long-term goals.

5.6.1.2. I follow through in a responsible way, keeping others informed and responding in a timely fashion.

5.6.1.3. I am respectful of established District processes and guidelines.

5.7.   <u>As a Representative of North County Fire Protection District, I will BE COMMUNICATIVE.</u>

5.7.1.   <u>In practice this value looks like</u>:

5.7.1.1. I positively convey the District's care for and commitment to its citizens.

5.7.1.2. I communicate in various ways that I am approachable, open-minded and willing to participate in dialogue.

5.7.1.3. I engage in effective two-way communication, by listening carefully, asking questions and determining an appropriate response which add value to the conversations.

5.8   <u>As a Representative of North County Fire Protection District, I will BE COLLABORATIVE.</u>

5.8.1.   <u>In practice this value looks like</u>:

5.8.1.1. I act in a cooperative manner with groups and other individuals, working together in a spirit of tolerance and understanding.

5.8.1.2. I worked towards consensus building and gain value from diverse opinions.

5.8.1.3. I accomplish the goals and the responsibilities of my individual position, while respecting my role as a member of a team.

5.8.1.4. I consider the broader regional and State-wide implications of the District's decisions and issues.

5.8.1.5. <u>As a Representative of North County Fire Protection District, I will BE PROGRESSIVE.</u>

5.8.2.   <u>In practice this value looks like</u>:

5.8.2.1. I exhibit a proactive, innovative approach to setting goals and conducting the District's business.

5.8.2.2. I display a style that maintains consistent standards, but is also sensitive to the need for compromise, "thinking outside the box" and improving existing paradigms when necessary.

5.8.2.3. I promote intelligent and thoughtful innovation in order to forward the District's policy agenda and District services.

5.9. <u>Enforcement:</u>

5.9.1. Any official found to be in violation of this Code of Ethics and Values may be subject to Censure by the District Board. Any member of any advisory Committee found in violation may be subject to dismissal from the Committee. In the case of an employee, appropriate action shall be taken by the Fire Chief/ CEO or by an authorized designee.[8]

This policy was last updated April 2009 and is specific about conduct, ethics, and values of their employees and representatives. It leaves little room subject to interpretation and does a good job of describing how an employee or representative should behave, be ethical, and act with high moral standards. The district's expectations are specific about behavior as an employee.

These two neighboring fire departments have specific ethics and core values for their employees to adhere to and follow. The message is clear; you must hold yourself to a higher ethical and moral standard. If you are new to the fire or EMS service, this may take some time getting used to. It will require a conscious effort on your part to follow these rules and act accordingly.

A code of ethics can only serve as a guideline. It is up to you, the individual who must decide where, when, and how you must act and behave, all of the time. These are your responsibilities as a public safety employee, and with some departments, your instructions for continued employment.

FIREFIGHTER CODE OF ETHICS

Now let's take a look at the Firefighter Code of Ethics. The International Association of Fire Fighters (IAFF) in its *Manual of Common Procedure and Related Subjects* contains this code, which helps union firefighters uniformly remember their career mission and goals:

It is a fundamental duty of a member of the International Association of Fire Fighters to serve humanity; to safeguard and preserve life and property against the elements of fire and disaster; and maintain a proficiency in the art and science of fire engineering.

All members will uphold the standards of their profession, continually search for new and improved methods and share their knowledge and skills with their contemporaries and those new to the profession.

All members will never allow personal feelings, nor danger to self, to deter them from their responsibilities as a first responder.

All members will at all times, respect the property and rights of all men and women, the laws of their community and their country, and the chosen way of life of their fellow citizens.

All members will recognize the badge of their office as a symbol of public faith, and accept it as a public trust to be held so long as they are true to the ethics of the fire service. All members will consistently strive to achieve these objectives and ideals, dedicating themselves to their chosen profession—saving of life, fire prevention and fire suppression.

AS A MEMBER OF THE INTERNATIONAL ASSOCIATION OF FIRE FIGHTERS, I ACCPET THIS SELF-IMPOSED AND SELF-ENFORCED OBLIGATION AS MY RESPONSIBILITY.[9]

A code of ethics does not stop with fire fighters; it applies to everyone as mentioned previously.

FIRE CHIEF'S CODE OF ETHICS

The Fire Chief's Code of Ethics was developed by the International Association of Fire Chiefs (IAFC):

- Recognize that we serve in a position of public trust that imposes responsibility to use publicly owned resources effectively and judiciously.
- Not use a public position to obtain advantages or favors for friends, family, personal business ventures or ourselves.
- Use information gained from our positions only for the benefit of those we are entrusted to serve.
- Conduct our personal affairs in such a manner that we cannot be improperly influenced in the performance of our duties.
- Avoid situations whereby our decisions or influence may have an impact on personal financial interests.
- Seek no favor and accept no form of personal reward for influence or official action.
- Engage in no outside employment or professional activities that may impair or appear to impair our primary responsibilities as fire officials.
- Comply with local laws and campaign rules when supporting political candidates and engaging in political activities.
- Handle all personnel matters on the basis of merit.
- Carry out policies established by elected officials and policy makers to the best of our ability.
- Refrain from financial investments or business that conflicts with or is enhanced by our official position.
- Refrain from endorsing commercial products through quotations, use of photographs or testimonials, for personal gain.
- Develop job descriptions and guidelines at the local level to produce behaviors in accordance with the code of ethics.
- Conduct training at the local level to inform and educate local personnel about the ethical conduct and policies and procedures.
- Have systems in place at the local level to resolve ethical issues.
- Orient new employees to the organization's ethics program during new employee orientation.
- Review the ethics management program in management training experiences.
- Deliver accurate and timely information to the public and to elected policy makers to use when deciding critical issues.[10]

The Fire Chief's Code includes the same ethics and morality issues plus more. Because of their position, they have a great deal more accountability for the overall department and organization on a much broader scale. They are responsible to the public, the elected officials, and to the employees of the department and must account for their actions and your actions as a firefighter. If you do something unethical or illegal, your captain, battalion chief, operations chief, and department chief must all answer for your mistake to the public, media, and elected officials. Think about it, how would you like to be responsible for what your friends do or don't do on a daily basis? Some of you right now are thinking, no way!

EMERGENCY MEDICAL TECHNICIAN/PARAMEDIC CODE OF ETHICS

Professional status as an Emergency Medical Services (EMS) Practitioner is maintained and enriched by the willingness of the individual practitioner to accept and fulfill obligations to society, other medical professionals, and the EMS profession. As an EMS practitioner, I solemnly pledge myself to the following code of professional ethics:

> To conserve life, alleviate suffering, promote health, do no harm, and encourage the quality and equal availability of emergency medical care.
>
> To provide services based on human need, with compassion and respect for human dignity, unrestricted by consideration of nationality, race, creed, color, or status; to not judge the merits of the patient's request for service, nor allow the patient's socioeconomic status to influence our demeanor or the care that we provide.
>
> To not use professional knowledge and skills in any enterprise detrimental to the public well being.
>
> To respect and hold in confidence all information of a confidential nature obtained in the course of professional service unless required by law to divulge such information.
>
> To use social media in a responsible and professional manner that does not discredit, dishonor, or embarrass an EMS organization, co-workers, other health care practitioners, patients, individuals or the community at large.
>
> To maintain professional competence, striving always for clinical excellence in the delivery of patient care.
>
> To assume responsibility in upholding standards of professional practice and education.
>
> To assume responsibility for individual professional actions and judgment, both in dependent and independent emergency functions, and to know and uphold the laws which affect the practice of EMS.
>
> To be aware of and participate in matters of legislation and regulation affecting EMS.
>
> To work cooperatively with EMS associates and other allied healthcare professionals in the best interest of our patients.
>
> To refuse participation in unethical procedures, and assume the responsibility to expose incompetence or unethical conduct of others to the appropriate authority in a proper and professional manner.[11]

Technicians, 1978. Revised and adopted by the National Association of Emergency Medical Technicians, June 14, 2013. Reprinted by permission.

IS IT ILLEGAL OR ALMOST ETHICAL?

A code of ethics is not law, but a high standard of conduct that fits the profession of public safety. Some departments require the code of ethics/core values to be followed to the letter and also as a requirement for continued employment. You break the code and you suffer the consequences by punishment or by termination. They are designed to promote high ethical standards and to create a spirit of professionalism. Many of these codes include such words or phrases as: "achieving excellence, responsibility to patient is paramount, ensure quality and equal availability to all, protect, respect, assume all responsibility for your actions, recognize a responsibility to participate in professional associations, and assumes responsibility to expose incompetence or unethical conduct of others."

By now, you have a good idea about unethical conduct of yourself and others. Recognizing poor decisions in yourself is one challenge, but recognizing poor decisions in someone else is another matter. Some departments include core values and ethical standards that include "your responsibility to report unethical conduct of others." Most of us can think of someone, in recent years, who makes an unethical decision on a regular basis. They bend the rules or stretch the truth to benefit their own personal goals and agenda. Perhaps, they just do not like authority and the idea that an organization is telling them what to do. If you work for a department that has ethical core values, then it is your duty to report those unethical decisions or actions. This is an uncomfortable position to be placed into. There are three distinctions here:

1. The unethical decision is against the law. This makes the reporting of that unethical decision easier and mandatory;
2. The unethical decision is in the gray area, much more difficult to define, and yet you believe this to be an unethical and bad decision;
3. The unethical decision was made by a close coworker/friend, in this case the reporting of this unethical decision is probably much more difficult to report.

Some department rules and regulations require you to report the incident; it's your duty and responsibility. Other departments may not have it stated in their rules, but I believe it is an unwritten rule that it is our responsibility to report unethical, immoral, and unlawful decisions. To help clarify the word unlawful, it could mean any of the following: criminal, dishonest, illegal, illicit, prohibited, and unauthorized. The bad decision may have been an accident and an innocent occurrence. But we, as public safety officers, need to recognize what the difference is between an accident, a one-time event, or something that just occurred. The individual that consistently makes poor and unethical decisions is the responsibility of all of us and reflects poorly upon all of us and the Firefighter/EMS family. You see, there is a trend with the repeated bending of the rules, stretching the envelope, and just seeing how far you can get. There is a behavior that exists, that may not get better with time. Quite simply, there are many people that are not a good match to work in the public safety sector. We are unique in our jobs, normal for us, but not for the general public. It is our responsibility to govern ourselves and not allow a consistently poor or an unethical decision scar, blemish, and mark the public safety family for years to come. We do not want to see our department name in the media covering that poor and unethical decision. These events break down the trust between Firefighters/EMS and the public, whom we serve. It is an absolute must, that the public trust their public safety officers. The only way to obtain that trust is to be consistently ethical, moral, and trustworthy, and yes, even likeable.

Some departments mail out customer satisfaction forms after the call. Just as a business would want to have further feedback, fire departments are asking for customer feedback. Most of the time, our customers appreciate the care they received and are even grateful. There are those, however, that are dissatisfied with just about anything. It is not likely we could satisfy all the people all of the time. It certainly is our goal but unlikely and unrealistic. There are many variables with this type of feedback that are out of our control. An example of this would be the transportation of the patient to the closest emergency department facility. That hospital could be closed and the patient would need transport to the next available facility. This occurs quite often in busier cities and metropolitan areas and is totally out of our control. How we can handle this situation, however, can be a manner of communication with the patient and family to explain why their loved one is in another city and two or three hospitals away. A valid question from the family is "why couldn't my grandfather just be taken two miles away to our neighborhood hospital?" This subject deserves a textbook all to itself, an explanation about the reality of our medical care system.

FOR THOSE THAT ANSWERED THE CALL

Fire Fighter's Prayer
When I am called to duty, God wherever flames may rage,
give me strength to save a life, whatever be its age.
Help me to embrace a little child before it's too late,
or save an older person from the horror of that fate.
Enable me to be alert to hear the weakest shout,
and quickly and efficiently to put the fire out.
I want to fill my calling and to give the best in me,
to guard my neighbor and protect his property.
And if according to your will I have to lose my life,
bless with your protecting hand my loving family from strife.[12]

SUMMARY

A code of ethics and core values for Fire Departments are an integral part of our behavior, the way we do our job, how we work with each other, and our interaction with the public. There is no doubt that we are held to a higher standard than most other professions.

One of this country's founding fathers had much to do with ethics, virtues, and public safety. Benjamin Franklin had a high level of commitment for the better good of all citizens. He was the founder of one of the first organized U.S. fire departments (Philadelphia), organized local law enforcement, and educated the citizens in prevention by reminding us "an ounce of prevention is worth a pound of cure." Just as Franklin strived to be a highly virtuous man, all EMT/paramedics, firefighters, and police officers must be professional at all times. We must have high standards of conduct, on and off duty, and high ethical and moral behavior. Public safety departments suffer the ramifications of illegal, immoral, and unethical decisions by employees. These decisions can have a lingering bad feeling and bad taste in everyone's palate. Remember, the news media is always ready for a good story. Not all people and not all "calls" act accordingly. Each is unique and presents itself with a different set of circumstances. That is why we as public safety officers must adhere to a common rule and code. . . . To be ethical and moral all the time.

NOTES

1. Walter Isaacson, *Benjamin Franklin, An American Life*. New York: Simon & Schuster, 2003). p. 132.
2. Walter Isaacson, *Benjamin Franklin, An American Life*. New York: Simon & Schuster, 2003). p. 264.
3. Walter Isaacson, *Benjamin Franklin, An American Life* (New York: Simon & Schuster, 2003).
4. Max Farrand, ed., *The Autobiography of Benjamin Franklin* (New York: Penguin Putnam, 2001).
5. "The Electric Ben Franklin; Franklin's Philadelphia, A Journey Through Franklin's Philadelphia." www.ushistory.org/franklin/philadelphia/fire.htm (accessed March 6, 2010).
6. www.ushistory.org/franklin/philadelphia/fire.htm. (accessed March 6, 2010).
7. City of San Marcos, California, "Mission Statement/Core Values." www.ci.san-marcos.ca.us/index.aspx?page=89 (accessed March 15, 2014).
8. North County Fire Protection District, "Code of Ethics and Values," in *Policy and Procedure Manual*. (accessed March 15, 2014).
9. International Association of Fire Fighters, "Firefighter Code of Ethics." www.iaff.org/ (accessed March 15, 2014).
10. The International Association of Fire Chiefs, "What Is the Fire Chief's Code of Ethics?" www.iafc.org/displaycommon.cfm?an=5 (accessed March 15, 2014).
11. Charles Gillestie, "The Code of Ethics [adopted by the National Association of Emergency Medical Technicians]. www.publicsafety.net/emtcode.htm (accessed March 21, 2014).
12. International Association of Fire Chiefs, "What Is the Fire Fighter's Prayer." www.iafc.org/displaycommon.cfm?an=5 (accessed March 15, 2014).

DILEMMA

As stated in the EMT/paramedic Code of Ethics, you assume the responsibility to expose incompetence or unethical conduct of others. Give an example from personal experience or something you have witnessed that would be incompetent or unethical conduct.

_____

_____

_____

_____

_____

_____

_____

_____

_____

_____

_____

_____

_____

_____

_____

_____

_____

_____

_____

_____

_____

DILEMMA

The Firefighter Code of Ethics states "I recognize the badge of my office as a symbol of public faith, and I accept it as a public trust to be held so long as I am true to the ethics of the fire service." Explain your contribution and your responsibility to uphold this part of the code.

_____

_____

_____

_____

_____

_____

_____

_____

_____

_____

_____

_____

_____

_____

_____

_____

_____

_____

_____

_____

_____

DILEMMA

You arrive on scene to a reported difficulty breathing at a convalescent hospital. The patient is found not breathing and the staff is performing cardiopulmonary resuscitation. You are told by the convalescent staff that there is a do not resuscitate (DNR) order; however, you do not have the DNR order in your hand. What do you do? What legal and moral issues exist?

_____

_____

_____

_____

_____

_____

_____

_____

_____

_____

_____

_____

_____

_____

_____

_____

_____

_____

DILEMMA

During a salvage and overhaul operation at a fire scene, you notice an engineer take a watch from a master bedroom dresser and put it in his pocket. Is this an unlawful act, an unethical act, or does it require further investigation?

_____

_____

_____

_____

_____

_____

_____

_____

_____

_____

_____

_____

_____

_____

_____

_____

_____

_____

_____

_____

_____

_____

DILEMMA

Describe how fire and EMS departments benefit and suffer from ethical and unethical employees?

_____

_____

_____

_____

_____

_____

_____

_____

_____

_____

_____

_____

_____

_____

_____

_____

_____

_____

_____

_____

_____

_____

_____

_____

The Process of Ethical Decision Making

7

CHAPTER OBJECTIVES

1. Understand the process of ethical decision making.
2. Apply the various methods of ethical decision making.
3. Understand the ramifications of not making ethical decisions.
4. Understand the difference between thinking and emoting.
5. Understand the importance of your demeanor in public.

© Flashon Studio, 2014. Used under license from Shutterstock, Inc.

Public safety is a difficult undertaking. The men and women who dedicate themselves to this endeavor put their safety on the line every day and they have to make decisions that could affect not only their lives but also the lives of fellow workers and the public. Firefighters and police officers are trained in the academy to make certain job-related decisions such as when and how to enter a burning building; what is needed for a search warrant; what is probable cause; when to make or not make an exigent search; how to ventilate a room; when and how to use a resuscitator; when can an officer make an arrest; and then they practice doing all of these things while still in the academy or at in-service training.

But where do they learn ethical decisions or how to behave ethically? They learn this from their trainers in the field or their friends and partners. Sometimes ethical decisions are based on the ethos of the department. Some cities' jurisdictions are less concerned with ethical behavior than others. Should this affect the safety officer's decision on how to behave? Should his or her peers feelings or beliefs be considered? More importantly, should his or her own personal beliefs be a factor in behavioral decision making? Should a police officer's code of ethics or a firefighter's code of ethics be considered? How about the public, should they be taken into consideration? The answers to these questions will be entertained in this chapter. A short answer would be yes and no.

PUBLIC SAFETY OFFICER CODES OF ETHICS

The rationale for public safety officer's codes of ethics is to support proper, thoughtful, and professional behavior. These codes cannot cover every possible circumstance that an officer may encounter. They are, however, excellent guidelines with which to begin thinking about ethical and unethical behavior. Whether they are beneficial or not depends on other variables, such as, moral fabric and the enforcement of the codes.

When looking at the police officer code of ethics and the firefighter code of ethics you will see many similarities. For example, the police code states that, "as a law enforcement officer, my fundamental duty is to serve the community."[1] The firefighter's code says, "We recognize that we serve in a position of public trust that imposes responsibility to use publicly owned resources effectively and judiciously."[2] A firefighter's code mentions that "I will keep my private life honorable as an example to everyone of my honorable calling as a firefighter."[3] The police code proclaims, "I will keep my private life unsullied as an example to all and will behave in a manner that does not bring discredit to me or to my agency."[4] The police code says, "I know that I alone am responsible for my own standard of professional performance and will take every reasonable opportunity to enhance and improve my level of knowledge and competence."[5] The firefighter code states,

"I accept as a personal duty to keep myself well educated and trained as an emergency responder."[6]

As we can see, there are many parallels in both the individual codes. These codes are standards of behavior and may be interpreted differently by individuals, although they appear to be clear.

Two surveys taken in 1980 and 1995 compared the rankings of the top twelve occupations based on how much trust the public had in each one. It seems the firefighters fared much better than the police. In 1980, the police were ranked in fifth place and the firefighters in third place, but in 1995, the police were ranked tenth and the firefighters first.[7]

There are many reasons for this difference. For instance, cops arrest people and deprive people of their liberty; they are called to referee family altercations; they carry guns and sometimes have to kill or injure people in the course of their duties; they give people citations for driving infractions, sometimes to firefighters, where firefighters do not engage in those law enforcement activities, which sometimes anger people. The public can forget that the police are part of the public safety team because much of their job is law enforcement and the people don't realize that this is part of what keeps them safe. Another reason for the change in ranking could be that the police need to pay more attention to ethics, as does the entire public safety community.

In the aftermath of a charge of inappropriate behavior by Los Angeles Sheriff's deputies working in the Los Angeles County Jails, the board of supervisors has voted to hire an inspector general to monitor the department. Max Huntsman, a former prosecutor, was named to the office with the intention to "Make civilian oversight of the sheriff's department a permanent reality." A blue-ribbon committee on jail violence urged the board to create the Office of the Inspector General in September 2012 after a nine-month investigation concluded that deputies engaged in "a pattern of unnecessary and excessive use of force" against inmates.[7]

The new chief of the San Diego Police Department, Shelley Zimmerman, has introduced a new camera program. The pilot program is going to start with ten officers. They will be wearing cameras on their persons that will record the officer's interactions with the citizenry. The program is the result of numerous complaints regarding officer's conduct with citizens. These cameras can protect the people and the police officers by providing concrete evidence of the behavior of all concerned.[8]

These new programs demonstrate to the public safety community and the general public that law enforcement is becoming more interested in behaving ethically.

IT SEEMED LIKE A GOOD IDEA AT THE TIME

How many times in your life have you said this or something similar, such as "I didn't think anyone would care"; or "What's the big deal?" or "I didn't mean any harm." Maybe some of you never had to say or think any of those things, but some of you have and at the time you did whatever it was, there is a good chance you weren't thinking.

Visualize this scenario. It's a slow Sunday night and you are an emergency medical technician (EMT) working in a large city that employs patrolling ambulances. You are assigned a district to patrol and the rule is you stay in that district to facilitate quick on-the-scene medical care when called. You are building a fence in your backyard and need to go to the lumberyard, which is out of your district, to pick up fencing materials. You figure, what's the harm? It's quiet and no one will notice. While you're in the yard you receive a call of a shooting in your district. You respond code 3 (red light and siren) but arrive too late and the victim has died. "It seemed like a good idea at the time."

Circumstances are different for public safety officers. If you were a truck driver or a salesperson taking time off to go shopping, it wouldn't matter; those occupations do not hold life or death in their hands, people in safety do.

Do you recall some of the cases we examined in chapter 2? Some, such as the Los Angeles Police Department Ramparts Scandal, The Rodney King beating, or the Jaycee Lee Dugard/Phillip Garrido cases, among others were very serious. Those cases involved people being needlessly beaten or police officers committing crimes such as planting evidence, robbery, or perjury. There were others such as the Porn Star Ball and the Bowling Cops that were almost humorous or seemed less serious because there were no crimes committed. It just appeared like poor judgment or a lack of discretion.

What public safety officers need to keep foremost in their minds is that there is no such thing as a "minor assignment" and all calls for service are important and they all demand our full attention. This doesn't mean the officers can't joke or have humor on the job, but it does mean that they have to exercise discretion.

There is an old Irish proverb that holds , "May you have the hindsight to know where you've been, the foresight to know where you're are going, and the insight to know when you are going too far."

DOING THE RIGHT THING

In his book, *Policing within a Professional Framework,* Michael E. Cavanagh used the phrase "Doing the Right Thing." He wrote that "Doing the right thing means behaving both within and outside of the agency in ways that clearly reflect its values, which are codified in its mission statement, code of ethics, and code of conduct. Additionally, it means obeying and enforcing the U.S. Constitution as well as criminal and civil law."[10]

Why is doing the right thing so important? It is important because if you, as a public safety officer, break a law, don't pay attention to a rule, or do something that calls negative attention to you or your department, it reflects not only on the department but also on the entire profession. If a cop or firefighter does something wrong in Florida, the reverberations are felt by every officer in the country.

Consider that in San Diego a retired police officer who operated a security business pled guilty in San Diego federal court to conspiracy to commit crimes against the United States and filing a false tax return, in March of 2014. The headline read "Retired Officer Pleads Guilty in Campaign Case." The article mentioned the fact that he was a retired police detective no less than four times.[11]

Remember that you not only represent yourself, you represent your department, your city, your state, and country. Because of your profession, you are a public person.

Take the case in Phoenix, New York, in which a firefighter was accused of stealing gasoline from the fire department. According to the article, Matthew Fratello, a firefighter for less than a year, was charged with theft for stealing seven gas cans full of gas. All together around twenty-one and a half gallons of gasoline was taken. The police arrested Fratello and he was dismissed from the department. Why is this relatively small theft case so important? Because the suspect was a public safety officer and the fuel belonged to the taxpayers.[12]

The fourth estate will ensure that the country will know about any transgression of public safety officers because they know it

Police Officer making a radio call.

© TRINACRIA PHOTO, 2014. Used under license from Shutterstock, Inc.

will sell newspapers. If a cop, for example, does something admirable, it is a small article buried in the back of the paper near the obituaries; if it is something negative, it is on or near the front page. Why? The public enjoys seeing someone in authority or someone who is successful suffering a setback in his or her life. It is likely more people know about Tiger Woods' transgressions than the tournaments he won.

SETTING THE TONE

Supervisors and administrators need to ensure that the men and women they are in charge of are doing the right thing. They need to set ethical standards and to see that they are adhered to. If employees are engaging in unethical conduct, there should be sanctions. Misbehavior is sometimes blamed on one or two "bad apples" and in some cases that may be true; however, it has been shown that many times the behavior has been overlooked or passively condoned. Maybe the excuse was that "it wasn't so bad. No one was hurt."

The administration of the department must create an example. The exemplary leader is a person who not only pays attention to the rules but also makes sure everyone else does as well. He or she should be above reproach. His or her personal life is impeccable. The supervisor becomes a role model for the other officers.

Sometimes, a shortcut may need to be taken to get the job done in a timely fashion and that may be allowable. It may be something that is innocuous, such as borrowing a camera from the photo lab to take photos of a crime scene and it would take too long to fill out the paper work. That could be overlooked. However, planting evidence on a suspect because you know he or she is guilty of a crime, even if it is not the current crime, is illegal and can never be allowed, under any circumstances. Query: What could be the long-term ramifications if the planting of evidence was discovered?

To be a good leader you need to think about all of the ramifications of your behavior, both in your professional and personal life. Others are watching you and they may be modeling your behavior. A good leader will never ask his or her charges to do something he or she wouldn't do. You want to create a milieu that encourages a positive attitude that will enable you and your team to realize the department's mission while adhering to its ethical values.

An article by David Rupkalvis in *The Graham Reader*, a Texas newspaper, states that Lt. Kyle Cornell was arrested for theft of $2,950 from the Graham Fire Rescue Auxiliary. The money was for the Muscular Dystrophy Association, which is collected by firefighters through their Fill the Boot campaign.

Chief Dennis Covey said that Cornell resigned when the thefts came to light. It is alleged that Cornell admitted the thefts saying he needed the money for personal debts. Lt. Cornell had served the people of Graham for thirteen years as a volunteer and eight as a paid firefighter.

Chief Covey said he was disappointed and shocked that Cornell was a long-time employee who had the trust of the people for years. He said the allegations had been hard on the other members of the department. "People first of all couldn't believe a guy of Kyle's nature could do something like this." Covey said. "He's always been well-trusted and well-liked. They couldn't believe he would do something like this without coming to ask us for help first."[13]

Here's a fire Lieutenant that has not only betrayed his department but also let all of the folks who worked with him and believed in him down. From the tone of the chief, it seems that if he had financial problems he could have talked to someone and gotten assistance. "It seemed like a good idea at the time."

We need to remember that a public safety officer, no matter what his or her rank, is a leader. Public safety officers are called into duty when there is trouble and others don't know how to deal with whatever the situation is. So people call the fire department or the police department or both because they expect these agencies to lead them from harm and to safety. To have a thoroughly ethical department, all aspects of the organization must stress the importance of always trying to do the right thing and that sets the tone for the behavior of all members.

THE PROCESS OF ETHICAL DECISION MAKING

Ethics is the discipline that provides a systematic approach for understanding and examining the nature of morality with the intent of promoting the overall welfare of the community.[14]

Jay Albanese in book, *Professional Ethic in Criminal Justice,* listed five steps to follow in solving ethical dilemmas. They are:

1. List the relevant facts (separating the irrelevant details from the central issues).
2. Identify the precise moral question to be answered.
3. List and think about the moral principles that might be used to support the positions to be taken.
4. Make and explain your decision (i.e., your morally permissible course of conduct).

5. Justify your conclusions using positive reasons and ethical principles in support of your decision, anticipating and addressing contrary views.[15]

Let's look at a situation, and try and arrive at an ethical decision using the steps previously listed.

A young man who is engaged to be married is seeing his fiancée's best friend secretly. One night, as he is leaving her apartment, he witnesses a mugging in the street. No one sees him, but he gets a good look at the suspect and walks away instead of waiting for the police. He is able to identify the suspect, but doesn't want to get involved because of his relationship with the best friend of his intended bride.

How does he resolve this dilemma? If he comes forward what are the possibilities? If he doesn't what are the ramifications? Is he morally required to go to the police? How would a utilitarian (John Stuart Mill) look at the situation? How about Aristotle or Immanuel Kant? How would the father of Situational Ethics Joseph Fletcher approach this problem?

Emotions versus Cognitive Processes

Emotions sometimes override our cognitive processes and that can cause problems with decision-making skills. Public safety officers should always maintain a safe distance between the task or clients and themselves.

TASK >>>>OFFICER
CLIENT>>>>OFFICER

The arrows in this case represent space. Officers must always maintain a professional distance or space from the folks they work for or with. They must never let their emotions intrude on decision making. This doesn't mean that they can't have empathy or sympathy for the person or the situation, but those emotions must be kept in check. To survive twenty to thirty years in public safety, officers have to be able to conserve their emotions. If officers became overly involved in every case they encountered they would exhaust their emotional reserves and become burned out. This is why officers must develop an emotional or professional space between their clients and themselves.

There was a case in Oakland, California, in March 2009, in which four police officers were killed. Apparently, according to the news reports, some of the responding officers let their emotions interfere with their decisions, and as a result they were disciplined and one retired. Now we can sit here and second guess like a Monday morning quarterback what these officers did or didn't do; however, any critique must take into consideration what was happening at the time and the fact that we weren't there.

There were a couple of articles in the *San Francisco Chronicle* on January 8, 2010, reporting on the shooting of four Oakland police officers in March 2009. In the first article by Matier and Ross, two officers, Sergeant Mark Dunakin and Officer John Hege, were killed while conducting a traffic stop on March 21. The suspect, Lovelle Mixon, a parolee, fled the scene and holed up in an apartment building on 74th Avenue in Oakland. Lieutenant Chris Mufarreh was one of the first supervisors to arrive and, according to the article, "self-assigned" himself to take charge of the situation and initiated an "ad hoc" SWAT raid on the apartment where they believed the suspect was hiding. During the course of the raid, two more officers, Sergeants Ervin Romans and Daniel Sakai, were shot and killed by Mixon.

Allegedly, based on an investigative report headed by a former Pasadena police chief, there were many mistakes made in the operation to apprehend the suspect. One of the mistakes was that most of the senior officers in the department went to the hospital to console the families of the first officers killed. The officers at the scene did not evacuate the other tenants in the building. SWAT members and hostage negotiators weren't yet on the site when the operation began, and there was no ambulance standing by. As a result of all this, Mufarreh and Captain Rick Orozco, who did respond to the area and apparently signed off on the raid, were given letters of discipline for the apparent bungling of the SWAT raid.[16]

The second article, this one by Chip Johnson, cautioned the police to curb their emotions. It states that while some cops were directed by department protocol, others were guided by their emotions.

Sergeant Ray Blackman was quoted in the article stating, "There is no argument that emotions played a role in the way some officers responded, but it's the difference between controlling emotions and removing them. You can never remove those emotions, but you have to control them."[17]

If you look retrospectively at this situation, you can visualize how things could have gotten mixed; how some of the decisions shouldn't have been made. We can do that because we are in a classroom reading a textbook. If you are on the line trying to arrest a suspect who has just killed two of your officers, you are frightened, angry, sad, confused, and frustrated. You want to get the individual and lock him or her up so others will not be injured or killed.

"Emotion" is defined in the *Merriam-Webster's Collegiate Dictionary as* 1a: disturbance, b: excitement, 2a: the affective aspect of consciousness: feeling, b: a state of feeling, c: a psychic and physical reaction (as anger or fear) subjectively experienced as strong feeling and physiologically involving changes that prepare the body for immediate vigorous action."

A short definition of "thinking" according to the same dictionary is "the action of using one's mind to produce thoughts." Another definition is "opinion, judgment <I'd like to know your *opinion* on this."

As we examine these definitions, can you see how they conjure up feelings? For example, each definition seems to justify itself. If you are emotional, you could be disturbed or excited and when you're thinking it is calmer, quieter, you are using your mind.

As Sergeant Blackman said previously, we can't remove emotions but we can control them. That is why we have to keep that safe professional space open between us and the situations and people we deal with while we are working. That space is what we use to think our way through a situation, even an emotionally charged one such as losing a comrade in the line of duty.

Another emotionally charged situation for many officers is a child abuse case. Crimes against children seem to affect people more because the victims are looked upon as being helpless and in need of greater protection. Many officers are parents as well and this can influence the officer's decision-making skills. Maybe the officer was abused himself or herself or the officer has had prior experience with child abuse victims and therefore has an emotional connection with this type of investigation. If the officer is not careful, his or her cognitive process may be overridden and the officer will respond emotionally, which could lead to trouble.

When we maintain the space, we can determine what the problem is and gather as much intelligence as possible, talk to others to get their opinions of the problem, look for any pitfalls, and determine the short- and long-term ramifications of our decisions. In other words, we think through the problem. We may still be angry, fearful, frustrated, excited, and disturbed, but we control those emotions while we are engaged in fighting the fire, caring for the injured, or working a sniper situation.

There was an article in the San Diego U-T on March 23, 2014, written by Jack Murphy that criticized the Navy SEALS who killed Osama bin Laden for firing approximately hundred rounds into the body of the terrorist. Again, when we criticize something like this we have to realize we were not there and have no idea of the level

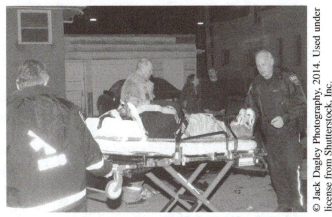

Man on stretcher.

© Jack Dagley Photography, 2014. Used under license from Shutterstock, Inc.

of emotion that was going on at the time. Mr. Murphy may have some idea, as at one time he was an Army Special Operations sniper and team leader. However, the amount of emotion attached to bin Laden and his activities has to be something that very few of us had ever experienced before. Mr. Murphy does make a good point when he writes that overzealous behavior should not be allowed to go unchecked because this kind of behavior can overtime create a unit subculture that could erode the viability of the unit. Remember in chapter 2 we discussed the "deindividuation" theory of Gustave Le Bon. Many times, in a group situation people lose their self-imposed controls and internalized moral restraints over their behavior. This very well could be what happened here. Query: How would you preclude this from happening?

Practice Makes Perfect

We can publish codes of ethics and write laws and regulations that forbid or discourage unethical behavior. We can tell people about the negative things that can happen if they engage in brutality or corruption. We can tell people not to act in certain ways, but these things would in many cases fall on deaf ears because the people we would be addressing would be thinking that they would never do anything wrong anyway. Most police and fire departments devote little time to ethics training. Police Officers Standards and Training (POST) in California requires eight hours of ethics and professionalism training, but some academies require more. There was a survey by the International Association of Chiefs of Police on ethics training in 1998. The association sent out 4,500 surveys and of the 900 returns, 70% of the responses reported that their agency had only four classroom hours or less for ethics; 17% stated that their departments had an eight-hour block for ethics.

H. Michael Drumm of the City of Markham (Illinois) Fire Department wrote a paper in 2000, titled "Identifying the Ethical Climate of the City of Markham Fire Department." The paper was written as an applied research project submitted to the National Fire Academy as part of the Executive Fire Officer Program. He used an anonymous survey. The results revealed that even though the department had a code of ethics, it is apparent that the members are not trained in understanding or using it.

The study found that: (a) the ethical foundation was weak, (b) the fire chief has to set the tone for the ethical operation of the department, and (c) ethics training and development should be a form of behavior modification.[18]

People coming into the public safety field should be made aware of the rules and regulations of the organization. Recruits should learn the right way to make decisions and this learning should be reinforced with continuous training after being hired.

When Aristotle spoke of moral virtue he said that, "[m]oral virtue develops as a result of habit by exercising them; it does not occur naturally."

Aristotle also said, "It is by doing just acts that the just man is produced, and by doing temperate acts the temperate man; without doing these no one would have even a prospect of being good."[19]

To do good deeds and exhibit ethical behavior, you need to practice; it requires an attitude and it becomes habitual. Moral virtue has to be learned and then practiced, much like becoming an athlete, actor, or musician. Moral virtue is not innate; we attain it by study, practice, or habit, and training. We have to remember that when it comes to behaving ethically we need to be constantly vigilant and remember that "practice makes perfect."

Values

What are values? Well, if you have a desire to be in good health or make a lot of money, those are values. You may think that education is important, so you value education. We may value having hair or being physically attractive. You may value a certain activity because you are good at it and it brings you pleasure. As we can see, not all values are of a concern to ethics. Values pertain to ethics only when we are trying to determine right from wrong.

We all have values that we've learned from our friends, families, religions, personal experiences, employment, subculture, roots, and political affiliations. These are important values but probably not the best ones to use when making ethical decisions. There are some values that are more or less universal and these are the ones we should examine when making ethical decisions as public safety officers. Values such as fairness, honesty, truthfulness, respect, responsibility, bravery, trustworthiness, and loyalty.

Sometimes values conflict. Some say that an honest man will never be wealthy, so your value of honesty may run contrary to your desire for wealth. Or to save someone's feelings you may have to lie.

Principles

We can convert values into principles in order to help us make ethical decisions. For instance, the Snohomish Fire and Rescue Code of Ethics says in one section that, "I will perform my duty with efficiency, good judgment and impartially to the best of my ability—accepting full responsibility for all of my actions." To accomplish this, we take the values of responsibility, fairness, and trustworthiness and convert them into the principle mentioned in the code of ethics. We have to have a consistency between what we say and what we do. The firefighter and police officers codes that we have examined are simply a way of values being placed into specific principles in the form of what to do.

Another Model for Making Ethical Decisions

Ethical decision making is the result of sound decision-making principles and the incorporation of ethical and moral values. Here is another process to be used when considering ethical questions:

1. Examine the situation and consider all of the elements as dispassionately as possible.
2. Investigate all of your options.
3. Decide on the ones that seem to be the most appropriate.
4. Fine-tune your selection by further examination of your choices. You may want to consult with others to gather input.
5. Decide on your final choice considering any difficulties you may encounter.
6. Consider the ramifications of your choice; the most positive or negative outcomes. Can you live with these outcomes?

Think of a personal ethical dilemma that you have experienced and using the process, try and reach an outcome that is compatible with your ethical beliefs.

WHAT GETS IN THE WAY OF ETHICAL BEHAVIOR?
Politics

The agency or city's subculture can hinder officers from behaving correctly. These may be ways of behaving that have been going on for years. Officers may have been taking gratuities or looking the other way when witnessing minor crimes or infractions.

In San Francisco, for instance, the district attorney didn't want officers to make arrests for prostitution. So some officers didn't enforce the law on prostitution, whereas others did. Who was right? The officers who didn't make prostitution arrests were obeying the district attorney. They didn't get disciplined for not making the arrests. The officers who did arrest the prostitutes were doing their job. They also weren't disciplined. In your opinion, who was behaving ethically? How did you arrive at your conclusion?

The officers might get the idea that if the district attorney doesn't think prostitution is important, they can pretty much do what they want. In other words, they can use their discretion when deciding whether or not to arrest the prostitute.

When exercising this discretion, the officer may elicit a favor from the prostitute and that would be unethical. But the officer's attitude could be "No one cares anyway." This would be a case of the political climate of the city affecting the behavior of the officers.

Politics can often affect an officer's career or perception. They may feel they are underappreciated because they didn't get the assignment they wanted or the promotion they thought they deserved. The officers could become frustrated because an arsonist goes free because of a technicality and is back on the street before the ink is dry on the arson report. These are stressors for public safety officers and they can react to these stressors in a positive way and as a result remedy the situation, or they can react in a negative way and exacerbate the problem.

If you failed to get the promotion you were trying for, you could examine your study habits or talk to some of the people who did get promoted and see if there was something you missed in your preparation for the examination. That would be a positive remedy. A negative remedy would be to start drinking on duty, taking bribes, or just not doing your job to the best of your ability.

If your arson suspect gets off on a technicality, you could perjure yourself and lie on the witness stand the next time you testify, which would be a negative resolution to the problem; or you could find out what your mistake was and learn a way of counteracting the technicality.

Public Safety Subculture

Public safety officers work in a close knot bureaucratic organization. In the case of the firefighters, they actually live together for much of their working hours. They sleep in the same building, share meals, watch television, even do the dishes, and clean the house together. The firefighters respond to emergency calls with each other and work as a team when putting out fires or answering a medical assistance call. Police officers ride together in patrol cars for eight to twelve hours a day, depending on what department they are working for. They spend more waking hours with their partners than they do with their spouses or significant others. The officers face dangerous situations together and are responsible for each other. In many departments, officers are allowed to pick their partners. The partners become close to each other, and in many cases the families socialize, so the officers know each other's spouses or significant others. They will know each other's children and the children will play together. You can visualize how public safety officers tend to think of their partners as family. Public safety officer are probably closer to their work mates than any other occupation.

As a result of this esprit de corps, public safety officers are reluctant to report their fellow workers for unethical behavior. Many officers believe that it is the supervisors or the command staff's job to ferret out the wrongdoers because they are getting the big money. The reality of the situation is that even otherwise ethical officers will look the other way at certain minor transgressions of the rules and regulations.

In order to provide some balance to the discussion of ethics and people in the same profession protecting their fellows, the authors need to call attention to the state of California legislature. There is a member who has been found guilty of eight felonies and he was allowed to take a paid voluntary leave of absence.[20] A public safety officer would have had to resign. This just reinforces the fact that public safety officers are held to a higher standing than elected officials.

The case of Frank Serpico, which was the subject of a movie starring Al Pacino, was a true story of a New York City police officer who refused to take bribes. There was no place for him to go because the corruption permeated the department; it was institutionalized. Finally, because Serpico would not back down, the mayor of New York, John Lindsay, formed the Knapp Commission in 1970 and the commission found that corruption in the New York Police Department was "widespread" and as a result a number of officers were terminated and some ended up behind bars.[21]

When Serpico testified in front of the Knapp Commission in December of 1971, he stated:

> "Through my appearance here today . . . I hope that police officers in the future will not experience the same frustration and anxiety that I was subjected to for the past five years at the hands of my superiors because of my attempt to report corruptions . . . . We create an atmosphere in which the honest officer fears the dishonest officer, and not the other way around . . . .The problem is that the atmosphere does not yet exist in which honest police officers can act without fear of ridicule or reprisal from fellow officers."[22]

That was 1971, and since then things have gotten better. Remember there has to be unwavering vigilance when dealing with ethics. We have to constantly reinforce ethical values and principles and continue to monitor ourselves to maintain ethical behavior.

Loyalty

In most cases, loyalty is a good thing, but sometimes our loyalty gets misplaced. We need to be loyal to the right things. If a fellow public safety officer is behaving unethically, he or she is violating his or her oath of office and is not being loyal to the profession or department. In *Merriam-Webster's Collegiate Dictionary*, the definition of "loyal" is as follows:

1. Unswerving in allegiance; as
   a faithful in allegiance to one's lawful sovereign or government
   b faithful to a private person to whom fidelity is due
   c faithful to a cause; ideal, custom, institution, or product
2. showing loyalty
3. obs: LAWFUL, LEGIMATE[23]

If we dissect this definition we can maybe determine who and what we should be loyal to. The first part of the definition states if we are loyal, we are faithful in allegiance to our government. And in most cases, if we are public safety officers, we are employed by a governmental subdivision. We need to be loyal to our constituents. The second section says "faithful to a person to whom fidelity is due." Is loyalty due to someone who is betraying our profession? Probably not. The third part of definition reads "faithful to a cause ideal, custom, institution, or product." Public safety officers have to be faithful to all of these. They need to be aligned with their department's mission to provide safety to the public and to live up to the ideals and customs of the job. And last but not least make sure that the product they provide is the best possible.

Officers should definitely be loyal to each other. They should be loyal to the profession and the members who subscribe to the rules and regulations of the department, the mission of the agency, and the code of ethics.

Belonging to the Group

There is nothing wrong with wanting to be one of the group. Most people want to belong. You can see this in every realm of life. Whether at school, at a ball game, or in a club, human beings want to relate to someone. In public safety, we also want to belong and not be an outcast. The question is who are the folks you want to identify with? Is it the ones who are in trouble most of the time: the drinkers, the shirkers, or the people who are corrupt? Or is it the officers who do their jobs, pay attention to the rules, and carry their load at work? You have to make a choice. If you engage in one act of corruption, they've got you. They can hold it over your head for the rest of your career. If you refuse, they may just ignore you and not approach you again. What you have to remember is that there is never a justification for unethical behavior, not even to be one of the group.

MISTAKES HAPPEN

All public safety officers are human (although there are some police dogs, who wear stars or shields). Human beings make mistakes; however, unethical behavior is never a mistake.

There was an officer who got into a minor traffic accident with a department vehicle. He struck the rear end of a car that was stopped at a stop sign. The woman got out of the car and recognized the officer's partner. The partner did not recognize the woman (she was a dental hygienist) who had cleaned his teeth a month prior to the accident. The officer who was driving said, "Oh you know this woman so there is no need to make a report. We will just exchange information." The partner told the officer driver that he has to make a report because that is department policy. The driver refused and so the two involved in the accident exchanged names and insurance information. It turned out that the bill for fixing the woman's car was several hundred dollars and the driver officer did not want to pay, he told her so when she called him, and hung up. The woman filed a report and the officer was made to pay the bill and got two weeks' suspension. Query: What is the moral to this story?

According to an article by Shaun Boyd in the *Colorado News,* the Mountain View Fire Department in Colorado has started a program in which firefighters can report their mistakes. The rationale for the program is to aid firefighter in learning from their mistakes.

According to the article, the Mountain View department made a mistake when they took off on an emergency call and trailed one thousand feet of hose behind them.

Luckily, there was no car behind them because the coupling for the hose could have gone through a windshield and caused a serious accident. The department wants to get the word out so that others will not make the same mistake.[24]

In another incident that took place in Charleston, South Carolina, in 2008, during a fire there were some issues regarding water supply and hoses, as well as communications and incident command. A federal agency reported that there was a breakdown in communications during the fire. The pump on one of the engines was not functioning properly and the engine company failed to locate a hydrant or to use large diameter hoses, which resulted in not having enough water on the fire. The result was nine fatalities.[25]

Consider this case: Two officers respond to a "man with a gun" call. The officers see a person standing on the street with a gun in his hand. They get out of the car and order the man to drop the gun. The man turns and points the gun at the officers; the officers fire and kill the man. Upon further investigation, it is determined that the gun is a toy and the "man" is a 14-year-old Samoan boy who is developmentally challenged.

What we've examined in this section are mistakes. Some of the mistakes were serious and people lost their lives. We also looked at a program that seeks to minimize mistakes and where we can learn from them. Mistakes can become training issues that can be addressed in the academy and at in-service training. But as mentioned previously, mistakes are part of being human and unethical behavior can never be justified.

HOW TO KNOW IF YOU ARE BEHAVING ETHICALLY

Teaching people to be ethical does not guarantee ethical behavior. There are people who understand ethics and still behave unethically. I'm sure Bernie Madoff, Martha Stewart, Kenneth Lay, and other administrative officers at Enron understood ethics, but they chose to not adhere to them.

If you know who you are and are true to yourself, you will probably know when you are behaving correctly. If you live by your values, you will be at ease with yourself. But if you feel troubled by your actions and experience anxiety because of them, there is a good chance that you are not doing the right thing.

If we look at any of the cases of unethical conduct that have been mentioned in this book, they could have been avoided if the actors had stopped and thought about what they were doing.

If we reexamine the case of the firefighter who stole the gasoline in Phoenix, New York, we can see that if he had considered thinking ethically, he may not have taken the fuel. Is stealing a good universal rule? Did it agree with any moral virtue? If you considered potential pain and pleasure, would stealing the gas bring the greatest total happiness? If he had thought about these things, he may have still been a firefighter and not awaiting trial for theft.

The Associated Press reported on January 27, 2010, that two off-duty Los Angeles police officers had been arrested for allegedly pistol-whipping another man during a fight. Apparently, one of the officers was having an argument with his girlfriend when the man intervened. Whittier police officer Mike Dekowski said that off-duty officer Brando Valdez turned on the bystander and punched him in the face and pistol-whipped him. Whittier police Lieutenant Carlos Solorza stated that the officers had been drinking and were outside of a café when the argument began. The officers are free on thirty thousand dollar bail for each, and the Los Angeles Police Department put them on administrative leave pending an investigation.[26]

Here is another case where the officers were not thinking. If you are a public safety officer, what should you consider before going out partying? Are you going to be working at this time? Do I need the tools of the trade? Who am I? Where am I going? How must I behave? You must remember you will be held to a higher standard. Remember: *Never* let your emotions intrude on your decision making.

Back in 2006, according to Laura Jesse of the *San Antonio Express-News* (Texas), three San Antonio Texas fire officials were to face a hearing on the accepting of gifts from a vendor who provided the department with bunker gear. Firefighter Jerry Cortes alleged that Lieutenant Jim Reidy received airfare, meals, hotel rooms, and gifts from the Total Fire Group. According to the transcripts of a hearing with the San Antonio Professional Firefighters Association, Lt. Reidy confirmed that he had received these gifts. Marty Sargent, who works for Total Fire, also implicated Fire Chief Robert Ojeda and Assistant Chief Carl Wedige, but there are no specific allegations regarding the two men. All of the gifts were unsolicited.

Sargent said that "We've built friendships with fire departments across the country, and I can tell you that never once did Jim Reidy ask us for any kind of gratuity. He never asked us for a meal, he never asked us for a hotel room; neither has Chief Ojeda, neither has Chief Wedige."

The City of San Antonio has an ethics code which states that a city official or employee cannot solicit, accept, or agree to accept a gift or benefit from a person or company that is already doing or is seeking to do business with the city, unless the gift is of nominal value or it is a meal worth less than $50.[27]

Here again appears to be a case where the officers were not thinking. Because of their rank, you would assume they would know the city's ethics code. What were they thinking? That no one would care? That no one would find out?

Why is this even a problem? Because accepting gifts could cause a conflict of interest. If you are in a position to purchase items for the city, you are obligated to get the best equipment available that you can afford. Maybe the company with the best equipment can't afford to give you gratuities, so you go with the company who can. The bidding process has to be fair and open to all without any consideration other than price and product. As a public servant, you have to remember you are representing the public and have to do your best for your constituency.

In situations involving questions of duty, there are three questions to ask:

- What does the law say you must do?
- What are the department rules?
- What do your personal ethics require?[28]

If officers ask these three questions of themselves, they will, in most cases, arrive at a decision they can live with and that won't cause them much anxiety. If we asked these three questions each time and made it a habit, the process would become part of our decision-making repertoire.

It's been said that many people are not capable of thinking when making decisions because they have not gone through the process. Ethical decision making is not included in the educational experience. Some of us get it at home or as a result of religious teachings, but ethical thinking is not included in secondary educational curriculum for the most part. So left to their own devices, they make decisions based on what is perceived as their own self-interest at the time. They only look at the short-term consequences rather than the long-term consequences. Hence, the saying, "It seemed like a good idea at the time."

If we look at our own self-interest closely, we would always consider the long-term consequences. If we remember this, we would always behave ethically. Let's consider utilitarianism for example; if we are going to make a correct decision we have to consider the ramifications, not only to ourselves but to others as well.

An example would be: An officer is thinking about committing perjury (lying on the witness stand after taking an oath to tell the truth) because the defendant is a serial child sexual predator and he needs to be incarcerated. But before doing this, the officer considers the long-term consequences of her action:

- She perjures herself. This is a crime for which she could go to jail and lose her job.
- Even if this doesn't happen, her reputation will be ruined and her credibility will be lost.
- The reputation of other officers will be smudged. People already are quick to believe officers are always lying on the witness stand.
- People will not trust the testimony of officers and will be reluctant to find defendants guilty.
- Citizens will not cooperate with public safety officers.
- This could lead to the demise of law and order and our society could end up in total chaos.

Now this does sound a tad draconian, but it is a possibility. There are countries in the world today where a total breakdown of trust and respect of public safety officers specifically and government in general has led to chaos. Two that come to mind are Mexico and Somalia.

The Mexican drug cartels have bought off many of the police officers, so people don't trust the police. As a result, no one will inform on the cartels. The officers who are not corrupt are being killed by the cartels. In 2008, six police officials were killed in one week in Ciudad Juarez. More than 2,500 people were killed in drug-related violence in Mexico in 2007.[29] There were one-thousand killings in Mexico during the first eight weeks of 2009. The local governments have fired more than six-hundred municipal police officers because they had links to drug cartels.[30]

On December 31, 2009, the U.S. Department of State issued a travel warning for Somalia. There appears to be nothing but total anarchy in this country. There is no functioning government and there are suicide bombers, clans fighting for territory, terrorists, and pirates.

The types of crimes that these groups engage in include: kidnappings, illegal roadblocks, banditry, and murder.[31] This is a country in which the government and public safety officials were corrupt and as a result, civilization broke down and now you have anarchy.

Because of the social chaos in these countries, the economy is in trouble, tourism has been negatively affected, and people live in fear and poverty. There is no one to call for assistance.

This seems kind of farfetched when we consider our system as opposed to the systems of other countries, but by illustrating this extreme we can begin to realize the consequences of our behavior and how important it is to always be thinking of what could happen if we had a breakdown of the government and other public services. A democratic society depends on the cooperation, involvement, and trust of its citizens. Public safety is the arm of government that is out there 24/7 and has the most interaction with the public. It is important that we keep this in mind.

ETHICAL CONDUCT TEST

Many people have given thought to the question: "Is what I'm doing right now ethical?" One way to test your behavior is to consider how you would feel if your family or the media found out about what you were doing. Would you be proud? If you would not want your behavior known to others, there is a good chance you are misbehaving.

Take the case of Senator John Edwards who tried to cover up an extramarital affair in an effort to salvage his political career. He knew he was behaving unethically. If he didn't, you have to be happy he didn't get elected president. He could have questioned his behavior at any time and come to the conclusion his behavior was not good. He could have asked "What is best for my candidacy and the country?"

Mark Sanford, the governor of South Carolina, had an affair with a woman in Argentina and lied about it saying he was hiking on the Appalachian Trail. He only needed to ask one question, "How would my wife and family feel about this?"

Tiger Woods, the number one golfer in the world and the highest paid athlete, had affairs with numerous people and as a result lost millions of dollars in endorsements. What if he had asked himself: What are the long-term ramifications of this if I get caught?

Now these successful men who were looked up to and trusted, they may be successful again, but will they ever be trusted again?

These men are public entities. Public safety officers are as well. They must adhere to the principles of the job and remember that they will be held to a higher standard and must conduct themselves accordingly.

> *If you tell the truth you don't have to remember anything.*
> *Mark Twain*

NOTES

1. International Association of Police Chiefs, "Police Officers Code of Ethics." www.theiacp.org.
2. International Association of Fire Chiefs, "Fire Chiefs Code of Ethics." www.iacp.org.
3. Snohomish Fire and Rescue, "Code of Ethics." http://snohomishfire.org.
4. International Association of Police Chiefs. "Police Officers Code of Ethics." www.theiacp.org.
5. International Association of Police Chiefs. "Police Officers Code of Ethics." www.theiacp.org
6. Snohomish Fire and Rescue, "Code of Ethics." http://snohomishfire.org.
7. Robert Faturechi, "Official urge cutting ties with sheriff monitors.' Los Angeles Times. 03/19/2014. P. AA1.
8. Mark Walker. "Police camera program to expand by summer" San Diego Union Tribune. 03/20/2014 p. B2
9. National Institute of Justice and the Office of Community Oriented Policing Services, p. 13 www.ncjrs.gov/pdffiles/crimepre.pdf.
10. Michael Cavanagh, *Policing Within a Professional Framework* (Boston: Pearson Prentice Hall, 2004), p. 3.
11. Kristina Davis, "Retired Officer Pleads Guilty in Campaign Case. San Diego U-T 03/19/2014. P. A-1
12. Debra Groom, "Phoenix Firefighter Arrested and Accused of Stealing from Fire Department." *The Post Standard.* 02/05/2010.
13. David Rupkalvis, "Texas FF Arrested for theft." *The Graham (Texas) Reader.* 01/08/2010 p. 1.
14. M.A. Lefton-Greif, and J.C. Arvedson, Ethical considerations in pediatric dysphagia. *Seminars in Speech and Language 18,* no. 1 (1997): 79–86.
15. Jay S. Albanese, *Professional Ethics in Criminal Justice: Being Ethical When No One is Looking,* 2nd ed. (New York: Pearson, 2008).
16. Philip Matier and Andrew Ross, "Two cops face Demotion." *San Francisco Chronicle* January 8, 2010, pc 1.
17. Chip Johnson, Lesson for the Police: Control Emotions. *San Francisco Chronicle.* 01/08/2010
18. H. Michael Drumm, "Identifying the Ethical Climate of the City of Markham Fire Department." www.usfa.dhs.gov/pdf/efop/efo21929.pdf 02/28/10.
19. Aristotle, *TheNicomachean Ethics* (New York: Oxford University Press, 1998). P. 35
20. Joel Anderson, *Smoke and Mirrors on Senate Floor.* San Diego U-T 03/27/2014. p. B 11
21. V.E. Kappeler, R.D. Sluder, and G.P. Alpert, *Forces of Deviance*: *Understanding the Dark Side of Policing.* (Prospect Heights, IL.: Waveland Press, 1994)
22. Knapp Commission (1971) V.E. Kappeler, R.D. Shuder, and G.P. Alpert. *Forces of Deviance: Understanding the Dark Side of Policing.* (Prospect Heights, IL.: Waveland Press, 1994).

23. *Merriam-Webster Collegiate Dictionary;* 10th Ed (Springfield, MA: Webster, 2001).

24. Shaun Boyd, "New System Helps Firefighters Learn From Mistakes." http://cbs4denver.com/local/colorado.News Denver.News.Boulder.2.548851.html 02/12/2010.

25. Shawn Smetana, "Former Firefighter: NIOSH Report Confirms Mistakes Were Made." www.wciv.com/news/stories/0508/518197.html 03/22/2010.

26. Associated Press. Wednesday 01/27/2010.

27. Laura Jesse, "Texas Firefighters Face Hearing in Gifts." *San Antonio Express-News* (Texas), 01/12/2006 p. 2.

28. Joycelyn M. Pollock, *Ethical Dilemmas and Decisions in Criminal Justice* (5thed.). (Belmont, CA: Thomson-Wadsworth, 2007), p. 210.

29. Ignacio Alvardo, "Top Mexican Police Officer Killed, Sixth in Week." Reuters. 5/10/2008.

30. Rick Jarvis, "Surge of Mexican Troops Leads to Lull in Drug War Violence." *USA Today.* 03/16/2009.

31. United States Department of State, Bureau of Consumer Affairs. Washington, D.C. 20520.

DILEMMA

You're a fire inspector and have been assigned to inspect a restaurant/night club for safety violations. You call the proprietor and request an appointment with him at the building and he suggests that you meet over lunch (on him) at another restaurant because he is closed during the day. What do you do? Can you accept the lunch? Why or why not?

_____

_____

_____

_____

_____

_____

_____

_____

_____

_____

_____

_____

_____

_____

_____

_____

_____

_____

_____

DILEMMA

You are investigating a murder case in which a young married mother has been killed and she was having an affair with another man. During the course of the investigation, you discovered through DNA testing that the husband was not the biological father of their child. By further testing you learned the boyfriend was the father.

Ethically should you tell the parties of the situation? Are you obligated to tell? What would Immanuel Kant decide?

_____

_____

_____

_____

_____

_____

_____

_____

_____

_____

_____

_____

_____

_____

_____

_____

_____

_____

_____

DILEMMA

You are a fire captain and one of the firefighters under your command is seeking to move to another department and wants you to write her a letter of recommendation. She has not been a particularly good employee. She comes in late often and abuses sick leave. Do you write the letter and get rid of her? What do you tell her?

_____

_____

_____

_____

_____

_____

_____

_____

_____

_____

_____

_____

_____

_____

_____

_____

_____

_____

_____

_____

_____

DILEMMA

You're a firefighter in a small city and one night you and your significant other go to a party at another firefighter's home. You go in to the bathroom and there is another guy you know from your engine company snorting cocaine. What do you do? Do you have an obligation to take any action? What would a utilitarian do?

_____

_____

_____

_____

_____

_____

_____

_____

_____

_____

_____

_____

_____

_____

_____

_____

_____

_____

DILEMMA

It is a cold and rainy night. You are driving down the street and while making a right-hand turn you sideswipe a parked car. There is no one around and no witnesses to the accident. What do you do?

Relate this scenario to Kant's "Kingdom of ends," which states that rational beings are united through common, objective universal laws that apply to everyone.

_____

_____

_____

_____

_____

_____

_____

_____

_____

_____

_____

_____

_____

_____

_____

_____

_____

_____

DILEMMA

You are working traffic and you pull over a motorist for speeding. You ask for the motorists driver' license, he hands it to you and there is a $50.00 bill attached to the bottom of the document.

What do you do? Is this a bribery attempt? Can you arrest the driver for attempted bribery? How do you proceed?

_____

_____

_____

_____

_____

_____

_____

_____

_____

_____

_____

_____

_____

_____

_____

_____

_____

_____

DILEMMA

You and your partner receive a family disturbance call, a husband and wife spat. Upon arrival at the home, you are greeted by the woman of the house and you recognize her as the girlfriend of another officer who is a friend of yours. The cause of the fight according to the husband is that she has been cheating of him and he has just found out.

Should you discuss this situation with your friend? Is it smart for an officer to get involved with a married person? Could this compromise your friend's career?

_____

_____

_____

_____

_____

_____

_____

_____

_____

_____

_____

_____

_____

_____

_____

_____

_____

_____

_____

Technology, Social Networking, and Ethical Judgment

8

It is easy to be wise after the event—Proverb

CHAPTER OBJECTIVES

1. Describe how computer technology has changed ethics.
2. Define the role of public safety officers and computer ethics.
3. Recognize the pitfalls of social networking.
4. Understand how technology can help or hinder you as a public safety officer.

© Emanuelle Tortora. Used under license from Shutterstock, Inc.

HAS TECHNOLOGY CHANGED THE WORLD OF ETHICS?

We are a society that is affected by mobile phones, BlackBerrys, iPhones, and laptop computers. It is hard to imagine life now without being able to "text" our family and friends. Text messaging, also known as "texting," refers to the exchange of brief written messages between mobile phones over cellular networks using short message service (SMS). In 2008, over 1 trillion text messages were sent throughout the United States, compared to 363 billion in 2007. This was a 37 percent increase in one year. Every American sends an average of 13 text messages per day. Text messaging is the most widely used mobile data service.[1]

I think it's here to stay in some form or another with sore thumbs and all. Technology is changing so quickly that in 2013, text messaging numbers dropped a little because of new technology like Apple's iMessage and Facebook. Smart phones only account for 50 percent of the total cell phone population. It has become a $150 billion-a-year industry by the end of 2013. Did you know text messaging was twenty years old in 2014?

Six billion text messages are sent every day and 2.2 trillion are sent every year just in the United States alone! And of course, we cannot forget globally, 8.6 trillion text messages are sent every year.

It is no longer a young person's thing to do. Statistics show that all age groups, and yes, senior citizens, are participating in this simplistic way to communicate. It's easy, fast, and you can say whatever you want without a facial gesture or verbal comment. In fact, text messaging and social media are the primary sources of intimidation and other forms of harassment.

In the United States alone, 75 percent of teenagers send sixty text messages every day. It has become the most popular form of communication among teenagers. It beats out the good old-fashioned talking face-to-face and the passé phone call.[2]

Texting is so popular that there are over 1,400 chat abbreviations. Here are some examples:

WOMBAT = Waste of money, brains, and time

ZZZZ = Sleeping (or bored)

WYD = What (are) you doing?[3]

Many studies indicate that texting is addictive. Experts say that there are four distinct symptoms to diagnosing texting as a mental illness: excessive use (neglect day-to-day activities); withdrawal (feeling depressed when not accessible); tolerance (over texting); and negative repercussion (social isolation). An interview with a texting addict, stated that "I text morning, noon and night, and it adds up to about 3,000 to 5,000 a month. It is bad."[4] I would add a fifth symptom, texting while in class! So let me ask the question, are you addicted?

And now for the ugly, dangerous, and sometimes deadly. We are talking about texting while driving. Texting while driving distracts the driver for almost 5 seconds. That is plenty of time to rear-end someone, drive through a red traffic light or stop sign, hit a pedestrian or bicyclist, just to name a few. Studies have shown that texting while driving is much worse than a drunk driver. That's right; this distracted texting driver has much slower reaction times than someone who is legally drunk. Around 39 states have made it illegal to text and drive, which, by the way, is very costly for the ticket. Just imagine how expensive, in many ways, it becomes if someone is injured, or worse, disabled, or killed by the distracted texting driver. How do you say, "Stay off the Slippery Slope" and "Do the Right Thing"? I have personally talked with drivers, including students, who have had close calls or actually had an accident. They now keep their cell phone out of reach while driving and/or in silence mode. If they must, they pull over to a parking lot and then make that all-important text or call. Here is a Socratic question: how did we ever get through the day before cell phones? When this technology addiction becomes deadly, it's a different story. Texting while driving leads to increased distraction behind the wheel. *Car and Driver Magazine* documented how dangerous it can be. Their test included rigging a vehicle with a red light to alert drivers when to brake. The magazine tested how long it takes to hit the brake when sober, when legally drunk at 0.08, when reading an e-mail, and when sending a text. The test vehicle was driven at seventy miles per hour on a deserted air strip. The results were as follows:

Unimpaired: 0.54 seconds to brake
Legally drunk: add 4 feet
Reading e-mail: add 36 feet
Sending a text: add 70 feet

In September 2008, California Governor, Arnold Schwarzenegger, signed Senate Bill 28 into law that "[p]rohibits a person from driving a motor vehicle while using an electronic wireless communications device to write, send, or read a text-based communication." He said "[b]anning electronic text messaging while driving will keep drivers' hands on the wheel and their eyes on the road, making our roadways a safer place for all Californians."[5] Studies show that when drivers text, their risk of crashing is twenty-three times greater than when not texting.

The National Transportation Safety Board (NTSB) blamed the engineer for the 2008 Chatsworth Metrolink train crash, which killed 25 people and injured another 135 people. This was one of the worst rail catastrophes in modern California history. The Metrolink engineer had been text messaging on a cellphone and the NTSB chairwoman faulted the engineer's "egregious" text messaging. The investigation showed that the engineer had dozens of texts during periods he was scheduled to operate trains. NTSB Chairwoman Deborah Hersman stated "this wasn't a one-off situation. This person didn't make a mistake. . . . He was almost text messaging more when he was on duty" than off duty. He had been counseled about this issue before but still "engaged in a pattern of behavior that was unsafe on a regular basis." NTSB investigators concluded that the Metrolink train ran a red light causing the Chatsworth crash.[6]

Texting has been banned in many schools because of harassment, bullying, threats to school security, cheating on tests, and plagiarism. Schools are also experiencing "sexting" among teenagers. Sexting is a slang term for the act of sending sexually explicit or suggestive content between mobile devices using SMS. Sexting becomes a legal issue when teens under eighteen years of age are involved. When recipients are over the age of eighteen, they are now in possession of child pornography material. This is illegal and is cause for prosecution. "Sexting" is becoming one of the most popular forms of communicating. Yes, no surprise this has become a common way for young adults to share. Around 80 percent have sent and received provocative text messages while 60 percent have exchanged photos and videos. According to Aristotle, young adults are driven by desire and they give in to temptation too easily. They have not fully developed their ethical judgment skills. Aristotle said another two or three decades of experience will be needed to fully develop these skills.

On a positive note, police departments around the world are turning to text messaging to help stop crime. Programs have been established in which you can text in a crime tip anonymously to help stop crimes. Public safety departments are developing text messaging for such emergencies as evacuations and Amber alerts. Texting a 911 message is now a reality which Verizon started in 2013. Many states are starting to accept these forms of emergency notification. In theory, it sounds good, but the reality and challenge is the timeliness, confirmation, location, and the actual message. With 1,400 chat abbreviations and the various text lingos that exist, the urgency may be lost in translation. Time will tell on this one.

Text messaging is currently used in the medical fields, as well, to improve treatment for addiction, diabetes, depression, and malaria. While in a different medical field, farmers are using text messages and SIM cards for cattle reproduction. Timing is everything.

Franklin Page earned his entry in The *Guinness Book of World Records* for setting a record texting on a touch screen device. He is able to type into his phone and send the message "The razor-toothed piranhas of the genera Serrasalmus and Pygocentrus are the most ferocious freshwater fish in the world. In reality, they seldom attack a human" in 35.54 seconds.[7] The new record holder in April of 2014 is Marcel Fernandes, a sixteen-year-old from Brazil. He typed the same twenty-five-word paragraph in 18.19 seconds. Who's next?[8]

In the mid-1940s, developments in science and philosophy led to the creation of the new branch of ethics which would later be called "computer ethics." The founder was U.S. scholar, Norbert Weiner, a professor of mathematics and engineering at Massachusetts Institute of Technology. During World War II, he helped develop electronic computers and other new information technologies. He predicted that after the war the world would undergo "a second industrial revolution"—an "automatic age" with "enormous potential for good and for evil" that would generate many new ethical challenges and opportunities. Today, the "information age" that Weiner predicted has come into existence.[9]

In 1976, nearly three decades after Weiner's book *Cybernetics*, Walter Maner noticed in his medical ethics course at Old Dominion University that problems became more complicated or altered when computers were involved. According to Maner, the addition of computers actually "generated wholly new ethics problems that would not have existed if computers had not been invented. He concluded that a new field should be called "computer ethics."

He defined this field as one that examines "ethical problems aggravated, transformed or created by computer technology." Some old ethical problems, he said, were made worse by computers, whereas others came into existence because of computer technology.[10]

In 1985, James Moor provided descriptions and examples of computer ethics problems, offering an explanation of why computer technology raises so many ethical questions compared to other kinds of technology. His explanation of this technology is that computers are "logically malleable. They can be shaped and molded to do any activity that can be characterized in terms of inputs, outputs. . . . The logical malleability of computer technology makes it possible for people to do a vast number of things that they were not able to do before. Since no one could do them before, the question never arose as to whether one ought to do them. In addition, because they could not be done before, no laws or standards of good practice or specific ethical rules were established to govern them."[11]

Information is so common place these days that we forget or never knew it was illegal before computers. The computer age brings with it positive and negative implications on society. As Aristotle noted, human beings are creatures of habit. Aristotle also believed that good ethical judgment depends on experience and that society is responsible for teaching appropriate behavior in children. How does this affect our decisions when computer technology is moving ahead by leaps and bounds? The following are just a few of the computer issues we deal with on a daily basis: censorship, cyberspace, copyright and fair use, hacker/security, hoaxes and viruses, junk e-mail, netiquette rules, and teacher-student netiquette.

The ethical bar will rise in the future. Part of the reason for this are advances in technology, increasing life span, and decisions that impact more people around the world. Ethical decisions will have greater consequences than ever before. Many consider that computer ethics should be regarded as global ethics. After all, it is the World Wide Web!

According to Dictionary.com:

Computing Dictionary

computer ethics philosophy

"Ethics is the field of study that is concerned with questions of value, that is, judgments about what human behavior is 'good' or 'bad'. Ethical judgments are no different in the area of computing from those in any other area. Computers raise problems of privacy, ownership, theft, and power, to name a few."[12]

Or as Moor believed, has computer technology generated many new situations and many new problems that are ethical dilemmas?

Consider this: a person living in the 1800s would learn in their lifetime the equivalency of what we read in a single Sunday newspaper! The copious amount of information at our fingertips is, to say the least, overwhelming. Good or bad, we can spend many hours surfing the Web, e-mailing friends, researching, using a new App, downloading music, or playing a game.

The first personal computer was marketed in 1977 by Apple. By the year 2000, approximately 60 percent of U.S. households owned at least one computer, which represented 168.6 million household computers. The general consensus in 2010 indicates that approximately 80 percent of all U.S. households have at least one computer. Within the last twenty years, most schools (private and public) are well integrated with computers. Most have computer labs for instruction and classes ranging from introduction to computers to PowerPoint, website development, and hacker prevention/security.

We are accustomed to speedy information and technology at the click of a mouse. Many cell phones today have the same information available, anywhere, any place. Computers and cell phones today are well integrated into our everyday life. It is easy to call, text, or e-mail someone a thought, a question, a picture, a joke, or a link. This ease of transmitting information instantly makes it even easier for us to share in a way that might not be ethical or moral. It sounded good at the time! Technology has made it much easier to communicate with a click of a button. Understanding the importance of what is appropriate, ethical, or moral while communicating with coworkers, friends, supervisors, and the public requires "thinking" before clicking.

We also need to take into account that most businesses, both private and public sectors, are using computers. Computers are a part of hospitals, schools, utility companies, government (federal, state, county, city), EMS, fire, and police. Computer-aided dispatch (CAD) is an integral part of dispatching 911 calls. A glitch with this system could mean the difference between life or death.

In the early twenty-first century, proprietary information has been printed on envelopes by private and public agencies. Mistakenly, social security numbers were printed on thousands and thousands of envelopes and mailed so everyone was able to see private social security numbers. This type of mistake actually affected a large number of retired firefighters. A retirement system incorrectly released social security numbers to the public.

THE EFFECT OF COMPUTER ETHICS

Computer ethics might affect public safety in ways that you haven't thought of. The London Ambulance Service is the largest ambulance service in the world, covering 600 square miles. It covers a residential population of some 6.8 million. In 1992, it handled, on average, about 2,300 medical emergency calls per day. The London Ambulance Service's Computer-Aided Dispatch Project (LASCAD) used computers in an effort to improve the efficiency and response times of the ambulance service. The primary goal was to replace the handwritten forms and human dispatchers of the existing service because these were thought to be too slow and more prone to making errors. The proposed LASCAD computer system was supposed to use faster and more reliable computer technology to receive emergency calls, gather vital information, and ultimately dispatch an ambulance to the emergency site.

On October 26, 1992, LASCAD was put into operation with catastrophic results. Sometimes multiple vehicles were sent to the same location, the closest vehicles were not dispatched, calls were put on a waiting list, and ambulances did not appear on the scene quickly. By the next day, the entire system had collapsed; a number of people may have died because they were unable to get to the hospital on time. After the LASCAD disaster, there were a number of inquiries into the causes. The general conclusion was that many different failures and mistakes led to the collapse.[13]

Because the system was not fully tested to a satisfactory level of quality before it was implemented, did the system fail on an ethical level? Was it morally wrong? Is what happened illegal, especially if a patient's condition was exacerbated, or worse yet, died because of the delays? Modern technology is a great tool and helps public safety officers to do our job; however, it also adds another level of checks and balances.

HISTORY'S SOFTWARE BUGS

Sometimes a bug's action ends up with deadly consequences.

In February 2010, automaker Toyota blamed a software glitch for braking problems in its 2010 Prius and the National Highway Traffic Safety Administration (NHTSA) opened a formal investigation into the braking system. Toyota confirms that the total number of vehicles recalled came to 8.1 million. Toyota said the recalls for the gas pedal-related issues could end up costing the company $2 billion.[14]

As reported by *Weekly Driver*, *USA Today* reported that Safety Research and Strategies, a safety research firm, has found 2,274 incidents of sudden unintended acceleration in Toyota vehicles causing 275 crashes and 18 deaths since 1999.[15]

In a follow-up to this debacle, in March 2014, Toyota admits to misleading customers and agrees to pay the highest fine ever imposed thus far of $1.2 billion. They were considered one of the most desired carmakers in the world. This criminal fraud charge lasted over four years with Toyota intentionally hiding and deceiving their customers, investigators, and the US government about their vehicles with sticky accelerator and floor mat problems. They admitted to this and deferred prosecution to pay out the hefty fine. Toyota has now stated, "In the more than four years since these recalls, we have gone back to basics at Toyota to put our customers first." Too little too late for the many lives lost and many injured. Must have sounded like a good idea at the time to "lie." This Toyota settlement should send a stern message to General Motors, who is under investigation and criminal probe in 2014 regarding customer safety fears.[16]

Back in 1985, a radiation therapy device malfunctioned and delivered lethal radiation doses at several medical facilities. The Therac-25 was an "improved" therapy system that could deliver two different kinds of radiation. Because of a bug called a "race condition," a typist could accidentally configure the Therac-25 so the electron beam would fire in high power but with the metal X-ray target out of position. At least five patients died and others were seriously injured.[17]

In 2005, a Las Vegas FM radio station falsely alerted cable companies and radio and TV stations in five counties to a national crisis that did not exist. The FM radio station tried to send out a message regarding an Amber Alert and instead transmitted an emergency action notification (EAN). This special code is reserved for the president of the United States to use in the event of nuclear war or similar extreme national emergency. It is believed that an internal battery had failed, which resulted in a hardware problem in the encoder-decoder for the Emergency Alert System (EAS). Because there had never been an actual activation of this system, the radio stations did not transmit this to the public.[18]

COMPUTERS AND ETHICS

In 1990, John McLeod devised a list of generic questions to help determine the ethical nature of actions within the computing profession.

TABLE 8.1

*Is it honorable?

~Is there anyone whom you would like to hide the action?

*Is it honest?

~Does it violate any agreement, actual or implied, or otherwise betray a trust?

*Does it avoid the possibility of a conflict of interest?

~Are there other considerations that might bias your judgment?

*Is it within your area of competence?

~Is it possible that your best effort will not be adequate?

*Is it fair?

~Is it detrimental to the legitimate interests of others?

*Is it considerate?

~Will it violate confidentiality or privacy, or otherwise harm anyone or anything?

*Is it conservative?

~Does it unnecessarily squander time or other valuable resources?

To be ethical, an action should elicit a positive response to all applicable primary questions (*) and a negative response to each clarification (~)[19]

In Chapter 1, we discussed ethics and religion and the *Bible's* Ten Commandments. After discussing the consequences of poor technology decisions, we can see why the Computer Ethics Institute developed the Ten Commandments of Computer Ethics. It has been an effective code of ethics for information technology. The Ten Commandments of Computer Ethics has been translated in fifteen different languages.

TABLE 8.2	

The Ten Commandments of Computer Ethics

1.	Thou shalt not use a computer to harm other people.
2.	Thou shalt not interfere with other people's computer work.
3.	Thou shalt not snoop around in other people's computer files.
4.	Thou shalt not use a computer to steal.
5.	Thou shalt not use a computer to bear false witness.
6.	Thou shalt not copy or use proprietary software for which you have not paid.
7.	Thou shalt not use other people's computer resources without authorization or proper compensation.
8.	Thou shalt not appropriate other people's intellectual output.
9.	Thou shalt think about the social consequences of the program you are writing or the system you are designing.
10.	Thou shalt always use a computer in ways that ensure consideration and respect for your fellow humans.[20]

Source: Computer Ethics Institute

After seeing how computer technology can affect public safety officers in many ways, can you see why a new set of computer ethics has been introduced with the computer age?

SOCIAL NETWORKING

Blogging is a form of Internet technology that lets individuals easily share information with a wide audience. In the past we called this "keeping a diary" or "keeping a log." Keeping a diary was usually private and a diary would be kept under "lock and key," only to be read by the author. Siblings loved to find their sister's diary so the secrets could be read and exposed. As you can see, the increase in popularity of blogs has created a new set of ethical dilemmas. Individuals must decide what they should and should not share in the public forums and employers must decide whether to regulate or censor what their employees are saying.

The spread of blogging is not limited to the private business sector. Government, including public safety, has seen the effects of blogging in the workplace as well. In 2004, a public safety communications center director was relieved from duty after sharing personal opinions regarding employees on his blog. Some companies have policies that require employees to clearly identify themselves on their personal blogs if they are commenting about the company. Employees also are required to write a disclaimer that their views are their own and not those of the employer. What are the requirements of your employer?

A quick Web search reveals blogs created by police officers, firefighters, EMS personnel and 911 dispatchers. In them, they share everything from their personal issues and opinions to details of calls they have handled. Blogs are also being used by outsiders to reveal the personal lives of public safety personnel, as well as to reveal inside information regarding police investigations.[21]

Public safety professionals are under scrutiny both on and off duty. Whether blogging takes place off duty or on duty, both the employee and employer could come under scrutiny. Because public safety employees have access to private and damaging information about victims, patients, and the public in general, releasing this information could have serious consequences and it could also be illegal. As an example, a vehicle accident could easily involve a lawsuit a few years later. All information gathered and put in a report now becomes part of a court record, including all computer and phone records. If public safety employees are allowed to post personal blog entries while using publicly owned computers then those entries could be considered public. The bottom line, just because you can say it, does it mean you should say it? Blogging done properly can be a great tool. If done improperly, it could be devastating and costly. Not to mention, you could lose your job.

2010–Facebook company statistics show there are more than 350 million active users and that 50 percent of the active users log on to Facebook in any given day and that more than 2.5 billion photos are uploaded to the site each month. Founded in 2004, their website states that Facebook is a "social utility that helps people communicate more efficiently with their friends, family and coworkers. Facebook is the second most-trafficked PHP site in the world."[22] 2013/2014 Facebook statistics:

> Total number of users: 1.28 billion
> Active monthly users: 1.23 billion
> Percentage of online adults who visit Facebook at least once a month: 72 percent
> Total number of daily active users: 757 million
> Daily active users in the UK: 24 million
> Number of users in China (even though it is blocked): 87 million
> Number of users in India: 100 million
> Number of users in Asia: 351 million
> The country with the most active users: Canada
> Average number of friends that teens on Facebook have: 300
> Percentage of teens who are friends with their parents on Facebook: 70 percent
> Percentage of users that are male: 42 percent
> Percentage of Internet users sixty-five years and older: 45 percent.[23]

If Facebook were a country, it would be the world's third largest.

1. China
2. India
3. Facebook
4. United States
5. Indonesia

Social media is no longer a fad. It has become a fundamental way people communicate.[24] Did you know there are more connected devices on the Internet than there are people on earth? That's an astronomical amount of connectivity!

In the past, our grandparents might have told us "think before you speak." Now, we can say "think before you tweet." Cornerback Antonio Cromartie of the

San Diego Chargers knows this all too well. In 2009, the San Diego Chargers ordered their star cornerback to pay $2,500 for sending out a message on Twitter criticizing the food served at the Charger's training camp. According to profoot-balltalk.nbcports.com, "As best we can tell, this is the offending tweet from July 31 at 3:46 P.M.: 'Man we have 2 have the most nasty food of any team. Damn can we upgrade 4 str8 years the same ish maybe that's y we can't we the SB we need.'"[25]

The tweet implied that if the Chargers did not have to eat the same nasty food for four straight years; they might have made it to a Super Bowl by now.

Cromartie said Chargers' coach Norv Turner pulled him out of a meeting Tuesday and notified him that he was being fined for his Twitter comments. Cromartie was also given a letter that spelled out the fine. Coach Turner said "We're trying to be open and give the fans a look at what we're doing, but certainly we're not going to go out of our way to give our opponents a competitive advantage or give them something that we feel should stay in our building. So that's been our approach with any forms of media that we're involved with."[26]

This subject has approximately 1,470,000 hits on Google. Why was Cromartie fined? Why was there zero tolerance on the matter? How would this complaint about the quality of food hurt anyone? Well, as you know, the "play book" is confidential and many things surrounded by a team's advantage or disadvantage remain confidential. In this case, this "tweet" was looked upon as an advantage given to other teams.

The National Football League (NFL) is trying to clamp down on players using Twitter. The league has outlawed players from tweeting during games. The Green Bay Packers have threatened to fine players who tweet during team meetings. The Miami Dolphins appeared to have outlawed it entirely. Again, the concern is that casual Twitter could inspire budding bloggers in their locker rooms to inadvertently disclose more than they should know about injuries, game plans, and what is said behind closed doors.[27]

So, again, think before you tweet and don't act on an impulse. Twitter can be more than just a service to post and receive messages to a network of contacts. This is a good example of one player or one employee being a small part of a bigger picture. One public safety officer tweeting statements regarding an event that is more of a personal opinion than a fact could send the wrong message. The news media would obtain this information and turn it into perhaps a bigger story. After all, they are always looking for a story. We must always consider what the perception will be. Your department may have a policy that restricts your social networking, just as the NFL. The public whom we serve expects professionalism, including leadership, trustworthiness, integrity, and fairness at all times.

Here is an example of social media that backfired on NYPD in April of 2014. The NYPD was searching for positive feedback on social media and received more than they asked for. To their surprise, most of the social media feedback on their request showed police displaying poor behavior. Twitter users jumped on the opportunity to post many negative photos that caught the police in a negative light and not doing the right thing.[28]

What's on "Your Space"?

EMS departments, Fire departments, and Police departments are checking "Your Space" as part of the hiring process! The question is: are you proud of "Your Space" and is it appropriate for your new position as a respected public safety officer. Is your content on "Your Space" something you would share with your grandparents? Employers are looking at Social Media to make hiring decisions. Is this legal or is this ethical? Once something is posted on a social networking site, it becomes available to the public. Therefore, it is not an invasion of privacy. Can public safety departments legally decide not to hire you based on a review of the contents of "Your Space"? The answer is yes, as long as they do not violate federal or state discrimination laws, such as race or ethnicity, when making the hiring decisions. Bottom line, do not post things that are embarrassing or damaging to your public safety career. On the positive side, use "Your Space" to highlight your education, training and experience. Be careful not to embellish, exaggerate, inflate, or overstate. These are easy things to do because your discussions are usually with friends. You may make a simple statement that I am a firefighter or police officer, when in fact you are in an academy and just starting your career. Remember, employers are not only looking for qualified applicants with education, training, and experience but also applicants who are making moral and ethical decisions. Departments are looking for common sense, the ability to use critical thinking (which also includes what we say and how we say it) not only in the interview but also on the Internet that everyone is able to see.

Social networking postings could affect your future employment as a public safety officer. According to the June 2013 CareerBuilder survey, almost 43 percent of employers reported that they used social networking sites to screen potential employees during background checks. Your social media profile can be a great benefit in your job search, or it can be a great disaster. Remember potential employers do check. Some things employers like according to a 2013 CareerBuilder study:

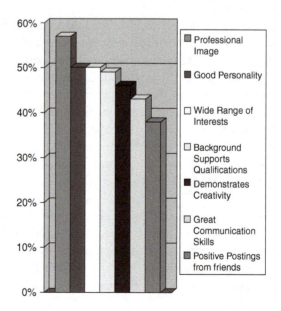

Examples of "inappropriate" content from jobseekers included: [29]

- Posting provocative inappropriate photographs or information, 50 percent.
- Posting content about drinking or using drugs, 48 percent.
- Bad-mouthing previous employer, 33 percent.
- Showing poor communication skills, 30 percent.
- Making discriminatory comments, 28 percent.
- Lying about qualifications, 24 percent.

When was the last time you did a World Wide Web search of a long lost friend? The social networking sites are the best way to keep in touch these days. This same social networking tool can also be your worst nightmare. If used improperly, the available information on these sites is accessible to future employers. That "dream job" you have been working toward for the last few years may not materialize. Put yourself in the employer's shoes for just a minute. You are interviewing 150 candidates for six openings. These are the first-tier possibilities after a lengthy process to establish a new hiring list. More detail will be discussed in Chapter 9 about the hiring process. For now, you have narrowed the candidates down to 15 and you must select the six best candidates. Social networking sites are a good possibility and source for departments to choose. Keep them clean, and informative with education, community service, and how you have trained for this public safety position.

SUMMARY

Computer technology has given us new opportunities and more choices than ever before. These choices often have come without standards, policies, boundaries, or better yet, any direction of ethics. Take for example, Napster, who allowed customers to download music, with online sharing. They did not consider the music industry source and the copyright laws. Their original service of sharing was shut down by court order.

Many ethical problems have come into existence because of technology. There are those that believe they are the same old problems with a new twist. Others feel computers have added a new realm of ethical problems because computers are malleable and can be molded to our own creative limit. There are no boundaries and the possibilities are endless.

Technology and social networking can be a great tool or a devastating tool if not used ethically or appropriately. It has become easy to click a button and send good, bad, or indifferent messages.

Unlike most humans, computers can remember things accurately and for long term. Details can be revealed years later, good or bad. Even though we might want to blog or Twitter someone about the details of the emergency call we just responded to, we must remember the victim or patient does not want the world to know about the details. Patient confidentiality laws are strict! In the computer world, the information is never forgotten and too easily shared. The philosopher Aristotle is known for saying "wisdom comes with age." As a public safety officer, we must consider our actions and the outcomes, in many instances, before we do them. We learn from our mistakes, and we grow from them. To apply critical thinking to our jobs as public safety officers is a requirement of the job. The public, the department we work for, our coworkers and ourselves expects no less. We must develop the skills necessary to know right from wrong and to expand our moral awareness and ethical values as police officers, firefighters and EMT/paramedics.

NOTES

1. "Americans sent 1 trillion SMS text messages in 2008." www.intomobile.com/2009/04/06/americans-sent-1-trillion-sms-text-messages-in-2008.html (accessed February 2010).
2. http://www.cnn.com/2012/12/03/tech/mobile/sms-text-message-20/
3. http://www.webopedia.com/quick_ref/textmessageabbreviations.asp
4. "Is text messaging a mental illness?" http://abclocal.go.com/kabc/story?section=news/health&id=6043089 (accessed February 21, 2010).
5. "SB 28 – California's Text Messaging Ban," www.drivinglaws.org/sb28.php (accessed February 21, 2010).
6. Los Angeles Times, "NTSB Opens Meeting on causes of chatsworth train crash." http://latimesblogs.latimes.com/lanow/2010/01/ntsb-begins-meeting-on-causes-of-chatsworth (accessed February 21, 2010).
7. Guinness World Records.
8. http://mashable.com/2014/05/16/world-record-fastest-texting-fleksy/
9. Stanford Encyclopedia of Philosophy, "Computer and Information Ethics," http://plato.stanford.edu/entries/ethics-computer/ (accessed May 16, 2010).
10. Stanford Encyclopedia of Philosophy, "Computer and Information Ethics." (accessed February 21, 2010).
11. Stanford Encyclopedia of Philosophy, "Computer and Information Ethics." (accessed February 21, 2010).
12. http://dictionary.reference.com/browse/compter+ethics (accessed May 16, 2010).
13. T. W. Bynum, and S. Rogerson, *Computer Ethics and Professional Responsibility* (Ames, IA: Blackwell Publishing, 2004). p. 129.
14. CNN, "A Timeline of Toyota Recall Woes," www.cnn.com/2010/US/02/10/timeline.toyota/?hpt=Sbin (accessed February 15, 2010).
15. "Toyota Recall: Safety Research Firm Reports 275 Crashes, 18 Deaths in 11 Years from Faulty Acceleration in Suspended Models." http://theweeklydriver.com/2010/01/27/toyota-recall-safety-research-firm-reports-275-crashes-18-deaths-in-11-years/ (accessed February 20, 2010).
16. http://www.forbes.com/sites/joannmuller/2014/03/19/toyota-admits-misleading-customers-agrees-to-1-2-billion-criminal-fine/print/
17. Wired.com, "History's Worst Software Bugs." www.wired.com/software/coolapps/news/2005/11/69355 (accessed February 15, 2010).
18. Wired.com, "Bogus Homeland Alerts Hit the Air". www.wired.com/science/discoveries/news/2005/08/68363 (accessed February 15, 2010).
19. Bynum and Rogerson, *Computer Ethics and Professional Responsibility*. p. 122.
20. Computer Ethics Institute, "The Ten Commandments of Computer Ethics." http://cpsr.org/issues/ethics/cei/ (accessed February 20, 2010).
21. S. K. Miller, "Ethics and Blogging in Public Safety," *Public Safety Communications*, March 2006. p. 2.
22. Facebook, "Factsheet." www.facebook.com/press/info.php?factsheet (accessed February 4, 2010).

23. http://expandedramblings.com/index.php/by-the-numbers-17-amazing-facebook-stats/ #.U4gN5PldV8E

24. http://www.youtube.com/watch?v=0eUeL3n7fDs

25. M. Florio, "Chargers fine Cromartie for Twitter Complaint." http://profootballtalk .nbcsports.com/2009/08/04/source-chargers-fine-cromartie-for-twitter-complaint/ (accessed February 6, 2010).

26. Associated Press, "Chargers fine CB Cromaratie $2,500 for Twitter post ripping camp food www.nfl.com/trainingcamp/story?id=09000d5d811a8aaf&template=without-video-with-comments&confirm=true (accessed February 6, 2010).

27. The New York Times, "The N.F.L. Has Identified the Enemy and it is Twitter." www.nytimes .com/2009/08/04/sports/football/04twitter.html (accessed February 20, 2010).

28. http://www.cnn.com/2014/04/22/tech/nypd-twitter-fail/

29. http://www.careerbuilder.com/share/aboutus/pressreleasesdetail.aspx?sd=6%2F26%2F2013& id=pr766&ed=12%2F31%2F2013

DILEMMA

Texting while driving in California is illegal. You are vacationing in another state where it is legal, will you text while driving? Explain why or why not.

_____

_____

_____

_____

_____

_____

_____

_____

_____

_____

_____

_____

_____

_____

_____

_____

_____

_____

_____

_____

DILEMMA

Describe how the *Ten Commandments of Computer Ethics* will affect your job as a public safety officer.

_____

_____

_____

_____

_____

_____

_____

_____

_____

_____

_____

_____

_____

_____

_____

_____

_____

_____

_____

DILEMMA

Give two examples of negative and positive outcomes of your social networking.

_____

_____

_____

_____

_____

_____

_____

_____

_____

_____

_____

_____

_____

_____

_____

_____

_____

_____

_____

_____

_____

DILEMMA

Can an employer be influenced of their opinion about your character on your social networking sites? Is there anything you can add that will complement your skills and education as a public safety officer? Explain.

_____

_____

_____

_____

_____

_____

_____

_____

_____

_____

_____

_____

_____

_____

_____

_____

_____

_____

_____

_____

_____

_____

_____

Ethical Questions and the Interview

9

CHAPTER OBJECTIVES

1. Describe the right stuff to be part of a winning team.
2. Understand different situational questions for the interview.
3. Define the cornerstone of the public safety officer.
4. Explain the relationship of core values and the interview.

WHO WANTS YOU ON THEIR TEAM?

Did you know over 65 percent of the workforce is dissatisfied with their job, a sad and unfortunate situation. Perhaps most of us have had such a job. We were not proud of, or happy with, the job, and it was "just a paycheck." Monday mornings are mundane for many, and TGIF became a popular saying. Wouldn't it be great if everyone looked forward to going to work? Confucius, a wise man, said "Choose a job you love, and you will never have to work a day in your life." This has significant meaning, whether you are in a job you dislike or a career you enjoy. The authors, Professors Peterson and Lofthouse, truly liked going to work and respected their jobs as a police officer and firefighter, and now they find teaching the subject matter is even more rewarding!

Most of us remember our school days during recess or P.E. class when a selection process took place. Two team captains picked from the student group who they wanted on their team. What really was the criterion; a friend, a good player, or an asset to the team? Perhaps the student was big and would make a good blocker. Whatever the reason, one point stands out, and they were picked to win. The winning team would have the bragging rights until the next recess or P.E. class. Most of us have a desire to be part of that winning team. We would like to be part of a department that represents a successful image in the community and to have the public's respect and confidence. We want to be proud of our job and career.

To work for the ideal company, you would probably look for an organization that is prosperous, flourishing, successful, and popular. Some people even give up pay for the feeling and recognition they receive working for this prestigious company.

Bottom line, employees want to feel they are part of a great team and part of the community. That's just part of a healthy work environment. It does not matter which profession you choose; it could be sports, doctors, attorneys, pilots, any well-known company, the fire/EMS department or police department. Usually, and we hope, they all have that image and reputation of a "winning team"; an integral part of the community.

The competition for these jobs is, at best, competitive. With any of the aforementioned professions few make it into those jobs. A recent survey stated that only 30 percent of the applicants make it to the police interviews, and only 5 percent are offered a job.[1]

Fire departments have similar numbers that reflect that public safety departments hire only the cream of the crop, the top candidates, and the best prepared.

The job requirements, experience, and education take years to acquire. This is nothing new within the public safety departments; there has been tough competition for decades. Hundreds, if not thousands, of applicants have applied and tested for these public safety departments and only just a few are successful.

What makes a successful candidate you may ask? Put yourself in the shoes of the testing department, looking for those qualified few that you would like to hire. You would establish the necessary requirements of:

- Education.
- Experience.
- And, yes, life experience.

Most departments would like to hire someone that has experience with life and has been around the block a few times. This may not be a written rule, however, this is the reality. These public safety jobs require more than education and experience, they require life skills:

- Maturity.
- Good communication skills.
- The ability to think on your feet.
- The capacity to work closely with others.
- Sound ethical and moral behavior.

These traits also take time to mature. Many times these conditions include a dangerous environment. That's not to say that all of our work is dangerous, that is just the critical part of the job. Because we spend so much time with our fellow public safety officers, they become our second family. Sometimes family does not see eye to eye on everything. We must learn to get along not only during the emergency but also in all other conditions. There is only one way to get life experience, and that is by experiencing life. There are some departments out there that look for maturity more than other qualifications. Because of the aforementioned characteristics, the only way to obtain these skills is by experiencing life many times, over and over. Most departments do not have the time to teach you these life skills; they would prefer to hire someone that already has them and can hit the ground running after they are hired. They are self-motivated, mature, and can do the job with little supervision. The testing process is expensive. Public safety departments require the best employee they can hire. The job as a police officer, firefighter, and EMT/paramedic are critical to the daily emergency functions and the public's life safety. Remember, more than likely that employee will be there twenty-five to thirty years.

WHAT ARE WAYS TO NOT MAKE THE TEAM?

Let's talk about the disqualifications for the public safety officer job. They are not in any particular order:

- Dishonesty during the application process.
- Criminal activity.
- Arrest record.
- Drug use.
- Driving violations such as driving under the influence (DUI).

You may be happy to know that many of your competitors are disqualified during the application process. Lying during any part of the testing process is a disqualifier.

Misrepresentation of yourself is a direct insight to the type of applicant/person you are. How honest, ethical, and moral are you? Many applications ask a simple question: "Have you ever been convicted of a felony?" Or, they just may ask a general question: "Have you ever been convicted?" Many applicants struggle with these two questions. They attempt, in their own mind, to justify their arrest record. If someone is having a problem with this simple question, then what kind of person would they be as an entrusted public safety officer? We have students approach us every semester asking the question, "Will a DUI hurt my chances to be hired as a public safety officer?" We are always truthful, and answer, yes. However, the next part of the question is totally up to you, the candidate. We will always ask how long ago this DUI was. This may have happened many years ago when you were much younger. By the way, it does not ever justify the DUI in the first place. This question does offer you an opportunity to discuss your arrest of the DUI with the interview panel. What have you done to correct and rectify this reckless behavior? The answer requires some soul-searching on your part, and a realization about the circumstances of this serious offense. You see, public safety officers should know better. Whether you are a candidate or currently working as one, we should know and recognize the seriousness of this behavior. Was it "sounded like a good idea at the time" to drink and drive?

Remember, one of the interview panel members may have personal experience with a fatality involving an intoxicated driver. As in Professor Lofthouse's experience, a young family member (along with a friend) was killed by a drunk driver who had been involved in many prior DUI offenses. Obviously, this type of irresponsible decision is even more personal when it hits close to home.

THE TESTING PROCESS

© wrangler, 2014. Used under license from Shutterstock, Inc.

The Climb to Success

Many departments these days are finding ways to reduce costs and, at the same time, trying to find better qualified candidates. One of the ways to do this is to require a standardized physical ability test certificate, which is given by a private company. The candidate bears the cost of this testing process, and in turn receives a certificate usually good for six months to one year. That way, the department does not bear the cost for that portion of the testing. The candidate just shows a current physical ability certificate and that qualifies them and satisfies that portion of the testing. Other departments are sharing the expenses of the physical ability and written exams. These usually are in conjunction with a joint powers agreement (JPA), which includes multiple departments.

On the written test, some departments are giving a pass or fail category. That way they are creating less cost, time, and work tracking that portion of the testing. They are also creating a testing environment that allows for testing of maturity and life skills during the interview process.

Written exams come in many forms and include any or all of the following:

- Reading comprehension/memorization.
- Writing, clarity, and spelling.
- Verbal comprehension/memorization.
- Math, fundamental, and algebraic.
- Critical thinking/problem solving.
- Spatial relations.
- Visualization, number, and letter recall.
- Human relations/public relations.
- Map reading.
- Mechanical aptitude.
- Fire fighting principles.
- Criminal justice principles.
- Fire behavior (structural and wild land).
- Police tactics.
- Emergency medical questions (EMT and paramedic).

There are many books available to help you, the candidate, to prepare for the hiring process. The written exam is an integral part of this testing process. The wide variety of knowledge that departments are requiring of the candidate is available for you to study before the exam. You may not know the exact question they will ask of you; however, you will have the basic concept and idea of what the answer to the question is.

That leaves the oral interview. Some departments are now weighting this part of the testing 100 percent. This is where the maturity, life experience, preparation, education, work experience, community service, and your personality count. The interview panel usually has about twenty minutes to find out all they can about the prospective candidate. The only way to accomplish this is to ask specific questions that seek to discover who the applicant is or who the applicant is not (who you really are). Public safety departments can teach you to be a better paramedic, a better firefighter, or a better police officer, but they cannot teach you to be more mature, moral, or ethical. Of course, these virtues do get better with time. The older we get, hopefully the more mature and wiser we become. Public safety departments are not looking for a perfect candidate; they are looking for a good solid base; that person who has the right combination of experience, education, maturity, and life skills at the entry level. This is something you must have learned and completed prior to your hiring. The only way to accomplish this is by having life experience that has afforded you the opportunity to have learned maturity and moral and ethical values. As discussed throughout this textbook, we recognize that ethical and moral attributes do not come easy. Most of us learn from our mistakes, and during this process, we become more ethical, moral, and mature. Public safety departments must hire the best applicant who already has high morals and ethical values with that right combination of maturity. The interview panel will ask of themselves, "Can this candidate do the job and work with us for the next twenty-plus years?"

WHAT IS YOUR RESPONSIBILITY?

Responsibility has a different meaning to each of us. Here are just a few of the words that come to mind when talking about responsibility:

- Accountability.
- Answerability.
- Conscientiousness.
- Dependability.
- Duty.
- Liability.
- Trustworthiness.

Legality fits into that responsibility mode as well. As previously discussed, legal is most of the time ethical and moral, but not all the time. A word that may or may not belong to this list is "burden." This is about those people you have worked with or possibly some or your acquaintances you could be responsible for. Are they more of a burden than anything else or are they an asset? Would you like them to be on "your team?" That is the question that a public safety department asks. Is this new prospective employee an asset to the organization; or do they have the possibility of being more of a burden? The testing process will help decide whether you are a future asset to the department and someone they would like to work with for the next twenty-five to thirty years. For now, I hope you are asking these questions of yourself:

- Am I an asset?
- Am I helpful?
- Am I a team player?
- Am I mature?
- Am I an ethical employee?
- Am I trained to do the job with my education and experience?

Only you can answer these questions, and only you can prepare for this career as a police officer, firefighter or EMT/paramedic.

Honesty, Integrity, Dependability and Professionalism are the "cornerstone" of the Public Safety Officer.

Here is an example from the San Diego County Sheriff's Department website:

Mission, Vision and Values

Our Mission
We provide the highest quality public safety services in an effort to make San Diego the safest urban county in the nation.

Our Organizational Mission
We earn the respect and the confidence of the public as a professional public safety organization. We are innovative and responsive to the needs of those we serve and work in partnership with our communities. We attract and retain highly competent and diverse employees.

Our Core Values
HONESTY   We are truthful in our words and in our actions.
INTEGRITY   As people of character and principle, we do what is right, even when no one is looking.

LOYALTY	We are loyal to our department and our profession and committed to protecting the quality of life in the communities we serve.
TRUST	We are confident in the integrity, the ability and the good character of our colleagues.
RESPECT	We treat everyone with dignity, honoring the rights of all individuals.
FAIRNESS	We are just and impartial in all of our interactions. Our decisions are made without personal favoritism.
DIVERSITY	We embrace the strength in the diversity of our employees and our communities.[2]

The hiring process for most public safety departments is similar. There will be a written, physical ability test, and an interview. Most of the time, there will also be a background check, credit history, department of motor vehicles (DMV) check of motor vehicle violations, medical exam, and drug testing. Today many departments also include a polygraph test and yes, they check "Your Space." As mentioned previously, remember we can control what our "Future Space" looks like, but we cannot delete or backspace what is already out there for the world and future employers to see.

In Chapter 8, we discussed how important "Your Space" is in reference to your future employment as a public safety officer. Employers are reading and viewing firsthand personal information. They can glean insight about you from these social sites, which, by the way, some of which could not legally be asked in an interview. In this case, just remember too much information is not in your best interest.

During the credit history check, departments are not able to see your FICO score; however, they can see your credit history. A credit history shows if a person pays their bills and if they are a potential negative risk. They are, again, looking for responsible future employees.

Departments need all the help they can get to determine your hiring qualifications and if you are the right person for the job. There are always some differences. For instance, some departments incorporate specific questions into their testing process that are specific department policies. They may also include their mission statement and core values just to see if you have done your "homework." There is that word again, homework and, as you can see, a good habit can serve you well into the future. As the prospective candidate, doing your homework to find out about the department you're applying for is not only a great idea but also a must. This is not only important to public safety departments but also to corporate America. Most departments and companies are more interested in a candidate/applicant who is well versed and interested in department/company history, statistics, mission statements, and core values. Go the extra mile to inquire and do your homework before the interview. How interested are you? Can you answer those series of questions about the department?

To prepare for the testing process, specifically the interview, we must look at what the public safety departments are trying to find out about you. What are your strengths and weaknesses? How do you talk about these traits in a way that separates you from the other candidates? Are you average? Are you a top candidate? The process of a 30–40-minute interview narrows your opportunity to make your case. Some departments only score the interview 100 percent. The written and physical ability test (PAT) is pass or fail. Make the time to polish, to practice, and to prepare for your "dream job." Most of us take multiple entry tests, and I can say every one of them is different. No two are alike. The only way to prepare for the multitude of department tests is to prepare yourself for every contingency. That is, to practice the strategies that makes you the "top candidate." During your time at the academy and college classes, recognize those who stand out. The ones who walk the walk and talk the talk. They are mature, a team player, they make time to always improve to help others, and yet are able to express those qualities in a humble way. You know who they are. I always believed, in order to improve yourself, you must have that team concept of like minds and career choice. If you want to be on a winning team, you first must be a player on that team. I always played any sport better with players better than myself. This is also part of the important aspect of team networking like college classes, academies, college public safety clubs, volunteering in your community, to name a few. After those classes/semesters, and after a couple years, you will find those networks of like-minded individuals to become the best you can be. And for those of you thinking that you would not want to share those nuggets of knowledge and information, consider how much information and nuggets of knowledge would you discover with those like-minded souls? "Esprit de corps" is a term you should learn, embrace, and be a part of! After all, as the old cliché says, "There is no 'i' in team."

WHAT ARE THE QUESTIONS DESIGNED TO DO?

During the oral interview you will be asked questions that involve ethical, moral, and lawful questions. You will also be asked questions that involve department policies and procedures.

Behavioral Interview Questions

Unlike traditional interviews, behavioral interviewing is based upon the fact that "the most accurate predictor of future performance is past performance in a similar situation." Currently, 30 percent of all organizations are using behavioral interviewing to some degree.[3]

With these types of interviews, remember (a) the situation or task at hand; (b) the action you took; and (c) the result or outcome. An example of this type of interview question is:

- Give us an example of a time that you had to go above and beyond the call of duty:

_____

_____

_____

_____

- Describe your example _____.

_____

_____

_____

_____

- What was your course of action? _____.

  _____

  _____

  _____

  _____

- What was the result? _____.

  _____

  _____

  _____

  _____

THE HIRING PROCESS AND THE INTERVIEW

We have all heard the expression that "you never get a second chance to make a first impression." This couldn't be truer than for your interview in the hiring process for your public safety officer position. How you dress, how you shake hands, what you say . . . and how you say it, all play a part. Because this book is about making the right decision, remember that you can shine with your answers to these questions that are asking about being untruthful, covering up for your coworker's poor decisions and then any actions that are illegal. Then, what about the department's policies and procedures, code of ethics and virtues? Does the department want you to follow these guidelines? Of course they do, and your answers should accordingly reflect this. After all this, remember to relax, be yourself, tell "your story" (who are you?), and correlate your current employment to the public safety officer position. Do you work at In-N-Out? Is your job about customer service, team work, and helping people? What are your goals? And last, but not least, be excited for this opportunity.

And the Question Is . . .

The following are examples of some *standard* questions that you will probably be asked in one form or another. (Of course these are all questions that you should have researched and prepared for in advance.) These questions are interchangeable and can be asked by any of the oral interview panels for public safety officer, EMT/paramedic, firefighter, or police officer.

1. Tell us about yourself.
2. How many stations are there in the department?
3. What makes you think you are qualified to be a police officer?
4. What type of community activities have you been involved in?
5. Tell us about your education.
6. Why do you think we should hire you rather than one of your competitors?
7. What makes you the best candidate for this position?
8. Why do you want to be a public safety officer?
9. What are your strengths? What are your weaknesses?
10. What are the attributes of a public safety officer? What is the most important one to you?
11. What will you bring to this department?

12. What can you tell us about _____ department?
13. If you were asked to choose a hero, who would it be and why?
14. What is our mission statement?
15. What are our core values?
16. How have you prepared yourself to remain calm and react effectively at emergency scenes?
17. What have you done to prepare for this position?
18. What is the job of a public safety officer?
19. What are your hobbies and what do you like to do on your days off?
20. Is there anything else you would like to add?

In regard to question number 1, this question is simply designed to learn more about you and your personal life (items that are not on your resume or application). This is your opportunity to tell the interview panel who you really are (i.e., you coach little league, you are a volunteer for nonprofit organizations such as Habitat for Humanity or Meals on Wheels, or you are on a recreational baseball team).

Question number 20 is a loaded question. The candidate should take this opportunity to discuss anything that requires further clarification of a question or statement that was not fully covered during the interview. This is also the time to give an outstanding closing statement about you that emphasizes your abilities and confidence in a nutshell.

HOW ARE YOU GOING TO ANSWER THE ETHICAL QUESTIONS?

It becomes more difficult when there are ethical dilemmas, legal and moral issues, and dilemmas that affect violations of the policies and procedures within the department. Remember, it is always necessary to answer a question ethically. There are not any "gray areas." Public safety officers are expected to make ethically, morally, and legally correct decisions in stressful situations. Public safety officers do not turn their cheek to look the other way. Sometimes situations may be ethical and moral dilemmas for others but not for you. This book has discussed scenarios in each chapter and you have had the opportunity to review the decision-making process. During your interview you can be confident with your answers.

The interview panel will be looking for your response to questions that relate to theft. Will you report a person for wrongdoing, perhaps one of your superiors? What is the right decision?

Because public safety officers work closely together, we might encounter situations in which you feel a paramedic is mistreating a patient. How will you react and what will you do next? Doing nothing is, of course, the easiest route to take but that would not be the right thing to do.

Maybe you are asked about the circumstances surrounding a crime scene and the suspect is complaining about how the police have treated him during his arrest. How do you answer this question? Are people treated differently? Does the suspect need to be examined for medical treatment?

Now, let's delve into the questions that require critical thinking about ethics, morals, and legalities:

1. You are at an off-duty party and see your supervisor using drugs. What do you say or do?
2. How would you handle an irate citizen?
3. What would you do if you see a fellow public safety officer put something in his pocket while at a fire scene?
4. How would you handle a conflict with a supervisor?
5. What would you do if you were given an order that places you in great danger or is morally wrong?
6. Define sexual harassment. What would you do if you were witness to someone being sexually harassed?
7. As part of the hiring process we will be doing an extensive background investigation. Is there anything in your past that you would like to discuss or explain to this panel?
8. Honesty and integrity. Define them and why are they important to you?
9. What would you do if you suspect a co-worker has a drug or alcohol problem on duty?
10. What would you do if offered a job at another department after we have hired you?
11. Are you currently on any other department eligibility lists?
12. How do you feel about the use of force?
13. Do you drink alcohol?
14. Have you ever used an illegal drug?
15. Have you ever been arrested?
16. Have you ever been involved in a motor vehicle accident?
17. Have you ever received a speeding ticket or moving violation?
18. What would you do if your supervisor gave you an order that you thought was illegal or morally wrong?
19. You are off duty at a very nice restaurant and notice that one of the exit doors is blocked. What would you do?
20. Another shift supervisor approaches you and asks you questions about a coworker. How would you handle this?

SUMMARY

The testing process for a public safety officer is challenging and stressful. There are many facets to the hiring process. For you, the candidate, to be successful you must follow a long and arduous journey. This journey includes many classes in your degree program. It includes work experience at other related jobs to gain knowledge about the profession to which you are applying. And, it also requires preparation for the hiring process; physical ability and conditioning; studying for the written examination; and homework for that elusive interview.

There are many difficulties in studying for this portion of the testing. It raises questions such as "How do I prepare to answer for the battery of questions for which I have no, or very little, experience?" After studying this chapter, you will have a much better idea about the challenges and the questions that will be asked of you. The interview is, by far, the least prepared for phase of the testing process and yet is the most important part of the public safety officer test. Most candidates think they can "wing it." While doing your homework and preparing for your chosen career as a professional police officer, firefighter, EMT/paramedic, you will understand the importance of virtues and ethics. Remember, honesty, integrity, dependability, and professionalism are the "cornerstones" of the public safety officer.

NOTES

1. "Police Interview Questions AND Answers-Police Officer Interview." www.job-interview-site.com/police-interview-questions-and-answers-police-officer-interview.html (accessed March 12, 2010 and May 1, 2014).

2. San Diego County Sheriff's Department, "Mission, Vision and Values. www.sdsheriff.net/about_mvv.html (accessed March 14, 2010 and May 1, 2014).

3. SUNY Brockport, "Student Life & Services." www.brockport.edu/career/behave.htm (March 14, 2010).

DILEMMA

You have been on the job as a police officer six months. You suspect that your training officer is intoxicated while on duty. What do you do?

_____

_____

_____

_____

_____

_____

_____

_____

_____

_____

_____

_____

_____

_____

_____

_____

_____

_____

_____

_____

DILEMMA

You are a senior firefighter and you observe your captain inviting a female visitor to his sleeping quarters on a regular basis. Who do you talk to?

_____

_____

_____

_____

_____

_____

_____

_____

_____

_____

_____

_____

_____

_____

_____

_____

_____

_____

_____

_____

DILEMMA

You are a paramedic and your coworker, also a paramedic, are responding to a call and you hit a parked vehicle. Your coworker wants you to ignore the incident. How are you going to proceed?

_____

_____

_____

_____

_____

_____

_____

_____

_____

_____

_____

_____

_____

_____

_____

_____

_____

_____

DILEMMA

You are a rookie police officer and you smell alcohol on your partner's breath. This has been going on for some time and you have chosen to not say anything. On this particular day you are involved in an accident that resulted in serious injuries to innocent bystanders. You are now faced with two ethical dilemmas. What are they? How will you proceed?

_____

_____

_____

_____

_____

_____

_____

_____

_____

_____

_____

_____

_____

_____

_____

_____

_____

_____

DILEMMA

You are on duty and you have a citizen approach you and she starts to complain about a fellow coworker whom you are not working with on that day. She gives you specific details about her encounter with your coworker. They are disturbing and difficult to believe. How do you answer her concerns? What's your next step?

_____

_____

_____

_____

_____

_____

_____

_____

_____

_____

_____

_____

_____

_____

_____

_____

_____

_____

The Future of Ethics

CHAPTER OBJECTIVES

1. Comprehend the importance of raising the bar in ethical behavior.
2. Understand how diversity can affect ethical thinking.
3. Recognize competing values, obligations, and principles.
4. Realize that ethical dilemmas exist.
5. Comprehend the difficulty of remaining ethical.

In today's society there is much distrust of our public employees. The public is demanding more transparency and accountability. We read everyday where a politician or an appointed public employee has misspoken or is involved in some kind of scandal. These are people we place our trust in and it appears they betray us.

On February 4, 2010, a principal of an elementary school in Oceanside, California, was found guilty of taking approximately $70,000 from the school district. The principal, Paulette Thompson, pled guilty to one count each of misappropriation of public funds and grand theft. Apparently she would wire the stolen funds to herself and members of her family and wrote herself personal checks.[1]

We cannot allow this to happen with public safety officers because they are what stand between us and chaos. It's not easy to maintain your own ethical standards when it seems like everyone else in the world isn't doing so.

COMMUNITY RESPONSIBILITY

Benjamin Franklin said in his speech at the close of the constitutional convention,

> Sir, I agree to this Constitution, with all its faults, if they are such, because I think a general government necessary for us, and there is no form of government but what may be a blessing to the people if well administered, and I believe farther that this is likely to be well administered for a course of years, and can only end in despotism as other forms have done before it, when people shall become so corrupted as to need despotic government, being incapable of any other.

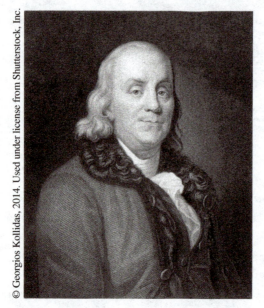

© Georgios Kollidas, 2014. Used under license from Shutterstock, Inc.

It sounds as if Franklin is saying that if we don't work together as a group and solve our problems with consensus, we will fail as a democracy and a country. This is especially true when working in public safety. Fire and police officials need the citizens and the citizens need them. For example, consider this scenario: a fire truck is dispatched to a neighborhood fire and people start shooting at it as it responds; how are the firefighters going to put out the fire? And how will the firefighters respond to the next emergency in that neighborhood? Will they respond or just say it is too dangerous? Is this ethical?

Another quote from Franklin comes to mind. He said, "We must hang together . . . else, we shall hang separately."

Someone once said, "People get the kind of policing they deserve." Maybe this quote could be expanded to say, "People get the kind of public safety, or the kind of government they deserve." What does this mean?

If the citizens of a community or neighborhood fail to take charge of their area and report crimes, code violations, hazards, victimization, and criminals to the authorities, that community will not be a safe place and fear and frustration will result.

An excellent example of a community that is experiencing problems is Vallejo, California, where because of budget problems they have had to lay-off police officers. Vallejo is a city of 117,000 people and encompasses thirty square miles. At one time the city employed 158 police officers and now they have 104. But because of further budget cuts, the city could end up with 89 officers; this in a city with a high crime rate.

Mat Mustard, president of the Vallejo Police Officers Association said, "There are certain times of the day when there are less than six patrol officers on the street-that's in a city of 100,000 people. We're concerned for the safety of the citizens and the safety of our officers."[2]

A councilwoman in Vallejo, by the name of Mari Brown, said that people should establish neighborhood watches and to protect each other by being alert. This is true not just when things are not going so well, but all of the time. If we as citizens looked out for each other there would be far less crime. It is our duty to look out for our fellow citizens. In areas where people do care for their community and each other there is far less crime. Citizens are at the very least responsible for their own well-being.

DESPOTISM

A despot would be a ruler with absolute power. Despots usually come into power in places where the citizens have little power or wealth. Some examples of despots would be Idi Amin, Adolph Hitler, Ivan the Terrible, Mao Zedong, Francois "Papa Doc" Duvalier, and Joseph Stalin, among others.

These tyrants became the sole voice of government in their countries and collectively killed millions of people, many of whom were citizens of the respective countries.

What Franklin could have meant by his aforementioned quote is if we become so corrupt as to be ungovernable, a despot will be needed to govern us because we are unable to govern ourselves.

What happens in despotic regimes? Stalin is alleged to have been responsible for the death of approximately 20 million people. He founded slave labor and persecuted certain ethnic groups, especially Ukrainians and Jews.

© Filipe Frazao, 2014. Used under license from Shutterstock, Inc.

Amin, the president of Uganda killed around 300,000 of his own citizens. He deported 60,000 Asians and as a result ruined the economy. He stole Uganda's money and when he left the country to live in Saudi Arabia, he took the money with him.

Pol Pot of Cambodia, a radical Marxist, slaughtered many of his own people. Khmer Rouge was the name of Pot's regime and among other atrocities he was responsible for the killing of 2 million people in Cambodia. He wanted to have an agrarian society and tried to do away with Cambodia's professional and technical class. He would kill anyone who was wearing eyeglasses, for example.

Duvalier appointed himself "President for life" of Haiti. Duvalier's gang called the *Tontons Macoutes*, were terrorists who killed many of Duvalier's political foes, as well as a number of private Haitians. He was corrupt and stole a fortune from the Haitian people. The country has never recovered from the vagaries of the Duvalier's regime.

If the citizenry does not become involved in the democratic process and actively participate in the government, including public safety, the government could become more corrupt, and as a result our way of life could be drastically modified. In other words, democracy would cease to exist in the United States, and we could have a despot as a leader. The people's involvement ensures the arms of government will not become corrupt.

A quote attributed to John Emerich Edward Dalberg Acton expressed the idea that: "Power tends to corrupt, and absolute power corrupts absolutely." He also said, "Great men are almost always bad."[3] The former British Prime Minister, William Pitt the Elder, said to the House of Lords in the United Kingdom something much the same as Acton. He said, "Unlimited power is apt to corrupt the minds of those who possess it."[4]

In the *San Francisco Chronicle*, on February 12, 2010, there was an article stating that thirty-one California lawmakers were going to be fined for taking unreported gifts from lobbyists. The gifts apparently included NBA tickets, meals, and stays at hotels. Assembly Speaker Karen Bass from Los Angeles received a $112.78 meal from AT&T, a $59.06 dinner from Chevron Corporation and $94.46 for a reception from the Pechanga Tribe, and failed to report she received them. According to the law, all gifts to elected officials should be reported. All of the state's lawmakers are required to receive training on the laws of the state on ethics. Why do people who know the law fail to abide by them? Probably because they can. Roman Porter, the executive director of the Fair Political Practices Commission, said "All the gifts to lawmakers were from sources that regularly do business before the legislature, so potential for public harm was greater."[4]

The amount of the gratuities given to the speaker was not great, but the fact that she failed to report them is serious. There could have been more gratuities that were undetected. The danger is that the acceptance of even inconsequential gifts could affect the decision-making process of the person receiving the gifts. It's called the "slippery slope," which can be defined as a perilous course that can lead to trouble.

If the people share in the governing of the community, they as citizens will support our politicians and public safety officers by assisting them in behaving ethically. Members of a democratic society control the public servants and can demand that they perform their duties in a timely fashion and abide by the rules and laws of the community.

DIVERSITY AND ETHICS

The United States is a diverse country. We have people living here that come from all over the world and as a result we will probably have different opinions on what is ethical and what is not.

When people come to this country they bring with them their ideas and experiences of authority and authority figures. The people who migrate from Mexico, for instance, to this country bring with them their attitudes about people in authority.

Students from south of the border have reported that when they crossed the line into Mexico to visit family and friends that the police have stopped them and given them a ticket for a bogus traffic violation, and then said that they could take care of the fine there on the street or proceed to the police station. If they gave the officer money, the ticket would be taken back and the motorist could proceed. Many of these students don't trust the police, even the police in the United States, because of their experience with the police in their home country.

Chinese also don't trust the police because of what goes on in China. An article in the *Wall Street Journal* reported that in Chongqing, a city in western China, the first of many trials may reveal how senior police officials plotted with local gangsters to operate rackets in one of the country's largest cities. Since the investigation in June 2009, hundreds of police officers, government officials, and gang members have been arrested. Some of the crimes that the defendants are charged with include bribery and extortion, as well as drug dealing and firearm possession.[5]

Pakistani police have been known to torture suspects to get confessions. There have been incidents of bribes being given to get the police to investigate crimes.[6]

© TonyV3112, 2014. Used under license from Shutterstock, Inc.

When we talk or discuss diversity we in most cases focus on race or ethnicity. However, there is also diversity in lifestyles that are brought about by age, socioeconomic situation, sexual persuasion, geography, and religion. All of the foregoing can affect an individual's ethics. Young people see things differently from people who are older. People of different religions have varied outlooks on morality. There are some who believe that abortions should be legal and other who are pro-life and against abortions. Some think we should have same sex marriage and others don't.

In a dropped wallet experiment done by Paul Kinsella in Belleville, Illinois: young people returned the wallet 56 percent of the time and senior citizens returned the wallet 88 percent of the time. Females appeared to be more honest than males in that they gave the wallet back 86 percent of the time where the males did the same 61 percent of the time. There were 100 wallets dropped on the street. The wallets contained $2.10 in cash, a fake $50.00 gift certificate, one fake grocery list, one fake receipt, one broken tooth pick, and a pinch of dust. All of this stuff was added to the wallet to make it look realistic. The gift certificate was added to offset the lack of cash in the wallet.[7]

Immigration

When we look at some of the immigration statistics provided by the U.S. Office of Immigration you can see how our country is changing demographically. In 2008, there were a total of 1,107,126 total people obtaining legal residence in the

United States. Remember, there are no statistics for undocumented immigrants. Out of that number 121,146 were from Europe and 369,339 from Asia. From the Americas, which included Canada, Newfoundland, Mexico, the Caribbean, Haiti, Jamaica, Central and South America, there were 491,045 folks becoming legal residents.[8]

Public safety professionals of the future will have to be aware of these differences and be able to deal with all of the population regardless of their personal feelings. Some departments are already preparing.

PUBLIC SAFETY RESPONSES TO THE CHALLENGES OF THE FUTURE

In 2008, the chief of the Washington, D.C. Fire Department, Dennis Rubin, initiated a program where firefighters and emergency medical workers would receive additional ethics, diversity, and equity training. He also required the members of the department to sign a statement of professional responsibility.[9] This type of training and accountability will probably become a regular occurrence in many organizations as the taxpayers are going to demand more of their public servants. Public safety departments are going to have to form a partnership with other governmental agencies and the various communities in order to dispel fears and concerns of the residents as well as the public safety officers. The programs should include training and education, outreach programs, recruiting and hiring processes, and a follow-up analysis to determine the viability of the process.

The town of Brooklyn Center in Minnesota has a program called "National Night Out," which encourages people to get out and meet their neighbors to help "Take a Bite out of Crime." This program is sponsored by Crime Stoppers. Brooklyn Center is also involved in a program called the Joint Community Police Partnership (JCPP), which is a collaborative effort involving Brooklyn Center, Brooklyn, Richfield, Hennepin County and Northwest Hennepin Human Services Council. The mission of the group is to encourage communication and understanding between the public safety officers and the multicultural community of these cities.

The motto is "Working together to build safer communities." This is done in three ways:

1. Improving the community members' knowledge and understanding of police procedures and laws.
2. Improving police officers' knowledge and understanding of diverse communities.
3. Providing more opportunities for positive interaction and two-way communication between police officers and community members.[10]

It appears that Brooklyn Center is on the cutting edge of community public safety. The city government is reaching out and providing vehicles for people to work and live together ethically.

The city of Gladstone, Missouri, has a department of public safety that appears to be on track to be able to provide exemplary public safety in the twenty-first century. Gladstone's department of public safety provides police, fire, and emergency medical services.

Their mission statement is a follows:

Courtesy of the City of Gladstone, Missouri.

> The Gladstone Department of Public Safety exists for the purpose of protecting and serving the people of Gladstone. Vital to this purpose are the values which reflect what the department believes in as an organization. These beliefs are reflected in the department's recruiting selection practices, policies and procedures, training and development, and ultimately, in the actions of its public safety officers in delivering services. Values reflect what the department considers important and determines the way public safety officers view not only their role, but also the people they serve. Moreover, our values serve as a linkage between ongoing operations of the department and the community's ability to not only participate in, but also understand the reason for Public Safety Department strategies. Our operational philosophy is based on the following values which we believe are conducive to a professional public safety department.

The first value is that the Gladstone Public Safety Department places a high value on human life. They consider this as their highest priority. For instance, police officers can use deadly force only when it is thoroughly justified and then only after all other means of apprehension have been exhausted.

The second principle states that the department must preserve and advance the principles of democracy. The organization believes that it is a privilege to be a public safety officer and that along with that privilege comes responsibility. Officers must consider individual rights and consider the values of our country when going about their duties.

Another high priority of the department is the prevention of crime. The department believes it is better to be proactive than to be reactive. In other words, it is better to prevent a crime than to solve it after it has been committed.

The Gladstone Public Safety Department believes that community involvement is crucial to the effective delivery of public safety. They realize that they cannot be effective without the involvement of the people they serve and they reach out to encourage public participation. Crime is a community problem and needs a collaborative effort to identify and solve.[11]

Accountability is a concern with this department and feels it must be answerable to the public it serves. This includes transparency and the ability to respond to the citizens concerns.

The Dallas-Fort Worth International Airport Department of Public Safety provides fire and police services to passengers and customers to the airport, which covers 18,000 acres and services approximately 57 million patrons each year. Their mission is to provide a safe and secure travel experience by minimizing exposure to crime and terrorism. They are geared to deal with current and future problems. The department is also concerned with the well-being of their employees and uses peer counseling and critical incident stress management (CISM). These programs are instrumental for the continued mental health of the public safety officers and will go a long way in guaranteeing ethical conduct.

Peer counseling is used in many departments today. Peer counseling brings together officers who have experienced a situation that is outside the realm of normal human experience with officers who have had like encounters, and they are encouraged to talk about their thoughts and feelings.

CISM is a program that involves members from other departments in the region and establishes a confidential outlet with which to discuss issues with individuals from other departments.[12] Public safety officers must keep their emotions in check while they are dealing with the various stressful situations they face on a daily basis. Peer counseling programs such as these give officers an opportunity to vent their feelings in a setting that is safe.

This is another department that is keeping current with the problems and concerns of the future by ensuring their officers are prepared and supported by services that are germane to their mission.

We all know that in the past the New York City Police Department has had its problems with corruption and other misbehavior. But we should also be aware that the majority of public safety officers in New York City as in other cities in our country are good honest individuals who are just trying to do a job.

The New York Police Department now has on its web page myriad information that informs citizens of workings of the police. If people look in the "frequently asked questions" section of the web page, they can find most of what they need to know in order to: make their home safe, make their business safe, and where they can get their vehicle identification number etched on their property. They will also tell the citizens about the programs they have that involve the community and what they are doing to improve positive police/community relations, which will contribute to the trust that is needed to perform the task of public safety. Taxpayers can also get information on where to sign up their kids for the police activities league (PAL), which provides sports and other activities for young people. One of the other activities is the Police Explorers Program which is a scouting program for young people who are interested in what the police do and may be interested in a career in public safety. The department also provides information on how to report crimes anonymously.

The New York police Department uses "zero tolerance policing." The is program was started ten years ago and focuses on "quality of life offenses such as urinating in public, public drunkenness, loud noise, graffiti, panhandling and other disorderly conduct." The theory being that if smaller problems are taken care of larger problems will not happen. The idea is if minor infractions will not be tolerated, the department sends the message that more serious crimes will not be condoned.[13]

This idea is based on a book written by James Q. Wilson and George L. Kelling titled *Broken Windows*, which in essence says "If we don't take care of the little things they will become big things." An example would be: There is a building with a few broken windows and if they are not repaired the place would look deserted so people would come by and break some more of the windows. At some point they may break into the building and occupy it. The building could become a fire hazard or a crack house.[14]

If the public safety agencies pay attention to the physical environment of the area in which they work they will be able to prevent crime and other safety hazards. If public safety officers demonstrate to the folks who live in these neighborhoods that they care; there is a chance that the citizens will begin to care and take pride in the community.

INNOVATIVE ETHICS PROGRAMS

There is an organization called The Williams Institute (TWI) for Ethics and Management that provides ethics programs for public safety in partnership with the FBI. Their philosophy is different from the traditional ethics training in public safety, which focused on fear, in that it concentrates on a personal responsibility model. TWI states that previously, public safety ethics training stressed paying attention to codes of conduct, rules, regulations, and laws, and if you didn't pay attention to the rules you would suffer the consequences.

They concede that rules and codes are necessary but what are more important are personal relationships and when people make decisions they should be responsible for them. Their clients include many institutions of learning, municipalities, and law enforcement and fire agencies.[15]

Ethics are about relationships between people. If we consider each other before we act, we will have a better chance at behaving ethically. Every time someone does something when in a group, that person must consider those who are present. If public safety officers are polite and respectful, they are promoting their profession, agency, city, state, or country because they are putting the welfare of the people above themselves.

Sometimes agencies try to legislate civility and for the most part it just doesn't work. Some agencies try to control the way officers approach motorists when stopping them for a traffic violation. This tactic is based on the fear factor and doesn't really change the officer's demeanor in any profound way.

There was an officer who was getting numerous complaints from motorists. Most of the complaints were for rudeness, so the department had him wear a tape recorder and turn it on whenever he stopped a car. He did this for about two weeks. After reviewing the tapes, he came to the conclusion that the way he spoke to the motorists was inappropriate. So he changed his approach and the complaints all but vanished. Sometimes we don't even recognize the fact that we are behaving in an uncivil manner, and we need to constantly monitor our behavior. Just remember: How would you like to be treated if you were in this situation?

John Hopkins University is offering programs through its Division of Public Safety Leadership that focus on police executive leadership and the training of public safety officers who aspire to administrative positions. These programs include courses on ethics, managing diversity, strategic thinking, decision making, and terrorism.

The program appears to be geared to the twenty-first century. The topics within the courses include: Is it possible to make a decision based only on the facts, or does the decision also reflect your beliefs, background, politics, or other factors? How much information is necessary before we can make a knowledgeable decision? Should an employee be held responsible for a well-thought out and well-researched decision that turned out having undesirable consequences?

The students explore differences in goals, values, beliefs, religion, race, and gender. They investigate factors that influence tolerance and intolerance. In the course titled "Ethics and Society," the students learn the "domino effect" of moral decision making and how their decisions guide and shape people, opinions, strategies, and operations. The course links personal decision making to service, teamwork, honesty, and building trust.[16]

This program is aimed at the public safety leader of the twenty-first century because it stresses ethics and diversity, two attributes needed to be effective in the future.

Rural public safety is ignored much of the time because most of the action and publicity is directed at urban areas. But today, crime and disasters can happen anywhere and often do. Criminals and terrorists may go to rural areas to hide or make plans for an attack, thinking that they will not be detected as easily. The University of Maine at Fort Kent has a public safety program specifically geared to people seeking a leadership career in public safety in "small town America." The institution is located near the Canadian border in the St. John River Valley. This venue gives the student an authentic taste of the rural life while learning the dynamics of working in a small department.[17]

Because of the way our world is today, we need educated and well-trained public safety officers throughout the country, not just in our major cities. This is a much needed program as our world continues to get smaller and more complicated.

ETHICS AND TERRORISM

The United States has experienced, in the past, other terrorist attacks such as the attack on Wall Street across from the House of Morgan on September 16, 1920, where a TNT bomb was exploded and killed about thirty people. The attack was never solved but it was believed that bolshevist or anarchist terrorists were responsible.

On January 24, 1975, a bomb was set off in Fraunces Tavern in New York City, and four people were killed. Responsibility was claimed by the Puerto Rican Group (FALN).

The U. S. Embassy in Tehran was seized by radical Iranian students on November 4, 1979. Fifty-two hostages were held for 444 days.

In 1983, there were three known attacks on Americans in the Middle East; the worst being a bombing of the Marine barracks at the airport in Beirut, Lebanon, where 241 Marines died. Within a few moments another explosion in West Beirut killed 58 French troops.

Libya was responsible for the bombing of a New York bound Pan Am flight in 1988 that killed 259 people on the airplane and 11 people on the ground. Some of the people killed were U.S. college students and service personnel.

The first bombing of the World Trade Center occurred in February of 1993; it killed 6 people and injured 1,040 people. Let us not forget Timothy McVeigh and Terry Nichols who were responsible for the bombing of the federal building in Oklahoma City. One-hundred and sixty eight people died, including 19 children.

There have been other attacks as well, but the one that really got our attention was 9/11. That incident changed the way we in the United States live. It will continue to affect us for years to come, maybe forever. Two-thousand nine hundred and ninety two people were killed that day and all of us were traumatized to a lesser or greater extent depending on our personal involvement in the event. The questions are: What is the ethics of terrorism? Are there any ethical responses to terrorism? Do we extend constitutional rights to terrorists? Are terrorists criminals or enemy agents committing acts of war?

PATRIOT ACT

There has been a profound change in the goals and mission of public safety since 9/11 and the passing of the Patriot Act. There appears to be a reduction of civil liberties, and law enforcement seems to be more prevalent. Federal money is now going to local law enforcement for training of public safety officers as first responders. Federal and local law enforcement are cooperating with each other more readily than in the past, and some say the nation is getting closer to a national police force. This is possibly an overreaction to the Patriot Act by some individuals and groups. Historically, there has been a resistance in the United States to any consideration of a national police department and that will continue to be the case. Remember that this country was formed by revolutionaries who had a great mistrust of government.

What is happening is a common reaction to an act of aggression by the various law enforcement agencies in this country against a serious threat. It stands to reason that first responders in any attack will be the local public safety departments because they are in the cities and areas that are vulnerable to assault. To keep the country safe will take a united front by all of those who are in the business of public safety.

On October 21, 2001, the Patriot Act was established by the Congress stating, "Uniting and Strengthening America by Providing Appropriate Tools Required to Intercept and Obstruct Terrorism." (USA PATRIOT).

According to a summary printed by the Republican papers[18] regarding the Patriot Act:

> There are articles that protect the civil rights of all Americans, including Arab-Americans. There are sections that allow the authorities to seize communications either oral or electronic, in order to produce evidence of terrorist activities. Another provision gives the Federal Intelligence Surveillance Act (FISA) the right to extend surveillance of non-U.S. individuals who are agents of a foreign power. A part of the act authorizes an attorney, investigative or law enforcement officer, who properly comes into contact with information from any wire, oral, or electronic device that contains intelligence or counter-intelligence information, to disclose it to officials. One section gives the power to the Director of the FBI to apply for a court order that would require the production of business records for foreign intelligence and terrorism investigations.
>
> The act provides a definition of a "terrorist organization" as a group: 1. so designated under the Immigration and Nationality Act or by the Secretary of State. 2. Two or more individuals, whether related or not, who engage in terrorist-related activities. In a related section, the act orders the Attorney General to monitor foreign students in approved educational institutions such as flight training, language and vocational schools.
>
> These are just some of the provisions of the Patriot Act. There are also segments relating to International Money Laundering, Bank Secrecy, Currency Crimes, Border Issues, Immigration, Removing Obstacles to Investigating Terrorism, among other things.
>
> In an attempt to protect the people there is a miscellaneous section, that states, the Inspector General of the Department of Justice is directed to appoint an official to investigate allegations of the abuse of civil rights, civil liberties, and racial ethnic profiling by government officials. There are also protections written in the section that protects the rights of any American, including Sikh-Americans.

It appears, for the most part, that the government is at least attempting to consider ethics in the war on terrorism. In February 2010, President Barack Obama signed a one-year extension for the Patriot Act. But there are questions as to how far this country should go in ensuring the constitutional rights to terrorists.

A utilitarian point of view could be that to reduce pain and increase happiness we need to keep the country safe. The outcome is important.

Immanuel Kant (formalism) might say that we shouldn't look at the consequences of our actions, but at the act. He also said that duty should be done. Duty is central to Kant's conception of ethics.[19] That being the case, it is certainly our duty to keep the country as safe as possible.

We mentioned previously in the book that Plato said "If you want justice, you must be moral."[20] Is holding someone incommunicado without charges moral? Is torturing an enemy combatant ethical? These are queries to be asked and explored?

Detention and Interrogation

International law states who can engage in combat and who cannot. To engage in combat, the combatants need to be armed forces designated by a state as such and they need to have a chain of command, need to wear uniforms, or have other unique ways of identifying them on the battlefield. They need to conform to the laws and customs of war. Based on the above description of those who can participate in war, the Al-Qaeda are considered unlawful combatants. Unlawful combatants can be detained and tried for the breach of the laws of war, criminal violations, and the nonobservance of humanitarian laws. Included in these transgressions are airplane hijacking, genocide, murder, and other atrocities, such as chemical warfare, and attacking civilians and other non-combatants.

Back in 2001, President George W. Bush decreed that the terrorists would not be protected by the Geneva Conventions, which is a law that pertains to prisoners of war, because they were not lawful combatants. He also stated that the acts by the terrorists were of grave concern and there was an extreme danger to the people of the United States. Because of the magnitude of the potential destruction, deaths and injuries, he also declared a state of emergency on September 14, 2001. As a result of this, the terrorists could be held indefinitely because an extraordinary emergency existed for national defense purposes.

The people covered in this document included members of Al-Qaeda, anyone who has engaged in, aided or abetted, or conspired to commit acts of international terrorism. It covered all of the bases to ensure that the country was as safe as possible.

The president also mandated that the prisoners would be treated in a humane manner, without discrimination due to race, religion, gender, and so on. They would be provided with water, food, shelter, clothing, and if needed, medical treatment.

When interrogating a criminal suspect, there are certain guidelines that are mandated by the Constitution according to the interpretation of the Supreme Court. If criminal suspects are in custody they have to be advised of their Miranda Rights before any questioning takes place. These are:

1. You have the right to remain silent.
2. Anything you say can and will be used against you in a court of law.

3. You have the right to talk to a lawyer and have him present with you while you are being questioned.
4. If you cannot afford to hire a lawyer, one will be appointed to represent before any questioning, if you wish one.

After the warnings you have to secure a waiver. To do this you have to ask two questions and receive an affirmative answer to each. They are:

1. Do you understand each of these rights I have explained to you?
2. Having these rights in mind, do you wish to talk to us now?

Prior to the 9/11 attacks, terrorists acts were considered criminal acts and in that the aforementioned standards would apply, but if the operations were considered acts of war, the United States could defend itself against further attack. As a result the due process rights of the terrorists could be suspended. There have been and continue to be myriad appeals and hearings regarding the prisoners being held at Guantanamo Bay, Cuba, and other locales. There have been allegations of torture and inhumane and degrading behavior. These allegations, if true, could be in violation of numerous conventions that have been put in place to protect prisoners of war. There is The Hague Convention, the four Geneva Conventions of 1949, the Third Convention Against Torture and Other Cruel, Inhuman and Degrading Treatment Pertaining to Prisoners of War, and the Fourth Convention that pertains to civilians. These were ratified by the United States in 1955.[21]

In 2008, the U.S. Supreme Court did find that the individuals incarcerated at Guantanamo Bay did have the right to habeas corpus to contest their imprisonment. Constitutional Article III, Section 9, says, "The privilege of the writ of habeas corpus shall not be suspended, unless when in a case of rebellion or invasion the public safety may require it." Habeas corpus allows a detained person to challenge the authorities to show cause for the imprisonment.

There is a debate going on regarding what constitutes torture. Some define an act as torture only when it is intended to perpetuate intense pain and lasting injury. Others describe it as being made to sleep on the floor or being deprived of sleep. It is considered improper for an orthodox Muslim man to be touched by a woman other than his wife, consequently some say that it is torture to subject prisoners to sexual humiliation, such as having females rub their bodies against them or dressing provocatively and being in their presence.

Another source of disagreement is whether to try the terrorists in a federal criminal court as criminals or at a military tribunal as enemy combatants. Some legislators are trying to pass bills that would forbid trying terrorists in any U.S. community and the Obama administration is saying the where and how to try them is under the purview of the executive branch of government and not the legislative branch.

What's Next?

The situation that exists since 9/11 is contentious and is being debated in government and in academia. Some say that the Patriot Act is diluting our constitutional rights, whereas others are opining that we need the act to protect the country.

What is ethical? Are we willing to give up certain rights to be safe? We've already given up some rights to be safe. This is called the "Social Contract Theory." This theory, developed by Hobbs and Locke, maintains that the individual gives up total freedom to be safe from others. Society provides safety and the citizens promise to obey the law.[22] To maintain a civilization, people need to heed the social contract. We all have to consider others because it is impossible to not come into contact with others when living in a society.

How far would you be willing to go in giving up your constitutional rights as outlined in the Bill of Rights?

The argument on how far we should go in protecting the country will continue well into the future and will depend on who you are talking to and what is going on at the time. We have to find a balance because we need to honor our Constitution while protecting our country and our way of life.

In this chapter we have explored how immigration, 9/11, and politics influence ethics and our thoughts regarding what is right. Public safety officers have to remain constantly vigil when it comes to ethics. They have to educate themselves about the differences in the various cultures they serve and remember to deal with their constituents fairly and equitably.

HYPOCRISY

You can believe a certain way and behave another way. This is called hypocrisy. Some studies say that there is not much of a correlation between beliefs and actions, whereas other studies state the opposite. We may believe that it is wrong to torture a person, but what if our loved ones are in danger and we need an answer to save them. What do we do?

Do you ever wonder if politicians who become corrupt are that way before they get elected or does the system contribute to their dishonesty? Politicians and others will say one thing and then do something else. Many say they are lying, but maybe after they get elected they come to the realization that to function, they must go along with the system. They may find they have to compromise their values. Maybe an elected official has a bill that would help her constituency, but she does not have the votes to get it passed, so she makes a deal with another politician to vote for his bill, if he will vote for hers.

This could also happen to public safety officers if they are not observant. Maybe a firefighter is taking fire department gas and putting it in his private vehicle. He knows it's wrong but he does it anyway because everyone is doing it. Should you do something because everyone else is? Maybe elected officials feel the need to compromise their values to get things done and to get reelected. But public safety officers don't because they don't stand for election.

SUMMARY

As we have gone through this book we've touched on the various aspects of ethics in general and public safety ethics specifically. As you probably surmised there are many pitfalls to be aware of when considering ethical behavior. Something may sound as if it is a "good idea at the time" but in retrospect it isn't. Whatever it is, even though it may look and sound as if it is just harmless fun, as we have seen in previous examples, if something negative happens during the time that you are not paying attention or goofing off, or it comes to light that you are being lax, it could turn into a scandal, or possibly someone could get hurt or die, or someone could lose their career.

When public safety officers are on duty (probably more than any other vocation), they must always behave in a way that engenders the public trust and instills in people the feeling of being secure when the officers are on the scene. Firefighters and police officers must always keep in mind that the citizens hold them to a higher standard than others, even other people who serve the public. According to a survey by *Forbes*, the firefighter is number one in status and the police officer is number seven. Another important aspect to keep in mind is that public safety officers need the people more than most other professions because they depend on the public's cooperation in order to do their jobs successfully.

We have department rules, we have codes of ethics, laws, and we have our personal ethics to consider when faced with a decision. The rules, codes, and laws do cover specific issues in most cases, but it is impossible for them to envision every eventuality. That is why public safety officers have to be constantly thinking about ethics because ethics are what they should use when faced with a decision.

Think for a moment about what you want your epitaph to say. Record what you want said on your tombstone. How would it be different if you were utilitarian, Kantian, or Aristotelian? This practice will help you clarify and prioritize ethical principles in your life.[23]

Because...

NOTES

1. Randy Kelp, "Oceanside Principal Gets Jail Time for Stealing Funds." *The Coast News*, February 12, 2010. P 1.

2. Chip Johnson, "Crime Wave Adds to Vallejo Troubles." *San Francisco Chronicle*, February 9, 2010. P. B 6.

3. John Emerich Edward Dahlberg Acton (1887). www.acton.org/research/acton/lol-lord-acton-quote-generator.php

4. William Pitt, the Elder, www.clpgh.org/exhibit/neighborhoods/point/point_n104.html "The Earl of Chatham and British Prime Minister."; Juliet Williams, "Panel Votes to Fine Thirty-One Lawmakers over Unreported Gifts." *San Francisco Chronicle*. 02/12/10.

5. James T. Areddy, "Chinese Trial Offers Peek Into Police Corruption." *Wall Street Journal*, October 12, 2009.

6. Z. Chatta, and V. Ivkovic, "Police Misconduct: The Pakistani Paradigm." In: *The Contours of Police Integrity*, edited by C. Klockers, S. Ivkovic, and M. Haberfield (Thousand Oaks, CA: Sage, 2004), pp. 175–194.

7. Paul Kinsella, "Results of the WalletTest.com Experiment." www.wallettest.com/Lost_Wallet__Test/Results_Page.html 02/23/10.

8. Homeland Security, *Yearbook of Immigration Statistics*. www.dhs.gov/files/statistics/publications/yearbook.shtm

9. Associated Press, "Chief Increases Ethics, Diversity Training for D.C. Firefighters." February 12, 2008. www.wtop.com/?nid=596&sid=1343692 WTOP.com 103.5 FM.

10. Brooklyn Center, "Minnesota Web page." www.citybrooklyncenter.org (accessed 02/15/10).

11. Gladstone, Missouri Department of Public Safety. www.gladstone.mo.us/PublicSafety 02/22/2010. pp. 1–3.

12. Dallas-Fort Worth International Airport Department of Public Safety. www.dfairport.com/dps 01/22/10

13. New York Police Department. Press release by Mayor Mike Bloomberg. 01/16/05.

14. James Q. Wilson, and George Kelling, "Broken Windows." The Atlantic Monthly, March 1982. Vol. 249 No. 3 pp 29–38.

15. The Williams Institute for Ethics and Management, "Ethics." www.ethics-twi.org (accessed 01/17/10).

16. John Hopkins University: Division of Public Safety Leadership. School of Education. http://psl.jhu.edu

17. University of Maine-Fort Kent. Public Safety and Criminal Justice. www.umfk.maine.edu/psa/default.cfm?ref=4

18. "Republican Papers." warrior69.tripod.com/id144.htm (accessed month day, year).

19. Immanuel Kant, *Grounding for the Metaphysics of Morals* (Indianapolis: Hackett Publishing, 1993/1785).

20. Plato, *The Republic*, Book II (New York: Oxford University Press, 1994).

21. Richard M. Pious, *The War On Terrorism and the Rule of Law* (Los Angeles: Roxbury, 2006), p. 181.

22. Joycelyn M. Pollock, *Ethical Dilemmas and Decisions in Criminal Justice* (5th ed.). (Belmont, CA: Thomson-Wadsworth, 2007), p. 64.

23. Jay S. Albanese, *Professional Ethics in Criminal Justice: Being Ethical When No One Is Looking*, 2nd ed. (New York: Pearson, 2008), p. 170.

DILEMMA

You are in charge of a diversion program for juveniles. This program takes young first offenders who have committed minor offenses (e.g., shoplifting, malicious mischief, and so on) and places them into community agencies with myriad programs such as tutoring, dental and medical programs, and cultural and recreational programs. You are asked to enroll a young boy into the program who has not committed any crime or infraction by a teacher at a school. The teacher thinks he would benefit from the program because he lives in a chaotic family and could use the structure of the community agency. What do you do? Is there an ethical question here? What is it?

_____

_____

_____

_____

_____

_____

_____

_____

_____

_____

_____

_____

_____

_____

_____

_____

_____

_____

_____

DILEMMA

You are a police detective and are interrogating a suspect about a homicide. Even though you have not found the murder weapon, which was a gun, you tell the suspect you have the gun. You know the make and caliber that was used because of a ballistics check. You produce another gun of the same manufacture and caliber of the murder weapon. And also tell the suspect that you got his fingerprints from the firearm. As a result of all of this the suspect confesses to the crime. Is this ethical? Why or why not? How do you feel about this tactic?

_____

_____

_____

_____

_____

_____

_____

_____

_____

_____

_____

_____

_____

_____

_____

_____

_____

_____

DILEMMA

You have a two-page paper due and you are busy. Another student says she will write the paper for you, and she does. When the papers are returned and graded you receive an "A," and she receives an "F" because her paper resembles yours too closely. What do you do? Why or why not?

_____

_____

_____

_____

_____

_____

_____

_____

_____

_____

_____

_____

_____

_____

_____

_____

_____

_____

_____

_____

DILEMMA

You're a firefighter and after your shift before going home you drop by your local lumber and hardware store to purchase some lumber for a deck your building in your back yard. After you pick out your boards you go to the cashier and the person working the register says "Since you're a firefighter you get 50 percent off."

What is your response? Is it ethical to take the discount? Why or why not?

_____

_____

_____

_____

_____

_____

_____

_____

_____

_____

_____

_____

_____

_____

_____

_____

_____

_____

_____

_____

_____

DILEMMA

You're an EMT assigned to communications and leave the communications center to have lunch. You are sitting in a restaurant having your meal and a woman collapses in front of you. What do you do first? What is the second thing you do?

_____

_____

_____

_____

_____

_____

_____

_____

_____

_____

_____

_____

_____

_____

_____

_____

_____

_____

_____

_____

_____

INDEX

CPSIA information can be obtained
at www.ICGtesting.com
Printed in the USA
LVHW021508081218
599762LV00001B/3/P